CIRCUS FOR EVERYONE

CIRCUS LEARNING AROUND THE WORLD

Molly Saudek training at the National Circus School, Montreal.
September 24, 1997.

CIRCUS FOR EVERYONE

CIRCUS LEARNING AROUND THE WORLD

Robert Sugarman

Mountainside Press

Shaftsbury, VT 05262

Circus for Everyone:
Circus Learning Around the World

Copyright © 2001 by Robert Sugarman

ISBN 0-9708693-0-4

Photos, unless otherwise credited, by the author.

Cover and book design by Paul Sugarman

Library of Congress Cataloging-in-Publication Data

Library of Congress Catalog Card Number: 2001089610

Mountainside Press
P.O. Box 407, Shaftsbury, VT 05262, U.S.A.
Phone: (802) 447-7094   FAX: (802) 447-2611

Printed in Canada

CONTENTS

Preface

Circus for Everyone chronicles a global phenomenon that developed in the last quarter of the twentieth century. Circus Learning has impacted educational systems, recreational activities, social service programs for youth at risk, as well as circuses. The book provides context for those working in these areas and insight for general readers into the ways art, economics and education interact.

The book is organized around Circus Learning activities: professional, touring youth circuses, community circuses, circus camps, circus residencies, inschool circus programs, year round independent circus programs, curricular and extracurricular college programs. It includes interviews with four circus professionals about their Circus Learning, brochure material from various circus programs, a listing by geographic areas of Circus Learning activities, and a glossary of Circus Learning terms.

Today's Circus Learning initiatives grew alongside the *new* circus movement that focuses on the art of circus performance, but the roots of Circus Learning lie in reforms initiated after the Russian Revolution. In 1919 the Soviet Union started a program of subsidized support for circus that grew to include the training of circus artists. Recent Circus Learning programs have been subsidized in a variety of ways - sometimes by sympathetic governments, sometimes by the programs themselves and the dreams and ingenuity of their creators. Unfortunately, in this time of instant communication, there is too little of it between the people and the organizations doing this work, especially in North America. While this study was being prepared, the situation improved with the establishment of the American Youth Circus Organization (AYCO) and the Flying Trapeze Association and the appearance on the Internet of increasingly rich Web sites by Circus Learning organizations.

The study was written at a time when circus was redefining itself in a continuum that extends from traditional presentations of unrelated acrobatic, animal and clown acts to unified theatrical forms enhanced by the latest technology and the latest ideas about people's place in the world. Although "circus" is still used in popular parlance to depict the unusual or the bizarre – basketball player Dennis Rodman's body piercing, tattoos and eccentric behavior are said to turn basketball into a circus, the gentrification of circus performance and the proliferation of circus training programs has begun to change ideas about what circus is.

This study is not about economics or the ways in which societies educate their young, but those forces do impact on how Circus Learning is conducted. The common denominator of all Circus Learning is people mastering physical skills, a process that requires intense training and commitment.

I thank many people who have generously shared work, ideas and time with me. Most particularly, I thank Alla Youdina, the first of the many gifted masters of Circus Learning I encountered. Her prodigious talent and openness to the possibilities of circus art led me to undertake this venture. She was also an invaluable source of information about Russian training. Carlos Cavalcanti supplied addresses of the Brazilian circus schools that appear in the Resource Guide. Nicholas Fersen translated Russian material. Ernest Albrecht brought The Russian-American Kids Circus and the Fern Street Circus to my attention and his book, *The New American Circus*, has been indispensable. Stuart Lippe provided many leads; more were found in Don Marcks' *Circus Report*. Richard Hamilton brought Hawaiian circus activity to my attention. Debbie Johnson led me to CirKids and Jerry Burkhalter. Fred Dahlinger, Jr. of the Circus World Museum answered historic questions and led me to several circus schools. Rob Mermin provided expertise when I was assembling the Glossary. Some material in this book appeared in somewhat different form in the journals *Spectacle, Bandwagon* and *The White Tops* and is included with their permission. I am indebted to my brothers, Marvin and Tracy, who have always led the way.

Finally, I thank my wife, Sally, for her continuous support and advice and for her enthusiasm for her own projects which has been an inspiration.

Robert Sugarman

I
Circus Learning

Learning is not discrete from life, although we often think it is. Perhaps it is the monastic tradition of scholarship from which our institutions of higher education evolved that makes us think of learning as cloistered - apart. Students and faculty in schools and colleges often dismiss the significance of where they are and what they are doing in relationship to the "real world." But when we learn, are we not engaging with the world? Is not that what learning means? The subjects of our studies are rooted in the world and the process by which learners extend themselves into the world through study is also real.

A further distinction has traditionally been made between learning - which is thought of as a mental process, and the physical experience of the world. Today the distinction between mind and body is less discrete than in the past. We now know we are holistic beings; physical health and mental health are not achieved separately.

A child takes its first steps. Kate Sugarman

One of the most exciting examples of learning - of mastering the possibilities of the world, happens when a child learns to walk. Those first steps are complex, difficult ventures into the unknown that require balance, thought, effort and courage. When the steps are achieved and a child proudly moves forward under its own power, the holistic nature of learning is demonstrated.

As a child does not stop learning having managed to walk, a student does not stop learning once the student leaves school and moves into a world which reveals itself to be no more real than school, only different.

Learning is a lifelong adventure. Writing this book has been such an adventure for the author, a retired academic whose area of specialization has, heretofore, been theatre. He was introduced to circus when he was six and has been a lifelong fan. That was the extent of his involvement until 1995 when he met Alla Youdina, then the Creative Director of New Circus Acts for Ringling Brothers and Barnum & Bailey Circus. Youdina was preparing an act not far from the author's home in Vermont. He accepted her offer to watch rehearsals and witnessed a group of young Russians, Americans and a Mongolian - strangers speaking different languages, learn together. Each was a unique personality with a unique way of learning which Youdina encouraged.

Bodies and minds had to be prepared for the demanding work. Each day began with a run up and down mountains at the ski resort where they were working; each day's practice started with a lengthy warm-up. Then they worked to bring to life Youdina's dream of butterflies and a spider on a giant web. As the act developed, the author witnessed the excitement he had seen when his granddaughters took their first steps. Mastery was being achieved; not just walking, but dancing, spinning and flying through space individually and as members of a team dependent on each other for their safety.

The author followed the act to Florida and watched it grow and modify as Youdina and the acrobats integrated it into the 1996 Ringling Brothers and Barnum & Bailey Blue Show. He continued to watch during the act's two year tour; the act wasn't learned and then repeated mechanically. Most performances were preceded by rehearsal; all by a thorough warm up. Each performance integrated learning and performance.

Intrigued by the process he had seen, the author set out to discover how circus performers came to be that; the first working title was *New Performers for a New Circus*. In recent years, the *new circus*, usually in one ring, placed greater focus on the performance of its artists than on spectacle. Where did those remarkable people come from?

At the same time, the author encountered Circus Smirkus, an international youth circus in Vermont's Northeast Kingdom with which Youdina also worked. In Bennington Vermont, where the author lives, Circus Minimus provided a summer program that taught circus skills to youngsters. It soon became apparent that all these activities were part of a resurgence of interest in what he came to think of as Circus Learning. This became the subject of the book.

Circus Learning continues the joyous experience the child has when starting to walk. It provides focused physical activity; it is a team sport that is noncompetitive. Rather than defeating another, one advances one's skills as far as possible alone and with a group. Each achievement becomes a plateau for further achievement. When one can juggle three balls - try four. Four? Try five. The only competition is with the participants' ability to transcend the limits of time and space. With Circus Learning, earthbound folk learn to fly and stop time. Objects can - when properly manipulated, defy gravity. Like dancers, circus performers demonstrate the ability of humans to extend the possibilities of the body, just as trainers extend the possibilities of animal achievement.

Circus Learning can produce legitimate self-esteem in those uncomfortable with academic learning which all too often is presented within traditions of class and caste. Circus Learning enables those who have fallen into social roles that make them outsiders find ways into community with their peers. This is not just true of children. First generation college students venturing into an unfamiliar campus environment find that mastering circus skills develops faith in their ability to cope with other learning situations.

Circus Learning is difficult. It requires focus, effort and the ability to move beyond failure. It teaches good work habits. In a world in which the media lull youngsters into passivity and computers encourage them to inhabit virtual realties, Circus Learning provides an authentic world in which the individual controls his or her actions. Perhaps that is one of the reasons for its new popularity

This study also considers how the methodology of Circus Learning can be adapted to other learning. We will note the importance of teachers whom students can trust and who, in turn, trust their students. We will see how clearly defined goals and clearly defined methods for achieving them make it possible to venture into unknown and frightening areas. Whether looking at professional training, children's training or recreational programs, we will try to discover the process that makes Circus Learning unique.

II
Professional

CIRCUSES

Ringling Brothers and Barnum & Bailey

In the Golden Age of the American circus, the Ringling Brothers show and the Barnum and Bailey show were leaders. In 1907, Ringling Brothers carried 1,000 personnel, 335 horses and 26 elephants on 92 railroad cars. Most mornings it erected a canvas city that featured a Big Top that could hold 15,000 spectators ranged around three rings and four stages. The circus performances emulated contemporary industrial giants in efficiency and magnitude. Most evenings, the canvas city was torn down, loaded on the trains and moved to the next town. At the end of the 1907 season, Ringling Brothers bought Barnum and Bailey, but the circuses operated separately until 1918. After the merger, the dominant position of The Greatest Show on Earth was unquestioned.

That position has been maintained in the face of changes in the world and in circuses. The Hartford Fire of 1944 crippled the circus which was already suffering from the loss of the cheap labor on which it had depended. Ringling Bros. and Barnum & Bailey folded its tents in 1956 and regrouped to play the indoor arenas that had arisen in the postwar building boom. For the next three years, except for three railroad baggage cars, the circus traveled by truck. It returned to the rails in a newly designed tunnel train of 15 cars in 1959. When ownership passed to a group headed by Irvin Feld in 1967, the circus added a second unit built around the German Circus Williams that included its charismatic star, Gunther Gebel-Williams. By 1978, the Ringling Brothers and Barnum & Bailey Red Unit traveled on 37 cars; the Blue on 38. The units continued to grow. The 1996 Blue Unit had 146 performers and a total company of 215 traveling on 54 cars. In 1999, both the Red and the Blue Units traveled on 56 cars. Through its history, Ringling Bros. and Barnum & Bailey, now a division of Feld Entertainment, Inc., has demonstrated a sense of tradition that maintained an identifiable mix of skill and spectacle; it also demonstrated willingness to adapt to changing circumstances.

As the largest and oldest circus in continuous operation in the western world, the Big One has become the establishment that advocates of the *new circus* attack for its perceived emphasis on spectacle and size at the expense of artistic excellence. Such attacks, like those of Animal Rights advocates on all circuses that use animals, are skewed by an unwillingness to see what is actually occurring. Feld and his partners not only added a second unit, they established Clown College to produce performers to augment the aging clowns on the show. When American impresario Steven Leber signed a fifty year contract with *SoyuzGostsirk*, the Soviet circus monopoly, that gave him exclusive rights to brings its performers to the United States, Ringling, under the direction of Irvin's son Kenneth, negotiated its own contracts with performers who, in post-*Perstroika* Russia were able to do so. Lacking Ringling's organizational and promotional skills, Lieber's Moscow Circus did not fare well playing arenas the Ringling shows use.

In addition, Ringling has developed new acts often incorporating the newly available performers from the former Soviet Union and its allied states. The key person developing new acts for Ringling until 1999 was Alla Youdina who had been working for *SoyuzGostsirk* when Tim Holst, Ringling's Vice President for Production and Talent, met her. Youdina, a former star of the Moscow Circus on Ice, retired as a performer in 1971 to raise her sons, but kept busy. She earned a graduate degree with a dissertation on theatrical imagery, became a dramaturg for the central theater authority advising companies on their selection of plays and working with playwrights before joining *SoyuzGostsirk* which transformed into *RosGostsirk*.

Alla Youdina

At the time she met Holst, Youdina came into possession of a letter that Rob Mermin, director of Vermont's youth circus, Circus Smirkus, had sent to "The Moscow Circus" hoping to link his fledgling operation to Russian circus tradition. While still with *RosGostsirk,* Youdina began working for Ringling Brothers Barnum and Bailey, America's largest touring circus organization, and for Circus Smirkus, one of the country's smallest. Eventually, she left *RostGostsirk* and became Creative Director - New Circus Acts for Ringling; Head Coach and

Creative Director for Smirkus. She joined Mermin in planning the year's
Smirkus program and trained acts during the two week rehearsal period which
in 1999 became three weeks. For Ringling, she joined in planning each year's
circus, created new acts, helped maintain those already created during their
two year tours, advised other acts on adapting to the needs of Ringling and
assisted Holst on his talent searches in Russia. The acts she created were characterized by vivid imagery and ideas. She said of her work with Ringling,
"This is why I am here, why Kenneth (Feld) invited me to be here, because all
my acts have ideas. This is how my brain works."[1] We begin our examination
of Circus Learning with a look at the way Youdina created The Spider Web act
for the Blue Unit of the Ringling Circus in the summer of 1995.

        The Ringling process for creating acts is far different from the method
that evolved over seventy years of subsidized Soviet circus. The Flying
Cranes, the last great act to emerge under the old system, took five years to
develop. Members of the act were graduates of the highly selective Russian
Circus School system that taught them circus skills, dance and gave them a
theoretical understanding of circus history and circus art. In contrast, Youdina
had four months to create The Spider Web.

        Youdina's circus career began when she joined the original Moscow
Circus on Ice at the age of sixteen. She performed with the show for more
than a decade becoming a featured artist who hung from a trapeze by one skat-
ed heel. When she joined the Moscow Circus on Ice, she was one of 5,500
people who competed for 18 spots in the show. Recruiting for The Spider Web
was far different; she and Holst found performers for the Spider Web where
they could. Most were strangers to each other and to some of the skills they
would be required to master; all were older than sixteen which Youdina feels
is the optimum age to start training for an act, but that assumes the person
already possesses basic skills.

        Oleg Sergatchiov, the Spider Web catcher, was a thirty year old med-
ical student when he found housing in a Moscow circus hotel. Its tenants told
him he had the body of a catcher and would be better off pursuing that. He
was assisting flyers when Youdina and Holst recruited him in Moscow. Katya
Odintsova, the act's butterfly, a Russian gymnast-diver, was working in a cradle act (two person trapeze) in Paris. American Joni Laskov and Mongolian
Gigi Batmunh were dancers on the Ringling show. Batmunh, like the
Mongolians Youdina used in the previous show's Bungee act, had benefited
from the circus and dance training the Soviets had established in Mongolia.
Russian Vika Volchek had previously joined Ringling working with animals

and had also done Spanish Web along with her mother. Cris Clark, an American, studied at the National Circus School in Montreal and worked with Circus Smirkus where Youdina found him.

Under very different circumstances, Youdina aspired to the excellence that was possible under a system where circus was an honorable lifetime career followed by paid retirement. That system was supported by circus schools that were fed by gymnastic and sports programs attached to communities and factories throughout the Soviet Union.

This is why circus in Russia (is) so much developed, because it was seventy years. You just know your acts, your skill, you just worry about your shape, your body, your brain, your attention and everything belongs just to that. Everything and all your life, the life of your family, everything belongs to that, nothing else. You sacrifice everything, but the government does everything for you. You have restaurant; they cook for you. You have transportation; they do this for you. They buy tickets for you and your family. You live in a hotel; you pay nothing. My sister, she was with animals twenty years - she has always five grooms to clean them. She had to be pretty, she had to train animals, she had to perform in the evenings - it was enough.[2]

Youdina was baffled by Americans who take to circus as a temporary activity and was appalled at those who, after signing two-year contracts with the Ringling organization, do not complete them.

They don't want to put their lives in it. Dilettantism - all around, everywhere. And circus doesn't like dilettantes. Circus needs real people, fanatics who will die here. Otherwise it's not interesting to spend your energy, your talent, your time, your knowledge - just for fun?[3]

Before recruiting performers for the Spider Web, Youdina had won approval from the Ringling management at its January planning session for an act that would employ traditional circus skills - trapeze; cloud swing (working on a horizontal rope); flying trapeze (flying from a trapeze to a catcher on another trapeze) and spider walk (upside down walk in which the performer is suspended from her feet.) All of this was to create an aerial fantasy about spiders, a butterfly and a giant spider web. The act was to be part of a section of the circus that had environmental themes.

The first problem was the web, itself. Youdina presented designs and models for a thirty foot web of rope-wrapped cable to the Hagenback-Wallace organization that creates Ringling props, but they were unable to build it. While Youdina and Holst were searching out people for the act, contracts were held in abeyance until the Web could be built. In May, Holst gave Youdina the go ahead to do it herself. With her sons Vanya and Grisha, one a graduate student of Economics in Moscow, the other a graduate student in Robotics, she built the Spider Web on the lawn of Circus Smirkus.

As she usually does when developing a new act, Youdina created The Spider Web first in her mind. She then did a series of drawings that showed what would happen during the act. Here is the first page of her notes for The Spider Web.

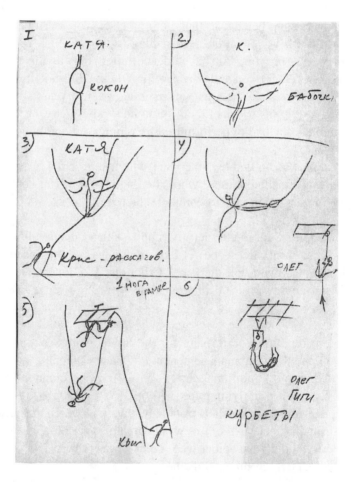

When the Spider Web performers assembled in the summer of 1995 in Vermont, they worked in the little Circus Barn of Circus Smirkus and at the gym of the Bolton Valley Ski Resort. Strangers had to become a team. After their work, Youdina knew the act was not guaranteed a slot in the new show. That would only come if the act met with the approval of Ringling management during November rehearsals in Tampa, Florida. Youdina's work was like a subsidized research project that might have commercial value; Ringling invested in the possibility of an act. If accepted, there would be last minute adaptations to fit the act into the program.

The performers strengthened their bodies with daily mountain hikes, stretching and warm-ups. Gigi Batmunh, a trained dancer, gave *barres* to increase the women's grace and strength. Before specific work began on the act, Youdina worked to make the troupe into a team that could trust one another absolutely.

Russian Oleg Sergatchiov and Mongolian Gigi Batmunh rehearse The Spider Web at the Bolton Valley Ski Resort, September 1995.

This work, it is not just their body. You teach them how to live together, how to keep team, how to shake hands with each other, how to help everybody with the act that day. The thing we do - stretching, it is like meditation and you tell them everything they can expect, what they will meet in circus life and how to prepare themselves mentally. They should be ready for this case and another case with body, with mind, with character together with the act.[4]

Watching her work, the author was struck by how gifted a teacher Youdina is. Although she had made drawings of what she wanted at each moment in the act, she was a sympathetic counselor adapting her goals to the capabilities of her performers. At the same time, she was never content with what a person was doing, but only with the further achievement of which the person was capable. With all her bi-lingual support, Youdina's response to difficulties her charges had was often a simple acknowledgment that, "Nothing is easy. I know it's hard. You must be unique; not everybody can do this."[5] She reminded them that circus performance is an art that demands the very best of which they are capable. Watching a runthrough in Tampa she commented, "They are too soft. They should be like tigers in a cage - aggressive. Otherwise you cannot make it."[6] Later she added

> You have to be aggressive. This is stage - you play aggressive; this is life, you be gentle. Some people mix up. Everything you have, you have to fight for. Circus is school of life. You must be aggressive with circumstance and gentle with partner who share in the fight.[7]

Her role is parental evoking the method of her mentor, Arnold Arnold (Barsky), creator of the Circus on Ice. "He was like my father, my grandfather and it was his style just to talk. And he was sometimes angry and so I can understand that sometimes maybe I am emotional and they think I am angry."[8]

Always there was the ticking clock. In Vermont, the whole day was built around the act, but once the troupe joined the show in Tampa, rehearsal time would be limited and the performers would be involved in preparing other duties in the show. Each member of the act would have to come a long way for it to work.

Youdina's certainty that the act could be achieved never wavered even as she had doubts if the finished act would be accepted. When a cassette arrived in Vermont with music for the act, the performers' work seemed more part of a performance. When the show's director, Danny Herman, visited with costume sketches, the sense of performance was heightened. Herman, a New York choreographer who had worked with Michael Bennett, was pleased with what he saw and encouraging. "I love hearing Alla talk about art," he said.

For the performers, it was intense, visceral learning. Unlike family acts into which young performers assimilate as they grow[9], The Spider Web was created as the skills were learned by its participants. It was analogous to learning the fundamentals of a language and then being required to converse on a high level of proficiency. Not surprisingly, as they were learning the act, some of the performers did learn each other's languages. Odintsova, who spoke no English when she started, was conversing comfortably in English the following summer. As Russian is virtually a second language on the Ringling shows, performers like Californian Janine Johnston in The Women of the Rainbow act Youdina created the following year, became proficient in Russian.

Having observed rehearsals in Vermont and Tampa, it was apparent to the author that the success of the act - the success of the Circus Learning that had taken place, was due, not only to the prodigious efforts of the performers, but to Youdina's unique skills as a teacher. The first attribute of her teaching is her mastery of the skills. She can do, or has been able to do, anything she asks of her students. The second is her ability to have a clear vision of what she is after. Third, is her sensitivity to the uniqueness of each of her students. When observing the Spider Web girls doing a *barre* in Vermont, she said

> Character is important in circus. You see, it's three girls and they do just *foutee* now and each *foutee* is different. Why? Not because of their bodies, because their brain is different and their character is different and I see this character immediately. They do just one *foutee* and I see why this is good, why this is bad. You can write whole story - biography, based on just one *foutee*.[10]

She noted of a performer,

> She is bright, but not so much concentrated. It happens often with people who are talented in many different areas. When you need to concentrate your attention, they cannot because they get everything so easy.[11]

Youdina's charm, sense of humor, and charisma make her students trust her as they push their minds and bodies into the unknown. Behind her stands a system of training that is almost gone, but her embodiment of that system supports her students.

It is always mind and body that are involved in Circus Learning. As Elvin Bale, the retired Ringling daredevil told the performer who would be shot from a cross bow in the circus that featured the Spider Web, "If you can see it in your mind, you can do it."[12]

Youdina's model for teaching is not the only one. In China, Circus Learning is less interactive. Children, apprenticed at a young age, leave their families to train and are seen as interchangeable elements in acts that are, themselves, interchangeable. When Chinese troupes join American circuses, they are only allowed to appear for six months after which they are replaced by virtually identical troupes.[13] Fellow performers have noted that the leaders of the Chinese troupes often identify troupe members by numbers, rather than names. The Chinese troupes live apart from other members of the circus and prepare their own food. Each performer carries an individual rice bowl identified not by name, but by number. For a teacher such as Youdina, such impersonality among her performers is not possible.

After The Spider Web became an effective part of the Blue Unit, Youdina was asked how much of her original vision of the act had been achieved. "Maybe fifty per cent,"[14] she replied. Her dream exceeded her performers' reach and the requirements of the show. For logistical reasons, instead of being in the center ring, the act played at the end of the arena where it was difficult for audiences to get a full sense of what had been achieved. Kenneth Feld considered the act exemplary of the acts his organization could produce.[15] During the run there were changes. Before the show opened, Laskov's husband was transferred to the Red Unit and she followed him after a Russian, Anna Vasilieva, was trained to replace her. At the end of the first year, Cris Clark decided not to continue with the act and the others covered his duties although the act was less strong without a second man.

The Spider Web in performance. credit: Ringling Brothers and Barnum &
Bailey

During the two year tour, Youdina helped Odintsova prepare a solo act in which she became Katya, Queen of the Clouds, in the next Blue Unit. In the new act, Odintsova did more with the cloud swing she had performed as the butterfly in The Spider Web and revived the one-arm planges (flips of the entire body while hanging from one arm) that Lillian Leitzel made famous in the 1920's and were later performed by Mickey King and Vicki Unus.[16] For the same show, Youdina helped Batmunh develop the spider walk she had done in The Spider Web into a solo act, Luna, Angel of the Air.

Another aspect of Circus Learning in the Ringling organization was Clown College that planned a gala reunion for its twentieth anniversary in 1987. In 1997 it graduated its last class and closed down. Over the years, the College graduated more than 1300 including MacArthur Genius Award Winner Bill Irwin, Barry Lubin - Grandma on the Big Apple and other circuses, Tom and Tammi Parrish who headed Clown Alley on the Blue Show until their retirement in 1996, and Tim Holst who went on to become Ringmaster, Production Director and finally Ringling's Vice President for Production and Talent. It also produced others, frequently criticized as "Cookie Cutter" clowns for their interchangeable identities and performances.

The somewhat hyperbolic program for the 1996 Clown College graduation tells how the College began.

The clown thrives today in the Greatest Show on Earth because of the wisdom and vision of one man — the late Irvin Feld. When he founded the Ringling Bros. and Barnum & Bailey Clown College in 1968, Irvin Feld ensured the smile of the clown would never vanish from the face of the earth.

When Irvin Feld purchased Ringling Bros. in 1967, he strolled into Clown Alley and found only fourteen clowns with an average age of 58. "The classic clowns had many years of success and wisdom to pass down to future generations, but there weren't any young faces to carry on the age-old art of clowning," he explained. "I was facing an endangered art form, and I knew it."

The following year, Irvin Feld founded Ringling Bros. and Barnum & Bailey Clown College in Venice, Florida at Winter Quarters as a training ground for clowns. He called on masters of merriment, including Lou Jacobs, Otto Griebling and Bobby Kay, to pass on their clowning skills to the young clowns in training. The first class of 1968 boasted a handful of fledgling students who were willing to break new ground and learn the art of clowning.

In the final years of the College its curriculum included pantomime, improvisation, makeup, prop building, costume design, choreography, juggling, unicycling, stilt walking, acrobatics and clowning. Auditions were held nationwide; in 1987 in Los Angeles, San Francisco, Chicago, Boston, San Diego, Dallas, Houston and Austin. The 34 selected studied, tuition free, 10-12 hours a day, six days a week from August second to October ninth when they presented a gala graduation performance. Based on weekly progress reports and the gala, some were given contracts to fill gaps in Red and Blue Unit Clown Alleys.

In its first years, the College headed by Mel Miller, a former Ringling clown who had gone on to be curator of Ringling's Sarasota Museum of the Circus, had 28 graduates. Like the then Ringling Clown Alley, all were male. The first Clown College class, according to that year's circus program, contained a priest who worked with handicapped children and who received permission to audit the course; two former teachers; a mailman; a minister; two professional actors; two acrobats; and several musicians. The special skills brought to College by the students were worked into their clowning.[17]

The effort to use Clown College to enhance each student's uniqueness, seems not to have continued, although over the years, Clown College, like the rest of the Ringling operation, became diverse in terms of gender and race. The year Clown College started, the move towards racial diversity was heralded by the arrival of the King Charles Troupe of African-American unicycling basketball players; the popular act was on the show for many years and returned in 1997.

The number of Clown College graduates climbed to 58 in 1979 and then declined. Bill Ballantine - clown illustrator, headed the school from 1969 to 1977 and recorded his experiences in the 1982 book, *Clown Alley*. Over the years the graduates brought youthful energy to the performances, but most did not move beyond the rudiments they had acquired in College. Many seemed more interested in a short term adventure than a career; turnover was substantial. While the College taught basic skills, it had not prepared its graduates for the rigors and isolation of touring nor given them strategies for developing their skills. Management, which had invested much time and money in the college - at the end its annual budget was rumored to be a million dollars, was frustrated. In 1995, Ringling sought a new direction that would create more individual performers and the directorship of the school was taken over by Smirkus' Rob Mermin and Dick Monday who was to found the New York Goofs discussed later in this chapter. That year's clowns did display a greater variety of makeups, but the problems continued.

Early in 1998 the College announced its closing. Kenneth Feld envisioned a new approach in *The White Tops,* the magazine of the Circus Fans Association of America.

Kenneth, who took the helm when his father died, declared that the new program "will be like a master's class in clowning." He said the whole idea, the challenge "is to create better acts that relate to the comedy of today."

He left it to spokesman (Rodney) Huey to explain exactly what this means.

"Audiences today, even eight year olds, are sophisticated and demanding," Huey said. "Clown College was the boot camp. Now we're moving to the real creative process for the best performance possible, less of the same clown look. We can find talent that's already working and bring them together with people on our shows and our creative team to develop incredible gags relevant to today. It's a way to get new, fresh ideas."

Now Feld envisions a higher calling for Clown College, a "graduate school" if you will. The new program, he said, will introduce clowns into the performance the same way the circus finds, trains and develops other acts. As examples, he cited the midair bungee ballet [Youdina], the aerial spiderweb display [Youdina] - and even Ariana, the Human Arrow [created by Elvin Bale.]

Quoting Feld, "We said, 'You know what? We can create clown acts the same way. But what we have to do is take discipline and the amount of time - three, six, eight months - it takes to create special clown acts and routines with existing talent."

Existing talent notwithstanding, Huey noted that during his travels looking for good acts, Vice President Tim Holst is keeping an eye out overseas for comedic talents.

In 2000, the Ringing Web Page stated:

It was decided last year to redirect the focus of Clown College by developing a Clown College Graduate Program consisting of a series of Masters of Comedy Workshops. These workshops will consist of the Ringling Bros. and Barnum & Bailey creative team working with clowns from both touring units of Ringling Bros., other Clown College Graduates, and new talent to design dynamic new routines for our shows.[18]

The plan, if implemented, seems not to have been effective as twelve of the fourteen clowns on the Ringling Red Unit left the show at the end of 1999, halfway through the two year tour.

The elimination of Clown College is less surprising as one considers how the role of clowns in the Ringling shows has evolved. Large numbers of clowns doing walk-arounds to distract from prop changes was a duty left from the Golden Age circus. With the high tech efficiency of contemporary prop changes and the use of lighting to direct audiences' attention away from them, clowns are less needed as distractions. However, they have proved useful in the Three Ring Adventure® preshow, especially as most of the clowns are American and able to speak with audience members more easily than performers for whom English is a second language. Another factor diminishing the need for clowns is that the Ringling shows, influenced by the *new circus* one ring shows, seldom have three rings occupied at the same time; the shows mostly focus on one or two rings. Clowning is often incorporated into acrobatic acts as with the King Charles unicycle basketball acts and the Russian comedy trampoline basketball act, The Torosiants, on the 1998 Blue Unit. As circuses trims operations in the face of the demands of bottom lines, fewer clowns are needed when some are part of existing acts. The Clyde Beatty-Cole Bros. Circus moved in that direction in 1997 when its dismissed its Clown Alley and replaced it - none too successfully many thought - with a family of South American clowns who did acts.

American clowning in recent years has followed the European model in which a clown is not just one of a group of pranksters, but an individual who has mastered many aspects of circus performance. The Russian clown Oleg Popov, Barry Lubin's Grandma, Ringling's David Larrible, are such masters. The problem for Ringling was finding a way to reduce the distance between neophytes and master clowns. Could the crash course preparation of acts that Youdina did be adapted to the creation of such clowns? If so, Ringling needs a master teacher in that area although the elimination of Youdina's position in 1999 as Creative Director-New Circus Acts, suggests that the Ringling organization was, as of this writing, less concerned with developing new talent than in hiring existing talent which is less expensive. Youdina was retained by Feld, Inc. as an independent contractor to assist when the occasion arises, but the organization has eliminated its continuing investment in training professional performers. The Ringling shows do introduce Circus Learning superficially with The Three Ring Adventure® in which performers introduce children to juggling and rolling globes and other equipment and allow them to try on costumes and watch clowns don make up. The immediacy of the Adventure, the direct contact with performers, has proved popular with audiences in demonstrating circus craft, but is no substitute for teaching it.

Feld Entertainment, Inc., also has an Educational Outreach Program headed by former clown Peggy Williams, a Clown College graduate.

I have a lot of latitude in my job and, in general, write materials and create programs, seminars and workshops that enhance any of our properties to audiences in schools, museums, newspaper departments, etc. Specifically for circus - I have developed the CIRCUSWORKS™ program and have presented it to over 25,000 educators of all grade levels all over North America in the last ten years. I have written and presented a 3 credit course on circus-in-the-curriculum at Fordham Graduate School of Education ('85-'88), and currently am reformatting many of those materials for online access at <Ringling.com/circusworks>.

Next week we are presenting (in Tampa) a prototype seminar based on the animals and careers in the circus - for about 1300 kids each time. Because of our curriculum materials, this qualifies as a field trip for the schools. We hope to repeat this around the country in conjunction with our show schedules when possible.

I also monitor all educator requests and create new materials in response to what teachers are looking for.[19]

In addition, Williams does hands-on circus education. In 1990, she taught clowning at the Belfast Community Children's Circus that brought children from Protestant and Roman Catholic communities together in

Northern Ireland and is discussed in Chapter Four. While there, she met Paul Woodhead, an Australian who taught acrobatics. She then went to Australia to help him set up a 4th-5th grade class in clowning that developed into the Dubbo West curricular circus program discussed in Chapter Seven.

The Outreach program Williams heads, while promoting the Ringling shows, integrates realistic information about circuses into the curriculum across disciplines. It also provides guidelines to help schools create their own circuses and presents educational materials on the Ringing Web site.

In the past, the Feld organization provided Circus Learning to develop new acts and clowns within its corporate structure. These activities benefited the entire circus industry. Newly trained performers moved to other shows after their stint with Ringling; Clown College produced more clowns than Ringling could use. Ringling Brothers and Barnum & Bailey, as has been noted, continues to occupy a preeminent position among circuses because of its adaptability to change. One hopes that its recent focus on the bottom line will be balanced by continuing long term investment.

Big Apple Circus

Circuses developed three rings for economic reasons; more rings meant more seats for the audience. The one ring circus was reintroduced for aesthetic reasons - to focus on performers rather than spectacle, to create a more unified performance and to establish a more intimate relationship with the audience. To sustain a one ring show, it helps to find a different economic base on which to operate. Some, like The Big Apple Circus, have become nonprofit performing arts organizations. This enables them to fund-raise and receive tax benefits that offset their diminished performance income.

Questions have been raised about the tax status of the Big Apple Circus. According to a *New York Times* account of the circus' new quarters in Walden, New York

A vocal minority is resentful that the circus, which enjoys non-profit status because of its children's educational programs, is likely to remove a building that once represented the village's sixth-largest source of property tax income from the local, county and school district tax rolls.

"I'm not opposed to circuses - why I even went to the circus in Moscow a few years ago," said David C. Lustig, Jr., 76, the owner of Lustig Realty on Main Street and a longtime member of the village Planning Board. "But that building could have accommodated another industrial plant."

Furthermore, he said, the wire factory employed more than 100 local workers who spent money 12 months a year in the community. The circus occupies the property for two months with up to 140 performers and crew members before it goes on tour. Three box office staff members and a caretaker remain.

For now, the Big Apple is still paying $45,000 in annual real estate taxes to the Town of Montgomery, Mr. Binder [Big Apple Circus Director and Founder] said, although the circus has challenged the payment under its tax exempt status. Besides, he said, "the factory had been closed for years," adding, "There was little hope of reviving the site.[20]

One element in Big Apple's nonprofit status is the unique relationship it maintains with the city for which it is named. Unlike circuses whose home bases are places to rehearse which they leave to perform, the Big Apple, despite its summer tours and the new Creative Center in Walden, New York, is very much a New York City circus. Its annual stand, alongside the building that houses the New York City Ballet and Opera companies, is its longest.

New York City's population, like that in much of the United States, is increasingly polarized between the affluent and the disadvantaged. The Big Apple Circus has established relationships with both groups that have benefited its nonprofit status. Members of its Board of Directors, drawn from the city's movers and shakers, are connected to people and organizations from whom they raise money. Over the years, Big Apple Circus has developed ancillary community service activities that help justify the organization's nonprofit status. The Clown Care Unit® works with sick and disabled children and their families in six New York hospitals as well as hospitals in Connecticut, Massachusetts, Washington and Washington, DC. The Unit

uses juggling, mime, magic and music. Specially trained professional performers make "clown rounds," a parody of medical rounds that bring laughter to youngsters who are often facing painful medical procedures they may not comprehend, and helps alleviate the fear and stress felt by their parents and caregivers. The more than 50 clown doctors now make 130,000 annual bedside visits.[21]

Circus for All!® "provides complimentary circus tickets to economically disadvantaged and physically challenged children and their families. During the 1996-1997 season, 10,000 tickets were distributed to needy groups throughout New York City."[22] Any free tickets offered to Big Apple Circus performances on the road are provided by local sponsors. Beyond the Ring[SM] brings training in circus arts to school children in East Harlem, one of the city's most needy areas. Circus of the Senses[SM] is an annual New York performance for hearing and vision impaired children and on tour where special funding has been developed. In 1999, Viveca Gardiner, Big Apple's Director of Special Projects, developed a *Big Apple Circus Study Guide: A Resource for Students and Teachers* that is provided to school children attending the circus or participating in Beyond the Ring[SM] to provide greater understanding of the classical [one ring] circus. The Study Guide may be downloaded from the Big Apple Web site.

The balance between community service and performance has evolved during the Big Apple Circus' unique history. The circus' co-founders, Paul Binder and Michael Christensen, met and learned to juggle in the seventies at the San Francisco Mime Troupe to which they were drawn by the Troupe's combination of physical theatre and anti-establishment politics. Christensen left to try his luck juggling in the streets of Europe. When Larry Pisoni, a Mime Troupe friend who was to found the Pickle Family Circus, failed to join him, Christensen invited Binder. Christensen and Binder performed across Europe for two years. They left the streets to work with Annie Frattelini's intimate, one ring Nouveau Cirque de Paris.

Binder and Christensen were fascinated by the dynamic of the one ring circus. After returning to the United States, Binder, soon joined by Christensen, became determined to establish a circus in New York that would combine what they had seen in the Fratellini circus with the creativity they felt emerging in New York's streets and parks. They described their proposed circus in their first fund raising proposal in 1977.

The signals of a rebirth of the traditional circus are already sounding in New York. The recent economic crisis has already undercut New York's established cultural institutions. At the same time, the streets and parks have become a stage where performers, in a renewal of ancient performing arts, are attracting large, enthusiastic audiences. The purpose of the Big Apple Circus and the New York School for the Circus Arts is to give this growing energy focus and purpose and to develop it under the auspices of trained professionals who respect the highest artistic standards.[23]

When Binder and Christensen started, they assembled a group of like minded people, many recent college graduates, who found themselves turned off by traditional careers and fascinated by circus as alternative theatre. To become a circus, the group needed to improve its skills and engaged a Russian immigrant circus couple, Gregory Fedin and Nina Krasavina, as mentors.

Fedin and Krasavina considered acrobatics the central discipline in the Circus Learning they provided the neophyte performers. They saw acrobatics, not in mechanical terms, but aesthetically as an interaction between performers and the surrounding space. The Big Apple Circus debuted on a landfill in Battery Park in an ill-fitting canvas tent that had been manufactured in the Bronx. The production was presented by the New York School of Circus Arts, Inc., an institution that was to mediate between the Circus and the city as it trained neophytes to become professionals as the first members of the company had become professionals.

Twenty years later, the Big Apple Circus tents had become gleaming, heated and air conditioned vinyl wonders manufactured in Europe. The Circus had abandoned its countercultural stance to become one the city's established cultural institutions. It no longer performed on a Battery landfill, but at prestigious Lincoln Center. The Circus Learning Big Apple provided no longer transformed New Yorkers into Big Apple performers. Instead, the Big Apple Circus performances featured the finest international acts and no longer reflected New York City's racial diversity or the energy of its streets. Ringling Brothers and Barnum and Bailey, with the Chicago Kids, the BMX Bikers and the Oxygen Skate Team of inline skaters did more in recent years to develop acts from racially diverse street performers than Big Apple.

The Big Apple Circus programs no longer lists the New York School for the Circus Arts School as its presenter. Binder and Christensen's model had been the School of American Ballet that trains dancers for the New York City Ballet. Like many analogies, this one did not work. The circus has no corps de ballet in which beginning performers hone their skills in a performance situation. Nor does Big Apple have the group of dancers with disciplined bodies who can be transformed into performers that Ringling Brothers and Barnum & Bailey has. Members of the Big Apple core company, who adapt their skills to each year's program, are already the equivalent of ballet's soloists.

Big Apple's Circus Learning shifted from its performance to its admirable ancillary activities. The one most germane to this study is the Big Apple Beyond the Ring[SM] residencies discussed in Chapter Six where the analysis of Circus Learning at the Big Apple Circus concludes.

Cirque du Soleil

At the dawn of the twenty-first century, Cirque du Soleil, created in 1985 by Canadian street performers Guy Caron and Franco Dragone, had become the most influential circus organization in the world. Much of the renewed interest in Circus Learning can be attributed to the elegantly theatrical Cirque du Soleil shows that gentrified the image of circus and made Circus Learning a respectable area of recreational study and even a path to a career.

The Cirque du Soleil production style combines hightech theatricality, elegant choreography, excellent execution of traditional circus skills which are all presented as elements of stories. Unlike other one ring circuses - Big Apple, Circus Flora and the Pickle Family Circus – that contributed to the *new circus* movement that focuses on performing excellence and unifying themes, Cirque du Soleil has not abandoned the Ringling emphasis on spectacle. Cirque du Soleil has made spectacle integral to its performances and has carried it to new levels in, above, below and around its single performing ring.

The rise of Cirque du Soleil can be linked to the affluence of the 1980's and 1990's. Cirque du Soleil shows are marketed as expensive luxury products. Their appeal is not to "Children of All Ages," but to sophisticated adults. In 2000, Cirque du Soleil's *Alegria* was playing indefinitely in Biloxi, Mississippi; *Dralion* was involved in a three-year tour of North America: *Mystere* was playing indefinitely at Treasure Island in Las Vegas; *O* was performing indefinitely in its own building at the Ballagio in Las Vegas; *La Nouba* was performing indefinitely in its own building at Walt Disney World in Orlando, Florida; *Quidam* was on a two-year European Tour; and *Saltimbanco* on a four-year Asia Pacific tour.

To staff its shows, Cirque du Soleil can not just book existing acts. It auditions throughout the world and transforms the gymnasts and performers it recruits into Soleil performers at its new corporate campus in Montreal. In the large, well equipped facility, future Cirque du Soleil performers receive personalized training from an international group of coaches.

Its success has not made Cirque du Soleil forget its beginnings in the streets. Its Cirque du Monde, discussed in Chapter Four, creates programs that bring Circus Learning to street children and others in need throughout the world.

SCHOOLS

Many schools that train professional circus performers were established in the last two decades of the twentieth century. They joined those that had been set up earlier in the Soviet Union and areas of Soviet influence. Listing the schools contacted for this book alphabetically in this chapter - rather than by location, suggests the diversity and the commonalities of programs in many places. The resource guide at the end of the book lists the organizations considered in this study and others, geographically.

The Actors Gymnasium

The Actors Gymnasium in Evanston, Illinois, established in 1995, is a school of physical theatre that teaches circus skills courses. Academic credit is offered through the Continuing Education Program at National-Louis University. The Actors Gymnasium also offers a two year Certificate Program in Circus Arts. (See Program Literature, p. 241 for details.)

The Certificate program calls for 32 class sessions. Sixteen are the twice-weekly Circus Arts; eight, gymnastics; two, physical comedy; two dance; two, either Monologue Writing, Adaptation for the Stage or Dance Theatre; and two elective sessions. The 1998 catalog listed twenty faculty.

The Actors Gymnasium is a project of The Looking Glass Theater that seeks links between physical and imaginative possibilities. In September 1998, Actors Gymnasium began the Circus Theater Performance Project to create an original theatrical piece that incorporated circus skills over a fifteen week period. Working with a core group of 10 adolescents who had developed circus skills, Sylvia Hernandez, co-founder of Actors Gymnasium and Thomas Cox, of the Looking Glass Theatre, created a version of a Siberian folk tale, *The Sun Maiden and the Crescent Moon*. Presented in December, "We sold to standing room only on both shows and it was well received."[24]

Non-circus courses at the school include acting, audition technique for the camera, capoeira - the Brazilian martial arts that is the basis of the act Alla Youdina prepared for the 1999 Ringling Brothers Blue Unit, contact improvisation, drum performance, flamenco, mime, music for the actor, puppet theatre, stage combat, tap dance and theatre criticism. A children's program includes dance, tumbling and physical theatre. In 1999 there was another one-term Circus Theater Performance project for nine to eighteen year olds.

Alla Youdina

Alla Youdina had just built a home in Greensboro Bend, Vermont when Ringling Brothers and Barnum & Bailey eliminated her position as Creative Director New Circus Acts. Situated at the top of a hill with a spectacular view, the home was also a training studio. The living room's cathedral ceiling supported a trapeze and the ground floor contained a large space for stretching and warm up. Youdina soon added an outdoor aerial rig and a pond for skating. The home became the base for her new work as a private teacher. Her neighbor's daughter was soon studying trapeze and in the winter Youdina, who had started her career with the Moscow Circus on Ice, was teaching skating on her pond and at nearby ski resorts.

Alla Youdina coaches a "Jane" for the Disney Jungle Ice Show in the living room of her Greensboro Bend , Vermont home, June 6, 2000

When Feld Inc. hired Youdina as an independent contractor to train twenty Tarzans and Janes for the Disney Jungle Ice Shows, she did the preliminary training in her home. The skaters, billeted at a nearby motel, learned to integrate circus and skating skills in the way it had been done in the Moscow Circus on Ice. One significant difference was that Youdina had even less time to train her ice show students than she had had when she creating acts as a member of the Ringling staff. Skaters, whose strength was in their lower bodies, developed their upper bodies as they took to the air in Youdina's home and on the outside rigging. Youdina, assisted by Velodia and Zena Augustov who had also settled in the area, trained two groups of ten before

Youdina followed them to Florida for the show's rehearsals.

Youdina's training facility was next used to train two Brazilian and one Russian aerialists for the 2002 Ringling Red show. Youdina, adaptable and creative, continues to thrive and to teach.

Arc en Cirque

In Chambéry-le-Haut, France, the Arc en Cirque professional training program prepares students for entrance to the Centre National des Arts du Cirque. Another Arc en Cirque program trains circus teachers. A third provides leisure programs for people of all ages and for those with disabilities. 500 students were registered in the programs in 1998.

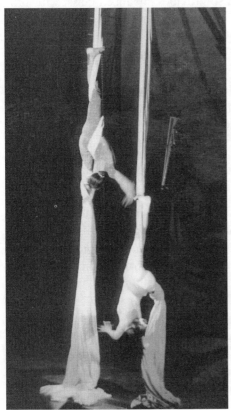

Arc en Cirque began in 1987 as a collaboration between a circus artist, some children and the French suburb of Chambéry-le-Haut. The school has since gained the support of many government and non-government entities including the French Ministry of Culture, the Chambéry town council, the County and Regional Councils, the Department of Employment, the Youth Mission, the Department for Young People and Sports, the National Department of Education, the Union of New Forms for Circus and the French and Rhones-Alpes Regional Federation of Circus Schools.

In 1997, Arc en Cirque moved into a building almost 4,000 feet square that contains three training halls. One, more than 1400 feet square and 24 feet high, is devoted to aerial work and acrobatics. A second, 338 feet square, is fitted with a suspended floor for dance. The third, 357 feet square, is for children's workshops. There are also changing

Arc en Cirque students perform a tissu act.
credit: Arc en Cirque

rooms, showers, dining rooms, a costume room, a circus library, an assembly and lecture room and a 59 foot circular Big Top that seats 300. The 11 teachers are certified in teaching circus, have first aid certification, and either five years professional experience or advanced diplomas. Guest lecturers from l'Ecole Nationale de Musique de Theatre et de Danse and professional artists supplement the work of the faculty. There is an administrative staff of three.

Arc en Cirque courses for performers include traditional circus skills, dance, theatre techniques, anatomy, physiology, social and labor law, history of circus, history of dance, *Son et lumière* techniques, makeup, and skills in finding employment. The teaching program prepares students for the *Brevet d'Initiateur aux Arts du Cirque(BIAC)* that qualifies people to teach beginning circus workshops to groups of eight children ages six and up. Both the performance and the teaching program require about 800 hours at the training center and 400 in professional placements. Grants and scholarships are available to French students. The school also provides advanced classes for professional performers

The leisure courses include *Discovery Courses* for children from four to 12, *Initial Training* for children above twelve, and *Advanced Training*. The goals of the *Discovery Courses* are to have children "play, learn together, progress alone and together, awake to the artistic dimension of Circus Arts, find out one's talents."[25] The weekly workshops for children four to six last an hour and a quarter; twelve children study with two teachers. The workshops for children seven to twelve last an hour and a half; three teachers coach twenty children.

Initial Training workshops have four teachers and a dance teacher for twenty children. The goals are to "learn together, progress alone and together – acquire circus technical skills – explore one's talents, explore one's vocations, participate in the cultural events around Circus Arts. Be involved in the creation of Circus Arts shows."[26]

Advance Training workshops have fifteen to twenty students with three teachers and a dance teacher. The workshops meet six and three quarter hours a week. The goals are "to sustain progression and to excel, explore one's vocation. To master the fundamental circus technical skills and further explore the particular circus arts discipline they have chosen. To find one's technical and artistic autonomy." [27]

Arc en Cirque has opened classes adapted to young people and adults who are physically or mentally disabled. The school is considering classes for the hearing impaired.

Arc en Cirque is developing networks with professional performance organizations and with other schools as it provides its students with placements. Arc en Cirque faculty develop circus classes and programs in schools in the area. "To allow access to circus arts to a wider public, Arc En Cirque sets up training sessions during week and school holidays."[28]

Blue Lemon & Ecole de Cirque de Bruxelles

Ecole de Cirque de Bruxelles has been training teachers of children since 1989. The school's approach, developed from research begun in 1981, integrates mastering circus disciplines and extending their possibilities. At the same time, Ecole de Cirque du Bruxelles encourages the development of creativity, cooperation, and communication. The one-year program involves 800 hours of study. 500 are devoted to circus skills, dance-movement and drama; 105 include psychology and testing, methods, group dynamics and anatomy; 30 are given to seminars on First Aid, games, movement, methodology, analysis of productions, and other topics. Student internships during the year include 50 hours of observation and teaching during vacations and 120 hours of teaching during the school year. Students are expected to train on their own 10 hours per week.

The school's l'Academie des Arts du Cirque provides a leisure program for young people. Those nine and up meet three hours a week during the school year. Half of the time is spent on circus skills, the remainder on acrobatics, dancing and movement, and acting. Those 14 and up meet four and half hours a week. Three hours are devoted to skills; one and a half to complementary activities. Auditions are required for participation in both programs. The Academie des Arts du Cirque sponsors a juggling meeting each November and a unicycle meeting each spring.

Ecole de Cirque du Bruxelles also operates Handicirque©, a program that introduces children with disabilities to circus skills.

Disabled persons are welcomed at Ecole de Cirque du Bruxelles where they are encouraged, supported and helped. Teachers give them the opportunity to enter the world of imagination. Little by little the barriers between abled and disabled is replaced by sharing and creativity.

Handicirque© integrates those with physical or mental disabilities so that the training contributes to the disabled person's well being.
While Handicirque© develops physical skills, it also enhances the
ability to work with others. Disabled students gain self-esteem as they
overcome fear, learn to dare and be creative and to develop new
awareness of their bodies' abilities. Our work is open and adaptable to
various situations. A playful spirit fosters confidence, respect and
pleasure. Skills include floor acrobatics with a partner; juggling:
scarves, balls, plates, diabolo; balance: ball, stilts, cable; trapeze; and
acting. The teachers have followed a year of specialized training at the
school.[29]

The school's Blue Lemon program brings together artists from
European and Canadian circus schools to produce circus shows, variety performances and shows for businesses. Blue Lemon also offers circus training
seminars.

Celebration Barn Theatre

Mime Tony Montanaro founded the Celebration Barn Theatre in
South Paris, Maine in 1972. It offers one- to four-week summer workshops
for adults in physical theatre. Studies include mime, acrobatics, juggling,
mask, movement, stage fighting, voice, and acrobatics. The focus is on group
as well as individual development. Students benefit most who come with projects to develop. Students in the Production Workshop consult instructors
when necessary and present their work to the group in the evenings. Students
are both professionals honing skills and those who do the work recreational-
ly. Celebration Barn Theatre is now owned by Carolyn Brett. There is a touring Celebration Barn Theatre Company.

Centre National des Arts du Cirque

The imposing home of the Centre National des Arts du Cirque in Châlons-en Champagne.
credit: Jacques Philippot

The French government opened a school to train professional circus artists in 1985. The original program was for four years; in 1998 it was changed to five years. Graduates receive a diploma granted by the Education and Cultural Ministries that is equivalent to the French Diploma of General University Studies (DEUG), a two-year degree. The highly selective program, like all public education in France, is free.

Soon after the Centre National des Arts du Cirque opened, the need became clear to organize the program in a way that would create better preparation for advanced work at the school. In 1998, eight schools offered the first two years of the program which lead to a Certificate in Circus Arts that corresponds to the French *baccalauréat* awarded when one leaves secondary school.

> The foundation course is a general course focused on helping students acquire basic circus skills (in acrobatics and in the different circus arts disciplines) and to explore artistic expression (particularly theatre and dance.)[30]

The final three years are held at the Centre National des Arts du Cirque in Châlons-en-Champagne. Beyond these nine schools, there are now over 500 circus schools in France offering recreational programs, teacher training programs and pre-professional training.

The selection process for the Centre National des Arts du Cirque is rigorous. About 200 students a year, between 16 and 23 years old, apply. The entrance auditions are open to citizens of any state in the European Union; candidates from non-EU countries may not exceed 30% of the students accepted. The school considers the number of years an applicant has studied dance or acting or acrobatics and the applicant's general cultural level. The

A juggler rehearses. credit: Catherine Noury

one hundred to 120 applicants chosen to continue the acceptance process are divided into four groups. Each group comes to the school for a day on a weekend in May or June for a pre-selection process that evaluates dance, acrobatic and acting levels. Sixty are selected to come for two weeks at the end of July during which they are evaluated for circus technique, acting, acrobatics and their ability to work with others. Eighteen are chosen to attend the school.

Some candidates may be awarded a place in the advanced circus arts course if they are between 18 and 25 years of age, have a *baccalauréat* or the equivalent, have had intensive training for two years in floor acrobatics, balance, trampoline, dance and theatre and have mastered the basics of a specific circus arts discipline.

The permanent faculty that serves the Centre National du Cirque and the preparatory school in Paris is between fifteen and twenty. It is supplemented by 100 to 150 others who conduct workshops, some of which run as long as two weeks. Workshop subjects include scenography, economics, circus history, various kinds of dance, different forms of theatre, English and music. The school operates a Training Center that serves professional circus artists and circus arts teachers. It also has a Library and Resource Center.

Circo Arts brochure

CircoArts

Based in Christchurch, a beautiful old English style city encapsulating the best of what New Zealand has to offer, CircoArts offers professional training in circus, clowning and street performance. CircoArts training prepares people for work in a wide variety of contexts: mainstream circus, new circus, street theatre/performance, corporate and private functions, hotel, cabaret, restaurant, institutions, festival, carnival and events.[31]

The school offers a one year Certificate in CircoArts for those who develop a range of skills and a specialty. It also offers a January Summer School. Applicants must be at least 17, have demonstrated interest in at least one circus skill, have at least three years secondary education, have demonstrated interest in drama, theatre music and/or gymnastics.

Circomedia

Circomedia is a performance school for circus artists, and a circus school for actors and dancers.
It is the only school of its kind in Britain where all the core staff are qualified teachers. It has developed its own Diploma in Circus and Physical Theatre and is the only centre offering this qualification …At Circomedia our training approach recognizes the needs of a new generation of performers wanting to combine circus with dance, theatre, cabaret and street theatre and to ground themselves in physical technique and skill. Circomedia offers training for the profession of Circus and Physical Theatre with a team of internationally respected tutors.[32]

Circomedia offers a one-year, full-time diploma course in Circus Skills and Physical Theatre and a three-month, full-time Introductory Course. Training is available in traditional circus disciplines and in Physical Theatre "for those whose interest is in creating pieces that convey moods, emotions and ideas rather than presentation of a skill."[33] The development of a new facility in 1998 enabled Circomedia to offer flying trapeze classes.

Circus Arts and Acrobatics, Inc.

The first ten week training session at Circus Arts and Acrobatics, Inc. began in April, 2000 in a newly renovated tile factory in Roseville, California. The school was founded by Maria Carrillo, a successful Silicon Valley entrepeneur who became interested in the flying trapeze at the San Francisco School of Circus Arts. Ms. Carrillo also founded The Flying Trapeze Association. She described the school and her plans for it three months before the school opened.

People are starting to sign up and in the meantime my bathrooms are being built and the offices and we're going to put the flying trapeze up this weekend. My trampolines are on order and so we are going through the whole start-up phase.

I am funding about two thirds of it myself and then I got a loan from the Small Business Administration. The facility has thirty-five foot ceilings. We're going to put a pit in so my net is actually going to be at floor level with a pit underneath it and mats all around so we will probably have a good forty to forty-one feet of air space. This was the only high ceiling I could find in the area.

When I started this, I was looking at people who get a Bachelors Degree in Dance or Theatre and I thought, "Why couldn't we offer an arts degree in Aerial or Acrobatic Arts and even Physical Comedy?" Then I did a lot of talking - mainly to Cirque du Soleil and the director of the shows at the Reno Hilton and some of the shows in Vegas and I said, "Would you guys look at someone who had a degree in acrobatics over someone who didn't?" Their response was, "Talent is talent." But we are going to approach colleges in this area and offer them physical education classes. As far as a degree goes, from a marketing perspective it was not worthwhile. It is something I am going to continue looking into, but it's not on the high priority list right now.

The faculty is not made up of people from the area. They are moving here for the school. Vladimir Chvalbo, the Director of Trampoline and Lilia Chvalbo, Trampoline Coach, moved out from Montreal. They were just tired of moving around with Cirque du Soleil. He was head acrobatics coach for *Quidam* and she was responsible for the continuing education of artists under 18. They wanted to settle down in a nice town and raise their kids so they moved out from Montreal. Laura Rappa, our Director of Aerial Arts, and Tony Steele, our Senior Aerial Advisor, moved out from Reno. Chuck Johnson, Director of Acrobatics, and Jeri Habberstad, Acrobatic Coach, moved here this weekend from Washington. There's a passionate following for this kind of institution. I'm getting people coming out of the woodwork; world class performers and teachers, who want jobs. I have a really great crew.

My background is not circus. I started my career building missiles for Lockheed and then for twelve years I ran clinical trials for start up companies in the Silicon Valley. My *forte* is business and in Silicon Valley I started high-tech medical companies and learned how to get the ball rolling. How to do financing, marketing, sales, advertising.

I did well on stock options in Silicon Valley. I'm not married, I don't have any kids, and I just decided to put my heart and soul and my check book into this. So I started with a healthy cash flow. Once you have that, for me the rest of it is like jumping through hoops.

I was flying at the San Francisco School of Arts. I love it. I love trapeze so much, but I am not a performer and I don't aspire to be one. So that's probably good for my school.

I have lots of things in the works in connection with the school. There are so many books I want to do about trampoline, acrobatics, flying trapeze, static trapeze, coaching handbooks. I'm even planning to take Tony Steele's *ABC's of Flying Trapeze* and turn it into an instructional video as soon as we get our rig up.

I am also starting a distribution function for Circus Arts and Acrobatics. We just signed a distribution agreement with EuroTramp® so I'm going to be selling competition trampolines. Along with that, I just hired a mechanical engineer to design all my circus equipment - trapeze bars, teeter boards, Russian Swings, and we are going to sell our circus equipment on line. I hired Svetlana Galova, from the Flying Cranes, to do our costume design and design our sportswear. She is our Director of Conceptual Design and is going to design our Flightights™. We are going to have a sportswear apparel line for aerial artists and acrobats.

Of course, this could blow up at any moment and go down in flames, but my safety lines are always tight.[34]

Two months before the opening date, fifteen students had signed up. The first were from Japan. Ms. Carrillo had made arrangements for comfortable living accomodations for her students at a nearby motel. Although the Circus Arts and Acrobatics Web page proclaimed "Welcome, One and All, to the newest form of recreation and exercise this side of the big top," the program also offered training for those who wish to pursue a career in circus.

Just before the school's official opening, Ms. Carrillo, in response to inquiries she had received, announced a new professional program beginning in June, 2000. (See Program Literature, p. 241.)

A month after the school opened, Ms. Carrillo reported that it was active and moving in new areas. An enhanced Circus Arts & Acrobatics Web site offered a virtual tour of the 30,000 square foot facility It also offered a variety of circus equipment including Flightights™, many kinds of trampolines, and a Flying Trapeze Rig Package that included installation and three days of instruction on equipment maintenance and safety.

> We just ran a ten week program at the Vencil Brown Elementary School with 35 fourth, fifth and sixth graders. Afterwards, they put on a children's circus; it was great fun. Today we start a summer program for the Parks and Recreation Department that will involve about a dozen classes.

> We have students signed up for the professional program that begins next month so that program is on its way. We have about 50 students using the facility. People drop in to try it out and every single drop-in has enrolled in classes. We are having the world's first Learn to Leap Night, June 17th. People pay $5 and they can swing on a trapeze or jump on a trampoline. We have had lots of birthday parties for Girls Scouts and Brownies. Corporations have approached us about doing corporate team building here.

> We are donating our services to a number of outreach programs for underprivileged kids. We work with the Rotary Club once a month at their recreation center and we work with a program for teen agers called The Star Enrichment Program.[35]

Circus Arts and Acrobatics was a unique Circus Learning institution that hoped to blend adequate resources, entrepreneurial spirit and standards of excellence. Unfortunately, the dream was not fulfilled. September 23, 2000, Ms. Carrillo announced the school's closing:

> It's official. After spending all week trying to adjust projections, cut costs and really try to negotiate a viable cash injection quantity, the bank has basically said NO to any additional funds being

injected into Circus Arts & Acrobatics. I will officially file bankruptcy next week. I'm sorry this didn't work out. There was so much left
to do and so many ideas that we just didn't have the time or money to
address. I feel like someone has awakened me from an intense dream
right in the middle of the night. No matter how I try to go back to
sleep, I can't bring the same dream back.[36]

The reasons for the failure of Circus Arts & Acrobatics are uncertain.
It started with what seemed adequate funding. Perhaps it grew too quickly
and in too many directions. It certainly lacked the governmental support such
schools receive in other countries.

Circus Sarasota School of Performing Arts

The National Circus School of Performing Arts was incorporated in
Florida in 1998 by performers Dolly Jacobs and Pedro Reis. Jacobs, a distin-
guished Roman rings performer, grew up in the circus; she is the daughter of
Ringling Brothers and Barnum & Bailey clown legend, Lou Jacobs. Reis, her
husband, is the school's Executive Director. An outstanding aerialist, he
began his career at a circus school in South Africa. He gave up performing
after a fall while with the Big Apple Circus. Their dream is to build a school
that trains professional performers as the National Circus School does in
Canada and the Centre National des Arts du Cirque does in France. The
Canadian and French schools are part of education programs that subsidize
higher education. The previous entry on Circus Arts & Acrobatics documents
another attempt to create a private professional circus school in the United
States.

The doors of the National Circus School of Performing Arts, which
had been granted status as a 501(c)3 nonprofit performing arts organization,
opened at the Ringling Museum in Sarasota for a seventeen day pilot program
May 1, 1998. Unable to find a permanent building, Reis and Jacobs had taken
out a bank loan to buy a 1400 seat European style, one ring tent that had
become available. Pitched at the corner of Interstate 75 and Fruitful in
Sarasota, the tent housed weekend shows that were fund-raisers for the school.
The shows featured Jacobs, the Flying Wallendas and others who were to be
the school's teachers when it opened in January 1999. Reis described his
plans for the school:

It will have basic acrobatics, tumbling, juggling, trapeze; we
may even be able to introduce some equestrian work. We'll start with

not more than twelve students in a five to six week program. It's a trial program - a testing ground for ourselves, not just the students.[37]

By January, 2000 the National Circus School of Performing Arts had changed its name to Circus Sarasota and had changed its mode of operation. Reis and Jacobs were still determined to establish a school that would be an important part of Sarasota, Florida which has a unique circus heritage. The name of the school would be Circus Sarasota School of Performing Arts. Sarasota was the home and winter quarters of Ringling Brothers and Barnum & Bailey for 34 years, starting in 1927 when John Ringling moved the show there. Other shows followed. Although the deterioration of the privately owned railroad tracks into Sarasota forced Ringling to leave the city, Sarasota's connection to circus is celebrated each January with the Sarasota International Circus Festival and Parade. Although some circus operations and many retired performers continue to make Sarasota their home, the role of circus in the community has waned. The Sarasota High School Sailor Circus[38] maintains an afterschool program and continues to present its shows in a tent on the school grounds, but the state owned Museum of the American Circus and the privately owned Circus Hall of Fame, have closed.

Like many performers with dreams that go beyond performance, Reis and Jacobs had to acquire business strategies that would enable them to achieve their goals. The source of funding was to be their performances, but they soon discovered that audiences were misled by the name National Circus School of Performing Arts into thinking that the performances, like those of the Sailor Circus, were amateur.   They changed the name to Circus Sarasota. During the first year, Circus Sarasota presented its performances in conjunction with the Ringling Museum. In the second year, Circus Sarasota was presented by the Van Wezel Performing Arts Organization that usually presented orchestras and touring performers. Reis and Jacobs postponed their plans for the school while they started a program to revive Sarasota's interest in circus in hope that would make the school possible.

The brand of circus Reis and Jacobs brought to the community was not the three ring extravaganza of the Ringlings, but a one ring performance. Their aim was like that of Paul Binder and Michael Christenson when they set out to introduce the one ring circus to New York, but Reis and Jacobs hoped to draw on Sarasota' unique circus heritage. Circus Sarasota's tent became the vehicle for a different kind of Circus Learning - not teaching circus skills, but teaching a community what circus art was.

Circus Sarasota sought, and found, foundation funding that enabled it to bring demonstration programs to schools and then bring the children to its tent to see a circus. Sue West, then Circus Sarasota's director of Marketing and Development, described the operation at the end of its second year.

Right now I'm finishing up a three-part program that started in the summer. The first part was the written curriculum for kindergarten through eighth grade that we developed in math, social studies and science. We introduced those into the school system and I had over 200 teachers involved. The second part of the program was educational; presentations in the school with some of our circus artists. In them, we talked about balance and demonstrated it with a couple that did plate spinning. We did juggling and had a clown who speaks fluent Japanese; while he clowned, he taught them some Japanese. We had an actor, Barney Fitzgerald, who had worked with us last summer at the Ringling Museum, play the part of Henry Ringling, the youngest brother. He talked about circus history and tied it all together.

We did it in assemblies. The show was about 45 minutes long so we did two in a day and usually covered a school. What was so amazing was that the kids were so intense. They didn't move. They didn't take their eyes off the action.

Right now we aren't teaching circus skills. It's more of just showing kids what's possible. What they can do if they work hard and that they can be whoever they want to be. It opens a lot of doors mentally for kids. I know we've touched some of them. They are totally in awe of what they see.

We did those shows right before Christmas. We spent two weeks and did about fifteen schools and now, since January we have entire schools scheduled to come to the circus tent to see a live performance. Originally when I worked with the school system they said, "Well, maybe you'll get a couple of schools interested." Well, the end result of our efforts is that I have 18 schools scheduled and over 10,000 kids.

We wrote six grants and the Venice Foundation funded the nine South County schools with $97,000. We wrote a grant for $97,000 and they gave us the full amount. Then we wrote five smaller grants and we got nine Sarasota North County schools. Out of the twenty-nine schools, we did eighteen.

Part of the funding in the grants was for bussing and I went ahead and did all of the scheduling. I hired a charter bus company and they worked with us and brought the kids in to shows. I think I spent over $35,000 on charter buses.

We have some follow up we'll do after the shows. I've got tons of letters from teachers and kids thanking us. We want to go back to the teachers and see what they felt about the program so we can tweak it a little bit before we do it next year. It was a huge undertaking. When you start something like that you don't know how big it's going to be. You plan for what will be big, but you don't have a clue until you're in the midst of it.

What we wanted to do is educate people as well as kids about the performing art part of circus. The shows for children were about two-thirds of the shows Circus Sarasota presented to the general public.

The Ringmaster this year is George Cahill who is Mr. Greenjeans on the new *Captain Kangaroo*. His script includes discussion about where the acts come from. We have a group from one of the new states in Russia. Every opportunity we get, we try to give the children a little more information than they had when they walked in. We spend an hour and a half and most of it is fun for the kids. This is the culmination of teaching them the curriculum in the schools.

A lot of people in town say to us when they hear we're going to build a circus school, "Hey, what about Sailor Circus?" The whole point is that Sailor Circus is an afterschool program for kids and it's amateur. It's a wonderful program. My daughter was in it for eight years so I know the program very well, but it doesn't give them what they need to be able to be a professional. They need the next step and that is what we would provide. So it's really a win-win for Sarasota because those kids that are committed to carrying on will be able to with us. As a matter of fact, Pedro trained one of the kids who went through Sailor Circus and he is now traveling with the Gatti Circus. He's a success story - he went to Japan for eight months last year. He's a flyer, but he does a lot of other things, too. He knows how to do all the rigging. He's learning what it takes to put a circus up and down. A lot of people can just come in and perform, but the people who are valuable are the ones who know the other stuff.

We do five year plans and we're three years ahead of where we thought we would be. We weren't planning on even starting a season last year then the tent became available and it was, "OK, let's hit the road." And now this program with the schools system is just huge! Pedro said to me. "I want you to schedule every day for January. Do you think you can?" And I said, "I'll see what happens." We had one day off the entire month of January. Between our regular season shows and our kid shows we will have done forty shows by Sunday night.

There are a lot of people who don't know the history and the heritage that is here in Sarasota. Part of our goal is to educate the entire community that circus is a good thing and it's an important part of Sarasota and it needs to be here and they need to support it.

Pedro has long range plans for a thirty acre campus where he would have his tent for the season and everything that went along with that, plus the school. We'll see what happens next year. We've done a lot better this year than last. Van Wezel helped us sell tickets and got us off to a really good start. We have changed our focus. We kind of put the cart before the horse when we started out with the NCSPA.[39]

Sue West left Circus Sarasota shortly after the interview. She turned her attention to Sailor Circus which was experiencing a major growth spurt after 51 years of operation. Aaron Watkin, Circus Sarasota's new Marketing Director, told of additional programs Circus Sarasota was developing. Laughter Unlimited is to be "a professional clown group that visits hospitals, nursing homes and other institutions, bringing smiles and laughter to children of all ages."[40] In the initial tour in the spring of 2000, a clown visited assisted living facilities.

We have two new programs this summer. The first is the world premiere of a clown and circus show called "Dan Rice and the American Circus." It will be a historic look at how the circus came from Europe to America as told through the eyes of Dan Rice. We're bringing in four clowns and another clown, an actor, to play Dan Rice. We're writing and producing the show over the summer. In the evenings, these same people will teach a series of clown workshops for four weeks in July. They'll teach juggling, clowning improvisation, mime and character development. The program will be divided into professionals, amateurs and children. It will meet every evening, six nights a week for three hours. The three groups will work separately and then come together to share ideas. Our winter show, "2001 a Circus Odyssey" opens November 26 and we are going to involve the schools again.[41]

Circus Sarasota production of Dan Rice and the American Circus, July 2000. Credit: Steve Meltzer

Certainly Sarasota is learning about circus from Circus Sarasota. Meanwhile, Circus Sarasota is continuing to define its mission. In addition to *Laughter Unlimited,* it started *Circus 4 U,* an outreach program for at risk youngsters in Sarasota and Manatee counties. One hopes that eventually Pedro Reis and Dolly Jacobs' dream of a professional school, the Circus Sarasota School of Performing Arts, will be fulfilled.

Circusschool de HOOGTE

The Circusschool de Hoogte in Leeuwarden in the Netherlands opened in 1996. The school offers a three-year professional circus training program for people 16 and up. It also has a program for children six to twelve and another for youths 12 to 16.

Admission to the professional program is based on an interview with the faculty. The first three months are probationary during which motivation, creativity and physical abilities are evaluated. If allowed to continue, the student completes the year during which he/she learns the basics of many circus skills including acrobatics, juggling, tightrope, tumbling, trapeze and unicycling. There is also instruction in ballet, modern dance and various theatre techniques.

After the first year, a student specializes in two disciplines. In the second and third year, students participate in the *Saltimbanque-group,* the school's circus-theatre show.

The faculty consists of two full time professionals who are former circus artists. Guest faculty teach ballet and mime. The School offers Weekend Workshops and an "Introduction Week" in the summer.

The Circus Space

The Circus Space in London, England has two great advantages. It is situated in a spacious historic building that has been adapted to the needs of circus training; the other is the position The Circus Space has in the circus life of the United Kingdom. The Circus Space students study in the midst of a professional circus context. Not surprisingly, The Circus Space assumed responsibility for training one hundred performers for the giant show that took place in London's Millennium Dome throughout the year 2000.

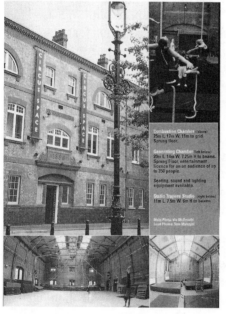

Circus Space brochure

Calling itself "The Powerhouse of Britain's Contemporary Circus", The Circus Space occupies the former Shoreditch Electricity Generating Station in Hackney on the northern edge of London. It offers a two year course for sixteen- to eighteen-year olds and in 1999 it began offering a two year degree for 18-25 year olds in Contemporary Circus in association with the Central School of Speech and Drama.

Charlie Holland, a juggler who is Program Director and Deputy Chief Executive, provided information about the facility while taking the author on a tour in February, 1998. The Generating Chamber, at that point the main space, is 55 feet long, 38 feet wide and 20 feet to the beams. There is also a static trapeze studio 30 feet long, 20 and a half feet wide and 16 feet high. The third space, the Combustion Chamber, was awaiting completion. It had a leaky roof, but housed flying trapeze equipment. By the end of the year, work on it was being completed to accommodate the Millennium 2000 students.

Describing the evolution of The Circus Space, Holland said

Circus Space was part of a regeneration program for the whole area. The funding came from a number of sources. The Foundation for Supporting the Arts gave us the first bit of money that was to be matched by the Urban Regeneration Scheme. The first bit of development was the static trapeze studio and the downstairs studio. Then we got some money from the Corporation of London and the European Regional Development Fund which took care of the frontage. We're trying to get National Lottery money so we can transform the entrance. We'd have a kind of atrium and the audience would enter into the auditorium.

We used to do a lot of work in schools. Now we're trying to go in the other direction and have things come in. We do fashion shows and corporate Christmas parties where we hire the space out. We need grants. We get a grant from the Arts Core which accounts for about a quarter of our income and the two year course is part of the Public Education system so a chunk of the tuition fees are paid for. We are now trying to get a two-year 16-18 year old program followed by a two-year 18-20 - approximate ages, so that one can do a four-year.[42]

The year after that interview, both programs were in place. The BTEC National Diploma, Performing Arts Circus, which is part of the Public Education system is described in Program Literature, p. 242.   S t u d e n t s who have completed that program, as well as others, can then participate in the BA (hons) Theatre Practice (Contemporary Circus) program which is also described in Program Literature

The Circus Space also offers adults more than fifty classes a week at all skill levels and two afterschool classes per week for children. It also provides individual tuition, short courses and plans to start teacher training.

Like many training centers, The Circus Space offers a variety of circus related services to its community. The studios and the Combustion Chamber are available for hire for rehearsals, photo shoots, TV commercials and West End show rehearsals. Circus equipment is available for rental. An agency, Acrobats Unlimited, is based at The Circus Space.

The school's integration into the British circus world is demonstrated by the way in which The Circus Space was utilized during the first six months of 1998. Those using The Circus Space included The London International Mime Festival; Average White Girl - a multi media exploration of female identity; Brit Circ - a multi media experimental circus performance; Live and Unstable, a circus performance that incorporated rock and opera; an Acrobatic Balancing weekend course; in March students from the two year course presented solo routines developed in collaboration with design students from the Central School of Speech and Drama; a cabaret; The Strawbery Clown Show; a five day course in acrobatic balancing; a program of Early Circus Films presented in conjunction with the National Film and Theatre Archive; the world premiere of Tango and Crash for a week; an aerial dramatic performance by Jeremy Robins and Lindsey Butcher who the following week presented a Creative Process Workshop; The Gandini Juggling Project involving six jugglers; performance by Albert and Friend Instant Circus, the UK's largest children's circus theatre troupe; Arboreal, a site specific environmental piece; and The Finale Show by students in the National Diploma in Performing Arts, Circus program.

For The Finale Show, students spent five weeks working with students from the Central School of Speech and Drama who collaborated on stage management, design, costume, props, sets, lighting and sound. At the same time, students at the end of the first year of the diploma program devised and toured a show to Hackney and Tower Hamlets primary schools. The final activity in June was a Try Out Cabaret in which novice and established performers presented new work with professional technical support.

The program at The Circus Space was dramatically expanded when it undertook recruiting and creating the one hundred person troupe for The Millennium Show. The first fifty students for the Millennium program started in the fall of 1998 and studied for a Certificate of Higher Education (Cert HE), equivalent to the first year of the degree course run in collaboration with the Central School of Speech and Drama. The second group, starting in April 1999, underwent training that was show specific; the students were not eligible for the Cert HE. Students in both courses received grants and help with accommodation.

The impact of the special Millenium program in the 1998-1999 academic year on The Circus Space was profound. The Combustion Chamber, whose finished state had only existed in computer generated projections when the author visited in February, 1998, was completed. The relationship with the Central School of Speech and Drama was strengthened. It enabled The Circus Space to create the four year degree sequence Charlie Holland discussed in his 1998 interview. After the Millennium Project, The Circus Space was positioned to continue to increase its role as a training institution firmly situated within the British Circus world.

Dell'Arte International School of Physical Theatre

Movement class at Dell'Arte International School of Physical Theater.
credit: Bob Pottberg

Dell'Arte was founded in 1972 by Carlo Mazzone-Clementi. Twenty years earlier, Mazzone-Clementi, along with French physical theatre proponent Jacques Lecoq, had been a member of a company co-headed by Italian clown and playwright, Dario Fo. In 1975, the Dell'Arte School moved into a former Oddfellows Hall in rural Blue Lake, California. The performing company began in 1977 "with the belief that outstanding professional theatre can be enhanced in a rural setting ."[43]

Dell'Arte offers training in physical theatre; has a touring ensemble, The Dell'arte Players Company; a summer festival, The Mad River Festival; and works with local schools in its Education Through Art program. In January and February 1999, Dell'Arte offered a Master Clown Workshop. Since 1996 Dell'arte has operated a residential program in Bali.

The goal of our trip is to introduce students to Balinese performing arts in a way that allows students to experience how the Balinese live and create, how family life and religious custom are woven into the creation of art. By studying the artists in their villages, using public transportation, learning the backroads, eating in village markets, you will have an experience of Bali very unlike the usual tourist experience.[44]

In 1998, Dell'Arte offered Summer Workshops in clowning, women in comedy, movement for actors, mask making, mask theatre, mime, spectacle and parades, generating new material, and big drums and wild dancing.

The Dell'Arte One Year Program's first term of ten weeks is called "the Education of the Self."

The development of awareness, of presence, of commitment, constructive use of voice and body; the self in relation to others (ensemble) and to the natural world. Principles of physical acting, corporeal mime, acrobatics, mask, Alexander technique, yoga, improvisation.[45]

The second 15 week term, "Truth and Size: The Styles," relates melodrama, clown and *commedia* to contemporary physical theatre. The final five week term, "The Audience," develops a show that tours remote mountain towns of northern California.

As the boundry between circus and theatre becomes less distinct, the role of schools of physical theatre is of increasing importance to both.

Ecole Supérieure des Arts du Cirque (ESAC)

ESAC, in Brussels, Belgium, offers a three year professional program in Circus Learning that enables students to develop skills and integrate them into the contemporary circus. Students acquire competency in one or two specialties, develop their own presentation of those skills and join others in end-of-year performances. Students study 35 hours a week, 1200 hours a year. In addition to circus skills, students study dance, music, design, drama, history of art, anatomy, diet, and career management.

The faculty is made up of practitioners from circus, theatre and dance. There are specialist teachers of balance, acrobatic dynamics, tumbling, juggling, and three teachers of aerial work. There are two dance teachers, two teachers of acting and a design teacher.

Class at ESAC. Credit: Xavier Claes

During the first year, students orient themselves to circus by developing strength and flexibility. They study acting, acrobatics and dance as well as aerial work, balance and juggling. At the end of the year, they choose the area – or areas - in which they will specialize. Second-year students continue the basic disciplines while pursuing their apprenticeship to their specialties. Third-year students perfect the specialties and develop their presentation of them.

Students receive evaluations four times a year in each discipline and written evaluations of their progress in their specialty. Second- and third-year students are able to study a musical instrument. First year students are offered courses in music theory.

The end-of-year performances are an important part of the curriculum. A different director is in charge each year. The performance is rehearsed six weeks.   Third-year students who present their specialties work with the director, a choreographer and a designer. Second-year students also appear in the production. First-year students work on the setting and assist the second- and third-year students.

The philosophy of the school is apparent in the questions it asks applicants. *What kind of artist do you wish to become? What is your idea of the circus of tomorrow?*

Escola Nacional de Circo

Escola Nacional de Circo in Rio de Janeiro, Brazil, is a tuition-free professional circus school that was established in the May, 1982 by the Brazilian Ministry of Culture. The School's goal is to enrich Brazil's circus traditions by helping its students achieve autonomy as circus professionals and as citizens. The school is situated in a four masted, 3,000 seat tent on a 7,600 square yard lot. In addition to the tent, which benefits from Brazil's year round moderate weather, there are classrooms, a workout gym, a dance room, a cafeteria, a physiotherapy room, a workshop for building and repairing circus equipment and administrative offices. The school offers living accommodations for students from other Brazilian states who would not otherwise be able to attend.

The school has three programs:

The Technical Course on Circus Arts is Brazil's only official professional circus arts program. In 2000 its curriculum was being evaluated to bring it in line with the requirements of Brazil's new education law. The program has a *Basic Module* that introduces students to circus skills and to the physical training that is needed for them; a *Professional Module* during which students develop competencies; and a *Specialization Module* in which students concentrate on refining one or two techniques. Workshops help students develop acts and create equipment for them.

New students are accepted each July on the basis of auditions and physical and psychological evaluations. In 1999, 350 applied to the school and 100 were accepted. At that time, 55 former students were working abroad in such companies as Cirque du Soleil and Ringling Brothers and Barnum & Bailey. In the year 2000, the school had graduated about 200. The minimum age for students is 12; there is no maximum.

The *Recycling Course* enables circus professionals to work on their acts. The three month course may be extended for an additional three months.

The *Basic Preparation Course in Circus Techniques* allows those in dance or theatre to develop projects that involve circus skills. This three month program can also be extended for an additional three months.

A student's perspective was provided by Patricia Martins. Martins studied at the school three years before being selected by Ringling Brothers and Barnum & Bailey, along with fellow student Helene Sadanha, to come to Vermont to work with Alla Youdina on a new aerial act, The Cube, for the 2001-2002 Ringling Red Unit. The third member of the act, Inna Pencheneva, was recruited in Russia.

People accepted in the school wear a school T-shirt that allows them to ride busses free for four years. During those four years, all classes and lunches are free. Most of those who audition have some experience in theatre, dance or copoeira, the African based

dance form that incorporates acrobatics. That's how I got into the school. A teacher, Silva, saw me trying to jump with some copoeira friends, and said, "Everything you are doing is wrong! Come to the Circus School and I can teach you to jump." I applied and was accepted.

Myself, I think too many are accepted. You must understand that in Rio we have a problem with many young people drifting into crime. After the slaves were given freedom,

Patricia Martins rehearsing for The Cube in Vermont

they had no place to live, no money and no opportunities. Many black people came to live in the small mountains we call *favellas* where life is very hard. The women work as servants taking care of houses and babies and the men work in hard jobs for little money. Many of the young people traffic in drugs. I think when people audition for the school the standards are not as high as I would like because the director and the teachers want to give young people a chance. Those who are in the school can use no drugs. Although the school is open to everyone, I never saw any rich students. I think that is because it is difficult for a circus artist to be rich so maybe rich people don't want their kids in the school.

When big circuses are in Rio, our director invites the performers to come to the School to practice. These professionals are a good influence on the students. There is no formal teaching of circus history, but we watch videos and our teachers tell us about it. We have classes that teach us how to put up and take care of tents.

Kids under twelve can only attend the school if they are from a circus family. I think that's wrong because the best athletes in the world start before they are twelve.

The School offers a certificate at the end of four years, but I have the impression it is not important. At every audition I have attended, no one cared about certificates. They just want to know what you can do.

While I was at the school, there were tests every semester evaluating our work. Some students drop out of the school. Most do it because of accidents that happen when they don't pay attention. If the students do not work hard enough, the director and their teacher send them to a psychologist. If it turns out that the students are lazy, they are invited to leave.

Because there are so many students, teachers have to divide their attention. We are not able to have more than four hours a day in the school. So, if I want to be a professional, I have just four hours a day, five days a week for four years. In The Cube I work with Inna, a Russian, who had many more classes than I had.

In the first six month semester at the school we experiment with everything. It is like a playground. In the second semester, we concentrate on just two or three things. The teachers like to teach and they are demanding. We do gymnastics every day, jumping, balance and aerial acrobatics. We have just one ballet class per week. We have a beautiful big tent to work in. I specialized in aerial acrobatics – tissu, web, trapeze and rings; and in working with fire. I practiced other things, too.

There are students from all over the world, especially from other parts of South America, because our school is free. The feeling at the school is very good. It is like a big family. There are many parties and everyone helps everyone else.[46]

There are examples throughout this book of Circus Learning addressing social needs. The Escola Nacional de Circo meets those needs while providing professional circus training. At the other circus schools in Brazil (see the Resource Guide, p.254.) the focus is on social service for young people, not professional training.

Espace Catastrophe

    Espace Catastrophe, in Brussels, Belgium, provides Circus Learning at many levels; it also assists performers develop, showcase and market their acts. While encouraging diversity in performance, the school has an embracing philosophy.

    The circus arts are in the midst of change. Today's circus artist goes beyond simple presentations and the purely technical to create links to dance, music and theatre. In this spirit, Catherine Magis, a multi-faceted Belgian circus artist, created Espace Catastrophe in September 1995.[47]

    The school offers four levels of training. *Discovery* involves the acquisition of basic skills; *Learning* builds on those skills; *Progress* develops the skills further; and *Specialization* completes the training. Training may be directed towards a career as a performer, towards human service work, or towards developing adult recreational activities. The school's facility includes the Hop Room which is 558 feet square with a twenty- to almost thirty-foot ceiling; the Amelikum Room that is 262 feet square with an eleven foot ceiling; and the U Room which is 200 feet square with an 11 to 20 foot ceiling.

    Full-time students take eight training sessions a week in circus skills, dance and acting. The school offers twelve-week sessions from September to December and from January to April. There is a nine-week session from April to June. Part-time training is available as is personalized advanced training adapted to individual needs. There are also intensive, short-term workshops. In 1999, the workshops were a thirty hour *Studio in the Street* about street performance; a fifty hour *The Object, the Other World of Clowns* in the context of a performance festival the school organized; and a sixty hour course in *The Clown, or Praise of Nonsense*. During 1990-2000, the school's research studios explored costume creation, juggling, games and musical instruments, and aerial dance. Espace Catastrophe's thirty-five full- and part-time faculty members come from Belgium, Bulgaria, Germany, France, Byelorussia, Spain, Chile, Brazil, Switzerland and China.

    Espace Catastrophe's festivals enable artists of various disciplines to work together to create acts. Outside companies also develop material for the festivals. In addition to developing acts, the school offers advice on management strategies, budgeting and grant and promotional writing. One of Espace

Catastrophe's 1999 Festivals, *It's Never Been Seen Before,* included performances in rooms, in cafes, on the streets, and in terrace concerts. There were also forums and debates.

The school's sponsoring organization, la Compagnie Catastrophe, is a nonprofit corporation. Espace Catastrophe receives small subsidies from the state, the region and the municipality of Saint Gille; four administrative employees are subsidized at 95% by the Brussels-Capital Region. Espace Catstrophe has developed sponsoring partnerships with press, television and radio organizations and with various companies. The school maintains national and international connections with circus, dance and theatre companies and with youth organizations.

National Circus School (École nationale de cirque)

Since 1989, the National Circus School in Montreal has occupied a spacious, historic building, the Dalhousie Railroad Station built in 1884 by the Canadian Pacific Railroad. The School was founded in 1981 by Guy Caron, co-founder of Cirque du Soleil, and Pierre Leclerc, a gymnast. In 1999, the National Circus School began granting its graduating Canadian students Diplomas in Collegial Studies in Circus Arts, accredited by the Quebec Ministry of Education. Eight years in development, the three-year program enables students to become proficient in many circus disciplines as they develop specialties and pursue academic studies. If work on a specialty is not completed by graduation, students stay on until they "get their act together" in a program called "Creating and Producing an Act." About 70% of the school's funding comes from government higher education grants to Canadian students.

The National Circus School in Montreal's Dalhousie railraod station.

Foreign students, about 30% of the student body, receive certificates at the end of a two and half year program. Foreigners are attracted to the School by its reputation which has been enhanced by its students' achievements in international festivals. Two won bronze medals at the November

1997 International Festival of Acrobatics in China and the following month one of them won a silver at the *Mondial du Cirque de Demain* in Paris. Molly Saudek, another National Circus School student, also won a silver at the Paris Festival that year for her tightwire act.[48]

Class at the National Circus School, September 24, 1997

A visit to the National Circus School's 1998 Spring Show, *Vice Versa*, demonstrated how effectively the School achieves its goal of developing circus artists. *Vice Versa* was directed by two faculty members, Pierrette Venne and Julie Lachance and by Guy Caron who returned to the School he cofounded. Kimberly Scully presented her bicycle act as a dance with a mechanical partner. The program credited her Technical Coach, Luc Tremblay, and her Artistic Counselor, Julie Lachance; both had worked with Scully since she had chosen the bicycle as her specialty. So it was with the other acts; each had technical and artistic coaches.

What infused *Vice Versa* and the School's work year-round is a vision of producing circus artists who can transform acts into something more than athletic or gymnastic tricks. Students at the School, like ballet or music students at their conservatories, master a difficult tradition as they develop abilities to create within it. The National Circus School respects tradition while it is open to new styles and rhythms of performance.

Music and ballet conservatory students usually begin their studies as children; students at the National Circus School have a variety of backgrounds. Some have done gymnastics, a few have worked with youth circuses, some have backgrounds in a specific specialty. Mark Pieklo, from the United States, who appeared in *Vice Versa* in a cradle act, juggled before coming to the school where he became interested in acrobatics and developed his body in the school's required acrobatics, balance and trampoline courses.

Unlike performers who grow up with circus families, students at the School must be oriented to the world of circus for which their immersion in the international teen pop culture has not prepared them. Pierrette Venne, acting and clowning teacher and Director of the School's Artistic Program, works to transform student attitudes in her acting classes and in the system of Artistic Counselors over which she presides.

The first year students come here, I like to get them to work in groups because in groups you have to develop generosity, humility. For me it is the values thing right from the beginning. Maybe I am an old time thinker, but it is important. The students want so much to be individuals right away in their own little world. For me they are too young.

It is too small to think only of their bike number or their trapeze number. The world doesn't go around like that. I want them to be curious about everything; to know how to work in groups. In the first year, we have in December the Evaluation Concept. For this, the group has to choose four or five different things, put them together and then show it to the School. Working in a group with a thousand ideas is difficult. The Artistic Counselor shows them when it is time to work together and when it is time that they work to be good at their own thing.

To me what is important is that when they go out from here they are autonomous, not only able to follow a director who tells them "Do this, do this," but they can understand the vocabulary and bring something to it.

I try to choose the Artistic Counselors from other fields - musicians, dancers, actors. The Artistic Counselor is not there to make their career, but to help them in the process; to give them cultural references so they are curious to go on with their creation when they are doubting if it is good and to reassure them everything is normal because the students want everything and they want it fast. They think it is easy, "Six months and I'll have it." So, when they realize it is not so easy, the Artistic Counselor supports them and says, "Welcome to the real world. It's not so easy. You can make mistakes and you can change your mind and you learn from it and you do not fix everything in three months, but creation is always moving and normal."

Sometimes they find it hard because they have to learn everything at the same time. They don't learn first the technical and then the artistic. We put the artistic consideration right there when they begin.

They are young and they zap very fast on TV. When I do acting class, it is OK when we move, but if I start to explain too long, I feel they are zapping me.

It's hard the first year because they only know two or three technical things so they have to work more on how to express them. They have to have a method to work; to respect the deadline, to respect all the other things. Sometimes they say, "I have to concentrate on my technique," and you say, "No, it is all at the same time."

We try to have them present things so we can integrate them and say, "Yes, yes." We try to accept as much as possible, but they have to learn to be directed, too. Creation is not to decide when and where you come in. Sometimes I tell them things and they look at me like I have an extra - - . I don't know if it is the new way they have been educated by their parents, but I am of the generation that can say, "No, it's not good." They are not used to that. They are not used to thinking that when they hear, "No," it is constructive.

I say to the students, "Use us. You are so lucky. Use the school; use everything." When the young people understand this and go for it, it is wonderful. Sometimes they are here a year and they don't do well, then in the show I see the lights in their eyes. They understand. It's the first time they put everything together. It's another thing when they arrive for the second year.

After they leave and don't have a job right away, they have to organize themselves. "Where will I find a place to train? I need my own trampoline. It's expensive. I need money." They organize themselves and they keep training. They do projects. They think, "Not only do I need a trampoline, but maybe a swing. I want a Chinese Pole and I can't find one. OK, I have to find a designer who will help me." Our kind of training is good; it is more complete. They can work many places. It is more than "I have my act. I have to send my video and the circus will answer me." For me it is important they work with many people with different visions, different ways, because that is reality.

I don't say any more Traditional Circus, New Circus. We need each other because we can not make New Circus if the traditional ideas don't exist. This school is different from a traditional school in Moscow even though they have dance and are so well trained. Maybe our mentality is different because we don't have any tradition. We say, "Let's do it the way we want to and the way we are." For us in Quebec - me - I have a European mentality and I'm North American. When I go to Europe, I realize how much I'm a North American. When I'm here, I'm so much a European. It is the mix that makes it very special.[49]

The acclaimed Cirque Eloize that now tours North America and Europe was started by Canadian students at the School. While they were establishing Eloize in Canada, a group of European students from the National Circus School established Cirque Pocheros in Europe.

In 1998, 46 full time students were enrolled in the professional program; an additional ten were in a high school program that provides academic education in self-paced fashion as well as circus training. The School is private; the tuition, by United States standards, modest. Students are responsible for their own food and housing which is not expensive in Montreal. Most students share apartments.

One reason for the school's success is the remarkable faculty-student ratio. The circus faculty is 19, the academic faculty, 16. There are three artistic counselors - one of whom, Julie Lachance, is also a faculty member teaching dance and tight wire. Five Russian members of the faculty were trained under the Russian circus system; Daniela Arendasova, director of the Education Department and teacher of contortion, is Slovakian. Ringling's former Creative Director-New Circus Acts, Alla Youdina, suggests that the number of Russians on a circus school faculty is a good indicator of the program's quality.

The mandatory circus curriculum at the National Circus School includes trampoline - fifteen minutes a day throughout a student's residence to help spatial orientation, acrobatics, dance, acting, music and voice. Academic classes include French Literature, Quebec Literature, Circus History and Career Management.

The weekly schedule for professional students calls for 30-45 hours of classes. Attrition at the school is slight. Christiane Barette, the School's Director of Communications and Marketing when the school was visited in 1997 and 1998, noted that, "I've been here five years and I can count on one hand those who have left. They did it in the first semester or the first year because they decided it wasn't for them. They decide on their own."[50]

Ms. Barette saw a greater problem standing in the way of students completing their work at the school.

The circus industry here in Canada has such growth that the students are solicited by the companies and the producers. The problem we have is they are lacking artists. Cirque du Soleil alone is looking for 300 artists by the year 2000. And I'm not talking about all the other producers around the world and all the agents that are looking for artists.

The kids say, "Well, if they find me good enough, maybe I'm ready." We have a problem keeping them and having them finish. That is our biggest problem at this time. They go out and work and then realize they should have completed their classes. "Why didn't I pursue the level of my act because then I would have a bigger role." They come back.[51]

Touring the school, Ms. Barette pointed out the room with exercise machines. "Here is the Torture Room. You understand why. Your muscles have to be toned. You have to be in top shape because you are demanding a lot of your body and of your soul as well because artistry here is equally important."[52]

Pierrete Venne brought her background in physical theatre, masks and *commedia dell'arte* to the School. "For me the circus is good," she says. "In theatre it is not so often we can use masks and in television it's too big so with the circus I find my family."[53] Daniela Arendasova, head of the School's Education Department, brought to the School her background in gymnastics. Her university studies included ballet, classical dance and choreography. Like Venne, she started with circus at the National Circus School.

When interviewed in 1997, Arendasova was excited by the evolution of the school's program.

This is now the second year of the implementation of the complete program. We don't have a generation that has finished the program. Before we had almost - but never a really complete program.[54]

She demonstrates a typical program by pulling folders of students.

In the first year, she has basic acrobatics, basic balance, acting, circus history, trampoline, dance, aerial flexibility and juggling. She has a choice for two hours of something she would like to do in the future as her discipline. Maybe in three years she will complete her work. Two hours the first year, five or six hours the next years and eight to ten hours the third year. Maybe she will do something very difficult and will need more time. Of course, she can stay. Many of the orientation classes to develop coordination and spatial orientation will be done in the first year. These disciplines will be replaced by others.

. . .this second year student continues her other studies and spends more time with her discipline.

. . .this third year student stays with acting, stays with dance and has two hours a day with his discipline plus some other disciplines of his choice. Here, trampoline because it is complementary for the preparation of his number. For Molly Saudek, whose discipline was tightwire, the complementary study was acrobatics.[55]

When asked about the balance between academic and circus courses, Arandasova replied:

This is something I changed this year and which I explore. Before, in the first year, it was fifteen hours of theoretical courses and ten hours of practical. The second year was to have ten hours of theoretical courses and the third year none. Now the first year is seven, the second year is eight and the third is seven. In this way the students have more opportunity to do more practical things and get into their specialty. We have an obligation from the Education Ministry - not just for us but for every college, for French, English and Philosophy. What I changed is that they start Philosophy in the second year, not the first; it works better in the second year. This way, they have two or three hours to choose their specialty. We haven't cut out anything, just moved it.

The students come here with an exact idea, but last year we had a student who at the end of her first year changed her specialty. That's why it is important that in the first year they find out what is right for them. A majority of the students are not trained when they get here. That is why there is orientation for everybody and there is no lost time even if they continue with something else. Everything they learn they use after in their discipline.[56]

Asked about the school's methods of evaluation, Arendasova explained

For the theoretical courses, it is the same as any other school - exams and so forth. For the practical courses, in the middle of the first session they have evaluations. The concern is their progress. It is just a description - not a score. We do use A, B and C. For example, I meet with one of my students and we have A for the specialty which mean the student is doing well; a B for attitude because it is fine; B for health - no injuries, no problems.

For the same student in acting, there might be a B for the specialty, a C for attitude because the student doesn't like it and A for health because there are no problems; no injuries, the student is not tired. From all of these we can see a portrait of the student and the teacher will see how the student is doing in other areas. Every teacher meets with each of his students and goes over the evaluations. The teacher may say, "You are doing fine, but if your attitude is more positive and you are more open to correction, you will do better. And your injury is coming along fine."

The students are prepared for the final evaluations because we have have been using the same evaluations all along.[57]

Students are not assigned specific advisors; the person in charge of the specialty the student is studying, usually functions as one. The School is considering a more formal advisor program. On rare occasions when students are not taking proper care of themselves, the health evaluations identify the problems.

Christiane Barette summed up the school's approach:

The philosophy of the co-founders was to create a new form of art. They wanted circus artists to be full-fledged artists and they wanted the artists to be able to express their artistic soul through circus. They based the training on that and it has evolved through the years.

Why did we fight eight years to get approval for our program from the Ministry of Education? Because we are convinced that classes like Literature and Philosophy - it's not so much that you talk about Plato, it's the fact that you are open to other things; that you know that people have thought before you. It is also to start a process of thinking that is important. We help them create their acts, but we are trying to make them responsible for their own artistry as well. When they are out there without us, they will have all the elements.[58]

Why is the program at the National Circus School so effective? What can be learned from it that can help other circus programs and other kinds of learning? The School has a remarkable faculty; having the best possible teachers is crucial. Some students can teach themselves, but they, too, need teachers who can challenge them. The School has a student-faculty ratio that keeps students in close contact with their mentors. The School has a wonderful facility in the Dalhousie Station, but the School was on its way before it moved into it. The Dalhousie facility, while excellent as far as it goes, is limited in space for the school's needs. What the facility has is a student-friendly, work-oriented design that enhances learning.

The School's continuous monitoring of students and discussing the findings with them is important. Making evaluations personal and interactive is another goal that could be pursued in non-Circus Learning situations. Most important is a clearly defined goal for learning. At the National Circus School it is the creation of adaptable circus artists; everything is part of this. Learning at the National Circus School is active, but so should it be elsewhere. Students benefit less when they are passive receivers of lectured material. Things must be taught, but students must be engaged in the process if the material is to be learned.

The National Circus School is open to students' developing interests beyond those that led them - and their parents - to choose the School. College age students are - in body and mind - flexible and adaptable to change. Just as Mark Pieklo developed his body in a new direction at the School when he discovered an interest in acrobatics, other students should be able to develop new interests; programs should be flexible enough to make this possible.

National Institute of Circus Arts

NICA LOGO

The number of circus training programs around the world that granted academic degrees grew as this book was being written. This suggests the increasing seriousness with which circus is being taken and the increasing employment opportunities that exist for skilled performers.

Australia, home of a number of traditional circuses as well as the *new* Circus Oz and the Flying Fruit Fly youth circus, became the site of a new degree granting circus program, the National Institute of Circus Arts (NICA). A facility was built in 2000 on the Prahran campus of the Swinburne University of Technology in Victoria. The course offered a three year vocational degree. Students who successfully completed the first level, *General Circus Skills*, would be awarded Certificate IV Circus Arts. Those who successfully completed level two, *Specialization in Skill Areas*, would be awarded the Diploma in Circus Arts. Students who successfully completed level three, *Creation of Performance or Individual Acts*, would be awarded Australia's first Bachelor of Circus Arts.

As she was engaged on a national tour to recruit students with backgrounds in sports, dance or circus for the Institute, Director Pamela Creed wrote:

> Modern Circus is experiencing extraordinary growth at an international level and Australian contemporary circus and physical theatre companies are in high demand both here and overseas. NICA will play an important role in this development over the next ten years.[59]

NICA's tuition is reasonable. Scholarships are available and international students are encouraged to apply.

NY Goofs

NY Goofs Ultimate Clown School, 1999. credit: Maike Schulz

Dick Monday directed the Ringling Brothers and Barnum & Bailey Clown College during its final three years. When it was disbanded, he returned to New York City and founded NY Goofs with Tiffany Riley. The Goofs became a performing group of fine professional clowns including, on occasion, Barry Lubin whose Grandma was featured on the Big Apple Circus for many years; and a teaching group. During the summers of 1999 and 2000, NY Goofs offered a one-week workshop, *The Ultimate Clown School.* The first year it attracted 12 students, the second year, 20. The possibility of two classes – one beginning and one advanced, was considered for 2001. In 2000, the program ran from 10 AM to six PM and culminated in a public presentation by fully madeup and costumed clowns of exercises from the classes. Classes included clowning; character development taught by Larry Pisoni, founder of the Pickle Family Circus; juggling taught by Hovey Burgess who was largely responsible for developing interest in Circus Learning in the United States; clown history, dance, movement taught by Barbara Carter; makeup taught by Mark Renfro of Ringling's Clown College; and improvisation. In the evenings, there were open workshops.

The NY Goofs does not have a permanent location and the decision whether its primary focus is performance or teaching has not yet been established. Dick Monday says, "We're teaching classes and workshops and we're performing regularly trying to make a living."[60] Asked about the possibility of trying to establish a private clown school, he said,

> I haven't dived out of the plane full force yet after being in charge of that incredible institution for three years. Before that, I had a fairly good theatrical and performance career in LA for fifteen years. Now, back in New York I feel a real drive to be a performer again and a writer and a director. It's a major decision. The first year has been interesting. I realize that being an educator and running an institution doesn't necessarily run in the same direction as being a performer. There are two different mind sets. I thought I could do both of them and I've learned that's not necessarily the case. I am getting a lot of urging from members of the community to take on a fulltime clown school and I think that would be great. At the same time, I need to be a little selfish before I say that's exactly what I'm going to do.

> What I haven't seen in this country is development of the trio format of clowning. The Goofs have spent months workshoping trio development. In America we've had a couple of great trios, but we always look to Europe to see the trio.[61]

NY Goofs also experimented with developing a full-length play, *Noses Off*, based on the career of the great American clown, Slivers Oakley. What is unique about the NY Goofs is that Monday and his associates are pursuing their own Circus Learning as they are teaching others. In both teaching and performance the goal is the same.

> We are working at developing new ways to approach comedy, develop relationships, heighten character, and utilize timing in solo, duo and trio clowning. By focusing on the theatrical and one ring environment, it allows us to think in subtler, less frantic, terms than in the three ring environment. As clowns, the circus skills are very important, but character is first on the list.[62]

The San Francisco School of Circus Arts

THE SAN FRANCISCO SCHOOL OF CIRCUS ARTS
and its
SAN FRANCISCO CIRCUS
IN ASSOCIATION WITH FRIENDS OF OLYMPIA STATION
and its
NEW PICKLE CIRCUS
present

YU SAN
(HARMONY) BLUELIGHT
NEAL CORMIER 1999

Flyer for the 1999-2000 Holiday Show presented by the San Francisco School of Circus Arts performing company

The San Francisco School of Circus Arts, like the Big Apple Circus, has roots in the counterculture street theatre of the 1970's. The San Francisco School of Circus was originally part of the Pickle Family Circus, like Big Apple, a pioneer of the *new circus*. The Big Apple's original plan was to move the energy of the streets into Big Apple performances through its New York School for the Circus Arts. The Pickle Circus did not start with an idea of a school. When it opened one, the school was to provide recreational circus skills training for children and adults in the Pickle training facility.

Judy Finelli, Pickle Family performer and Artistic Director from 1987 to 1990, founded the Pickle Family Circus School in 1991 with another Pickle performer, Wendy Parkman. The school acquired a large brick building that had once housed Polytechnical High School. Finelli was the first Artistic Director of the school, Parkman succeeded her. In 1990, Finelli had brought Lu Yi, former Artistic Director and star of the Nanjing Acrobatic Troupe, to the Pickle Circus. When the school separated from the Circus and was renamed the San Francisco School of Circus Arts, Lu Yi became one of its most important teachers.

The school now offers professional training as well as children's classes, many of which are taught by Parkman who embodies the history of the school. "I was lucky to be part of a wave of circus interest that hit San

Francisco in '74 and '75 - it was a circus renaissance. In those days circuses were part of social and political movements."[63] In addition to her duties at the San Francisco School of Circus Arts, Parkman assists student circus groups at Oakland's Prescot High School and Lincoln Middle School in Alameda.

The children's courses at the San Francisco School of Circus Arts are beginning and advanced. There is an introductory Circus Arts class for students ages 5-12.

The basic elements of circus are taught in an environment which is fun, supportive and cooperative. This program uses Circus Arts and circus equipment to allow children to explore their abilities, giving them an opportunity to grow in confidence and self-esteem. Each class consists of a warm-up, tumbling and work on circus equipment such as Trapeze, Mini-Tramp, Rola Bola and Globe.[64]

There is also a class in Chinese Acrobatics for children 7-17. The school offers scholarships to children who otherwise could not attend. A dozen child and teenage students of the school perform as The San Francisco Circus which was started by Lu Yi in 1996; the focus of the performances is acrobatics. In 1998, San Francisco School of Circus Arts also had a summer Circus Day Camp.

Adult classes are now attended by the majority of the more than 200 students at the school. The classes include Circus 101, an introductory class; Conditioning and Body Awareness; Theater and Dance (Clowning and Physical comedy, Dance/Movement for Circus, Stage Combat); Trapeze and Aerial Skills (Flying Trapeze, Static Trapeze, Rope and Aerial Hoop); Trampoline; Juggling; Acrobatics (Chinese Acrobatics, Chinese Poles, Chinese Hoop Diving, Teeterboard, Doubles and Hand to Hand, and Contortion.)

The Principal Instructors in the winter of 1999 were Lu Yi who has 40 years performing and teaching in Nanjing and with Big Apple and Circus Oz; Scott Cameron - Flying Trapeze; Jim Donak – Trampoline; and Richard Lane - Stage Combat. The 1997 catalog listed twenty instructors.

Unlike the degree granting, well-funded National Circus School in its comfortable building in Montreal, the San Francisco School of Circus Arts operates in austere quarters. "The brick gym, built in 1912, is so cold that parents bundle up in winter coats, gloves and scarves when they come to watch their children train."[65] The San Francisco School of Circus Arts offers courses, but it is up to individuals to create their programs with the school's advice. (See Program Literature, p. 243.)

The San Francisco School of the Circus Arts shares its space with the New Pickle Family Circus and with Make*A*Circus "America's original participatory circus/theater dedicated to empowering and celebrating children and their communities." Make*A*Circus, started in 1974 by Englishman Peter Grankham as a version of London's Circus with a Purpose, offers a Clown therapy program for adults and children who are physically and emotionally challenged, a Teen Apprentice program that employs at-risk teenagers, School Tours and other special events. Make*A*Circus continues the social activism that was part of the impetus for the Pickle Family Circus in the 1970's and offers students of the San Francisco School of Circus Arts ways to use their skills in the community.

The State College of Circus and Variety Art (GUTsI)

Circus arts – especially satiric clowning - are part of Russian folk tradition. When the Byzantine church took root in Russia, tradition says that it encouraged folk artists to perform in front of churches to attract people to them. Eventually, the story goes, the church and the government grew unhappy with the popularity of the irreverent performers who were forced underground.

At least as early as the eleventh century, Russia had its own mimes and minstrels, the *skomorkhi*. These itinerant showmen displayed trained bears and performed as comedians and acrobats; they were quite similar to the medieval mimes of Western Europe, and cross influences are quite probable. They performed not for the rich but for the common people. Later they also came to be called *vatagami*, meaning "for the masses," and were sufficiently political for the government to fear their popularity. In 1648, just one year after a bloody revolt in Moscow, Czar Alexis I (father of Peter the Great) issued an edict banning the performances of the *skomorokhi*.[66]

When the circus was introduced to Russia at the end of the eighteenth century, it incorporated the satiric folk tradition. The Durov brothers' entered the rings in pre-revolutionary Russia introducing themselves as "King of Jesters, but never the King's Jester! The Jester to his Majesty the People!"[67]. Their trained animals parodied those in power. The musical and acrobatic team of Bim-Bom offered topical parodies from 1891 to 1946.

After the Russian Revolution, Anatoli Visilievich Lunacharsky, the People's Commisar for Education, drew on this tradition to further the Revolution. However, clowns would no longer wear masks and the heavy makeup associated with bourgeoise performance under the Czars. There was also to be a positive aspect to circus – acrobatics would demonstrate the beauty of the new Soviet people. Lunacharsky laid out the goals of the new government's circus program in an article "The Problem of Revitalization of the Circus" in the third issue of the magazine, *Messenger of Art* in 1919.

Among the basic components of the circus spectacle, Lunacharsky listed the display of human physical beauty, courage, daring as well as clowning of all kinds, especially its satirical aspect. As he put it, 'Clowns dare to be publicists.'[68]

That year, the Ministry of Education established a government bureau, *SECCIRCA,* to oversee circus. In 1931 the State Association of Musical, Stage and Circus Enterprises, *GOMETs,* integrated the administration of circuses with that of the philharmonic and stage organizations.

Training programs were established in 1928. The Workshop of Circus Arts, *WCA,* retrained established circus artists while the Workshop of Courses of Circus Art, *CCA,* trained new performers with a three year curriculum. After the first *CCA* class graduated, training was expanded in the Technical Institute of Circus Art, *TICA,* that erected a training arena that was the site of a student showcase, The Regional Circus. *TICA* became the State College of Circus and Variety Art, *GUTsI,* in 1934. A seven-year physical education and acrobatics division for children was established in 1960. *GUTsI* added a stage-craft department in 1961. Throughout its existence, *GUTsI* granted over 2,000 diplomas. Many graduates became masters of the Soviet Circus and were widely known abroad. *GUTsI* helped establish circus schools in Hungary, Bulgaria, East Germany, Poland, Mongolia, Cuba and other countries.

American Leon Harris visited the children's acrobatics school in Moscow in 1970.[69] He noted that one applicant in seventy was accepted. Students at the school continued their academic studies while developing skill in acrobatics, gymnastics, balance and juggling. They also studied dance and all aspects of circus. There was one teacher to each five or six students. Students studied six days a week from 8:30 to 3:30 and had at least two hours each day in the rings.

At 14 or 15, after the eighth grade, students entered *GUTsI* where they were joined by other students who had demonstrated outstanding talent. Graduates of the preliminary program skipped the first year of *GUTsI*. 500 students studied at *GUTsI* with more than 120 coaches in a building with two training rings. GUTsI, financed by the national educational system, was operated by the national circus system, *SoyuzGostsirk*. The first two years of study developed skills in all the circus disciplines while students learned about the history of the circus and the history of art. A panel of experts then assigned students areas of specialization. At the end of four years, students participated in a graduation performance, received a diploma and were guaranteed employment in 73 circus buildings throughout the Soviet Union. After twenty years, performers received a pension whether they continued to work or not. An additional appeal of circus training in Soviet days was that it offered young people an opportunity to travel outside the country as circuses, even in Iron Curtain times, were Soviet cultural ambassadors throughout the world.

The national circus organization, later *RosGostsirk,* maintained the quality of circus performances. While some *GUTsI* graduates went directly into performance if their acts were deemed ready, others, whose acts needed work or who had lost act members to the Soviet military, worked in Studios maintained by the circus system. There, acts received additional coaching, costuming, design and whatever was necessary. In pre-*Perstroika* days, the budget for the Studios was large. In addition to developing individual acts, the Studios produced entire shows such as the Moscow Circus on Ice and magic shows that employed fifty or sixty performers

Since *Perstroika,* much has changed. The government program to prepare youngsters for *GUTSi* has been eliminated. Business and computers now offer young Russians more remunerative ways to travel; a career in circus offers no certainties. Graduates of *GUTsI* are no longer guaranteed work. Some are offered one year contracts by *RosGostsirk* which manages slightly more than half the circus buildings it controlled before the newly independent republics reclaimed their buildings. The remaining Russian circus buildings are not in full-time use.

Currently, the circus program operated by North Korea's Ministry of Culture echoes that which existed in the days of the Soviet Union. The 500 performers in Moranbong Circus are divided into troupes at Moranbong and Pyongyang where performances exalt the government while demonstrating the physical grace and artistry of its citizens.

Behind North Korea's skilled circuses is a highly selective and regimented government training program. Children are taught circus routines at an early age in primary schools. After six to seven years of training, the top students are selected to join the Pyongyang and Moranbong troupes.[70]

The Russian circus training system that provided a model for circus schools throughout the world, continues. There is still a free, four-year degree program at *GUTsI* for which Russian students audition. However, as educational subsidies have been cut, the number of students has shrunk to approximately one hundred. The hardships of life in the new Russia affect *GUTsI*. Practice sessions used to last as long as three hours; they are now limited to half an hour because of the expense of electricity. The school has opened its doors to foreigners whose dollars help subsidize the diminished program. Meanwhile, Russian coaches, trained under the old system, bring their commitment to circus art to many of the new schools the Russian circus system inspired.

Ward Alexander's College of Complexes Circus and Carnival Studios
This whimsically titled venture is the retirement activity of Ward Alexander, a former sway pole artist and catcher in flying acts. Alexander now owns title to the Flying Wards acts in which he used to perform. His twelve acre site in Newbury, Florida features sway pole, flying and cradle rigging, a circus ring and a stage. Alexander creates Flying Wards acts that perform overseas where the pay is better than in the United States. He offers other professional training on an ad hoc basis. Although his priority is professional training, he also offers one week introductory courses in circus skills. Alexander is also a show painter, rigger and tattoo artist. All these services keep his retirement active.

Zippo's Academy of Circus Arts (ZACA)
Martin "Zippo" Burton is is a clown whose work is featured in Zippo's Circus which tours the United Kingdom. Burton also heads Laughtercare that brings clowning to hospitals and Zippo's Academy of Circus Arts (ZACA) which he established in 1992 and described in a 1999 Email response to an inquiry:

Zippos Circus, Victoria Park Finchley,
September 19, 1999

Zippo's Academy of Circus Arts offers an intensive six months training course in circus skills. Performance forms a vital part of the training. It is my belief that we all tend to be a little lazy and that knowing you are going to be performing in front of the public tonight is a great incentive to get you working hard on act/costume/props/skills.

Basically, months one and two are spent gaining a foundation in a wide variety of circus skills, getting fit and learning to live on a circus. At this time ZACA is based alongside the main commercial circus.

Months three and four, the students, their teachers, trainers and crew go off on their own, performing at weekends while traveling around Britain. Most of these gigs are of the state fair/country fair show type and each student contributes to the show what they can. There is no pressure to perform if the student is not ready, although every student is encouraged to have a go.

Months five and six are back with the main circus and each student, who by now is focussed and has a much better idea of what circus is all about and what part they want to play in circus. During these last two months, each student specializes in their own chosen act(s) and at the end of the ZACA course we present a showcase performance to an invited audience of agents, circus directors, friends and family and those student who want to go on and work in circus are introduced to all the agents/circus directors with a view to getting contracts.[71]

This survey of professional circus learning which is far from complete, suggests the range of training available for those who wish to enter the world of circus and physical theatre. It also suggests how significant direct government support or indirect support in the form of education grants are to professional training programs.

III
Touring Youth Circuses

Touring youth circuses provide unique opportunities for Circus Learning. Young people experience circus life both as support personnel and performers while presenting performances under a wide variety of circumstances. At the same time, they assume responsibilities for sustaining a traveling community.

CIRCUSES

Circus Ethiopia

Circus Ethiopia was begun in 1991 by Marc La Chance, a Canadian who had arrived the previous year to teach at the International Community School in Addia Ababa. While bicycling to work, he was struck by the needs of young people he passed in the streets. When young Ethiopian Jews, waiting in a compound for flight to Israel, were entertained by some acrobats, their interest was aroused. With La Chance's help, practices began. At first the goal was learning skills; performances came later and Circus Ethiopia developed.

Circus was new to Ethiopia and has had profound meaning, especially for poor children who find in circus a sense of community and focus for their lives. The success in Addis Ababa was emulated elsewhere in the country. In 1993 Circus Jimma started and in 1994 Circus Tigray and Circus Nazareth. The four circuses make up the Circus In Ethiopia Association sharing resources and ideas. By 1998, six additional Ethiopian circuses had started. Each follows the same pattern; after-school rehearsals during the week and performances at home and on the road on the weekend. Performances are accompanied by messages about sanitation, AIDS, polio, land mines, violence and poverty.

Circus Ethiopia has developed its own style of performance. According to Aweke Emeru, director of Circus Ethiopia

When we started Circus Ethiopia, we began by copying Western Circus tradition. However, today we are evolving our own Ethiopian form of circus, combining many of our own cultural traditions. For instance, the western circus focuses traditionally on the individual act with the drum roll highlighting the individual drama and danger. Our style is more of a group activity, with less emphasis on individual acts of daring. We also incorporate many traditional cultural elements of dance and song in our routines.

The most important thing we are aiming at is to build our own circus centers where we can live and work, where different ideas and energies of different people come together. With the help of circus, we want to show our culture to other countries, but to achieve this, we must live together. We are getting land in the four cities where the circuses are established and with the help of the international tour revenues and friendly organizations we are planning to establish the circus movement in a permanent way. Within these centers we also want to establish training facilities for many different jobs for our youth.[72]

In each location the circus has become a kind of family serving youngsters from a variety of religious and economic backgrounds. Each circus has three components:

The Performance Group performs every week free of charge in open spaces. Performance Groups also tour internationally. Companies, drawn from the four circuses in the Association, travel abroad under the name Circus Ethiopia. They have performed to great acclaim raising money to support their work. At home, the 160 boys and girls aged 8-21 in the Circus in Ethiopia Performance Groups follow their regular schooling and receive tutorial classes provided by the circus. Members of the Performance Groups receive transportation allowances, medical care, and meals. When needed, Circus Ethiopia provides accommodation near the Circus Compounds.

The Circus Schools, which include living accommodations and workshops for learning trades, teach circus skills to children from the community. The teachers are members of the Performance Groups.

The Street Kids Program is for homeless and working children who rehearse three times a week. Performance Group members are the teachers; students receive a meal at the end of each practice and transportation money.

One of the overseas supporters of Circus Ethiopia is Cirque du Soleil. Since 1991, videos and music from Soleil performances have set standards for the work in Ethiopia. Beginning in 1993, Cirque du Soleil supplied shipments of costumes and sound equipment and has held benefit performances to aid Circus Ethiopia.

Ethiopia, which had no tradition of circus, now has a thriving one that is true to the nation's culture.

Circus Smirkus

Pirates juggle in the 2000 Circus Smirkus show
"The Voyage of the Pirate Queen."

The performers in Circus Smirkus, based in Greensboro, Vermont, officially range in age from ten to nineteen, although the requirement is flexible and some as young as nine have participated in the six week tour in July and August. There are usually about thirty young performers in the troupe as well as some adult coaches. Shows are given in a tent; performers live in host homes along the way. Sometimes Smirkus alumni arrive during the season and work their way into the show as Toby Ayer, then a student at Oxford, did in the '97 season. Midseason he was helping with rigging, by the end of the tour he was juggling. Rob Mermin, the show's director, usually appears.

Head Coach and Artistic Director, Alla Youdina, took leave from the Ringling organization each year for the two-week Smirkus rehearsal until she took a leave from Smirkus at the end of the 1999 season. Until then, she kept in touch with Mermin during the year as they planned the show. This became easier when Youdina built a home near Smirkus in 1998.

Coaches not involved in the tour help staff the Circus Smirkus Camp that opens after Circus Smirkus starts its summer tour. The quality of Smirkus coaches was demonstrated in 1998 when they joined Mermin in an off-season, indoor show, *Rockin' Robin's Rock and Roll Circus.* Chimgee Haltarhuu, a veteran of the Mongolian Circus and Ringling, did hand balancing with her 13 year old son Tamir, a Smirkus performer. She also did hula hoops and foot juggling. Velodia Augustov, of the Moscow Circus, did a comic slack wire act and partner handbalancing with his wife Zena who did a one armed handstand on his head. Together they presented a remarkable display by house cats and a mongrel dog; the animals participated in Augustov's Perch Pole act. The coaches demonstrated how attractive and effective mature circus performers can be. They were joined by another Smirkus coach, former Ringling clown, Troy Wunderle and his wife Sara. Troy, sometimes aided by Sara, conducts Smirkus' school residencies in the winter. (See Chapter Six.)

In 1998, the eleventh year for Circus Smirkus, the show performed under a handsome new Italian Big Top that replaced the small tent whose many holes had been patched with stars relating them to the star-filled Circus Smirkus logo. Five new performers were selected by audition or from video tapes if the applicants were too far away to attend auditions. The new "Smirkos" joined twenty-five veterans who come from as far off as England and Israel. Performers pay tuition although the application makes clear that "No one is denied participation because of financial need."

In the 1990's, each year's show was built around a theme. In 1999 it was Robin Hood. That show became the subject of a 15 part television documentary, *Totally Circus*, that ran on the Disney Channel in the summer of 2000 and was repeated twice. In 1998 the theme was *The Circus Smirkus Rock and Roll Tour;* in '97, *The Tenth Anniversary Birthday Party Tour.* Some themes develop from guest performers. 1992's *East Meets West* brought together youngsters from the Great Y Circus in Redlands, California and from Moldavia, Russia and Kazakstan. In 1990 it was *Moscow Youth Circus Meets Circus Smirkus.* In 1998, after months of negotiation, Circus Smirkus included Chinese performers who arrived just before the show opened. As an institution with slender resources, Circus Smirkus has to raise special money to pay the expenses of foreign guests. The Freeman Foundation awarded Smirkus $37,500 to bring the Chinese. Through the changing themes and guests, regular patrons watch continuing acts develop: Chris Grabher and Lisa Taylor-Parisi's double tightwire act, Sam Johnson's slack wire, Tamir Bayarsaihan's balancing and acrobatic skills.

A Smirkus performance is a communal effort. People featured in one act reappear handling rigging and props in the next. Although many performers develop specialties, all are generalists and appear in many acts. Acrobatics and juggling are shared activities and clowns reappear in other guises. The show opens with a *charivari* in which the entire company presents an array of acrobatics. Mermin, a fine clown, acrobat and musician, usually appears through the show and is often responsible for a quiet moment toward the end of each performance. One year he played a soulful cornet while keeping a feather aloft with the breath from his instrument; in the tenth anniversary show he was surrounded by his performers as they basked in the glow of the show's birthday cake. Good clown that he is, the quiet moments are never saccharine, but welcome changes of pace.

The 1998 Rock and Roll show was preceded by performers introducing audience members to circus skills, something Smirkus was doing before Ringling Brothers and Barnum & Bailey started its Three Ring Adventure®. The show's acts included three people on a Gym Wheel to surfer music; three people doing rolla bolla on surf boards; team juggling; single trapeze, two-person Lyre; two-person strap act; a clown car routine that involved most of the company; chair balancing; slack wire that included unicycle and hand balancing on the wire; two-person tightwire danced to fifties music; and a fourteen-person cradle and strap act. The Chinese guests did contortion and hand balancing.

Amanda Crockett, who became a Smirko the summer after graduating high school described the Smirkus Experience:

There is a magic about that place that I, and so many others, are addicted to. It is family. It is home. And it is an interesting phenomenon. . . . people spending ten months of the year looking forward to, and preparing for, those two months of Smirkus. The summer becomes the main part of the year and all else becomes less important. After a summer at Smirkus, your priorities change, the way you view things and approach challenges change, I believe. It's part of being/becoming a "Smirko."[73]

Circus Smirkus and other Vermont institutions created during the Vietnam War era - Ben and Jerry's Ice Cream, The Bread and Puppet Theatre - made their idealism integral to their success. Bread and Puppet is still animated by its original ideology thanks to the continuing control of its founders Peter and Elka Schumann. Ben and Jerry's, while continuing to support community activities like Circus Smirkus, experienced identity problems as the operation grew and Ben and Jerry stepped back from direct control which was assumed by the Unilever Corporation. How much of the ice cream company's counterculture ideology will survive remains to be seen. Circus Smirkus, like Bread and Puppet, is still under its original management, but its slogan has shifted from "Vermont's Own Home-Grown Country Circus" to "A non-profit organization serving youth, communities and business."

Things may change as the Circus and the Camp grow in the wake of the attention derived from the *Totally Circus* documentary. There are plans to make Circus Smirkus a year-round operation. Whether Mermin will always appear in the Circus is uncertain. His presence brings performances continuity and the traveling Smirkus community consistent leadership, but touring means he can not be as involved with the Camp as he wishes. He used to do the Smirkus school residencies before he trained Troy Wunderle to conduct them. When Mermin relinquished his role in the performances of Circus Smirkus during the year he was co-director of Ringling's Clown College, the show, still good, lacked his presence. Circus Smirkus is very much a projection of his imagination and persona which combine openness and gentleness with rigor and a strong work ethic. At times he seems a guru of a sixties commune, but one with a firm sense of direction. As Karen Saudek, two of whose children spent years with Smirkus has said, "Rob is a major Pied Piper."[74]

Mermin's leadership is reflected in the daily community meetings Smirkos hold to keep everything on course. Mermin describes them this way:

These meetings are held in the barn studio every evening after dinner and chores and in the circus ring on tour. The council leader is whoever takes the "council club" - an old juggling club from the first season. It is quite fun to watch the mood of the council takes its flavor from each different leader, especially when a ten year old, filled with purpose and sudden authority over the teenagers, takes the club in all its solemnity.

Everything and anything can be discussed and voted upon, from variable age-level bedtimes to personal problems, chores and the show itself. Since there are three times as many troupers as adults, it is not easy to pull rank and majority rules. It is understood that rules are really guidelines for survival in these close living and working conditions. The first rule is this: we are willing to make changes in rules easily, if we are willing to change back easily if it doesn't work.

As circus proprietor, I often make quite natural attempts to swindle, sucker or bribe the meeting into agreeing with my opinion, but these are kids: they see right through me.[75]

Alla Youdina experienced culture shock when she first encountered council meetings.

When Rob called his first council meeting with the American kids when they were in Russia, it really shook my system. We only have meetings from the top down called in a crisis, and we only listen. I thought anxiously, what is the crisis here? But the kids sat around and talked to Rob, the boss, so boldly. None of the Russians understood what was happening. Now I see it is just a natural expression of their feelings and Rob accepted it, even asked for it.

Since that beginning there has been a growing spark of mutual understanding. I share Rob's dream to more and more share cultures and art and to find an outlet for talented people to showcase their creativity through groups like Smirkus. Our goal is always to reach one creative horizon and then naturally see the next horizon, always moving horizons. In Smirkus we are always striving for higher standards of art and for higher values in living together, so for us each summer is always like a new horizon.[76]

Circus Smirkus performances are integrated presentations of themes. This allies Smirkus with the *new* style of circus performance associated with Cirque du Soleil and Big Apple. More important than the themes is the idealism that animates the Circus Smirkus training and performances. Mastering skills is never enough, it is employing them in an endeavor that enriches the performers' lives and that of their audiences. Time will tell how the proposed changes will affect the unique Smirkus identity .

The Flying Fruit Fly Circus
The Flying Fruit Fly Circus - Ordinary Kids Doing Extraordinary Things, is a year-round operation in Australia that has its own training school. Begun in 1980, The Year of the Child, as a circus project of the Murray River Performing Group, The Flying Fruit Fly Circus soon established its own identity and was touring. The school, first known as The Acrobatic Arts Community School then as the Flying Fruit Fly Circus School, was estab-

Flying Fruit Fly Circus program cover

lished in 1987 in conjunction with the Wodonga High School in Albury, Victoria. The school features a full academic program as well as circus training. The idealism that animates the circus and the school can be seen as one looks at the school which is

a Victorian State School that caters for students from Year 3 to Year 10. AACS is an exciting innovation in Australian education, utilizing a combination of standard education and the amazing performance and life experience provided by a life in the circus.

Students can start at any level after Year 3. However, as circus performers, the most benefit is gained if you join before year 8. Any child with an interest in circus skills is invited to enter the school by participating in the Community Intake Kids Scheme (CIKS) and a special orientation program. This project entails intensive training sessions and, on completion, assessments are made. Selection and recommendations will be given to each participant at this time.

Prospective students and their families must also be prepared for hard physical work, a strong commitment and a challenging academic program.[77]

Tim Matthews, Coordinator of the School, adds:

The Victorian government funds our school under an extraordinary model. No other schools are funded quite as generously as we are, which is fine, but we never have enough to realize all our ambitions anyway. Students pay a school levy and a transport levy. The school is about six kilometers away from our training facility, which is a nuisance. It is, however, in the next state (New South Wales) which is OK since it enables Fruit Fly to tap another source of government funds. Students don't pay a fee for training, although that very matter was raised for serious discussion at a recent Board meeting. Economic climates have a way of sneaking up on one!

The balance between academic and circus is achieved in two ways. One, some circus training is included in the school curriculum. It stands next to English, Maths, Science, etc. Further training is delivered outside school hours. During school time, training tends to focus on physical conditioning and skill acquisition. Afterschool training is directed towards act development and rehearsal.

School staff includes two teachers of classes at year levels 3-6 (ages 8-12) and 3.5 teachers of subjects (in Victoria's current vocabulary "key learning areas') to year levels 7-10 (ages 13-16.) Circus staff includes directors of training, performance (Artistic Director), business/marketing. There are then three further trainers, another administrative officer, and a tour manager. Whilst school and circus are legally and financially quite separate entities, we are close in practice - to say the least!

There are no specific grants for students. Their funding is guaranteed at school by virtue of being enrolled. Their funding at circus is a permanent struggle. Our students are, roughly speaking, too young to access state and federal training budgets, already catered for in education budgets, and are funded for performance (not training) by state and federal arts budgets.

School staff accompany tours acting in a variety of capacities, but attempting to include a variety of recognizable educational activities. Life in the performing arts is, I think, an education in the real world of work of necessity. Sometimes the textbooks do come out, however.[78]

The commitment to academic education is strong. "The curriculum is designed to ensure that when students have fulfilled their work obligations, they can transfer successfully to complete their V.C.E. in Victoria and the H.S.C. in New South Wales."[79]

The school is more than a school that has added circus to its curriculum. It stresses students' understanding the consequences of their actions with strong emphasis on conflict resolution. The school encourages self-discipline, respect for the rights of others and is committed to equal opportunity, inclusiveness and social justice. Parents are involved through a weekly newsletter and school committees as the school believes education is a responsibility shared by families and school. The program links intellectual and problem solving activities with self-expression and creativity. The goal is not creating circus professionals, but providing students the ability to determine their future. The school works to respond to individual needs while teaching students to work in groups.

The Flying Fruit Fly production, *Outburst: Children of the Sun* began a two year tour in 1997. The performance included poles, trampoline, group bicycle, rolla bolla, cloudswing, silk, juggling, solo trapeze, double trapeze, chair balancing, and casting. While the Outburst company numbered 26 ranging in age from 9 to 17, 53 "Kids in Training Back Home" were at the school. The Flying Fruit Fly circus training staff in 1997 was ten supplemented by three guest trainers.

The Flying Fruit Fly Circus has integrated foreign trainers into its program. In 1983, the Nanjing Acrobatic Troupe of China started a training project with Flying Fruit Fly and other Australian circus performers. In 1987, eight Fruit Flies spent three months in China training with the Guangzhou Acrobatic troupe. In 1991, Fruit Fly hosted the first National Training Project for circus performers and trainers from all over Australia. In 1992, trainers from The Moscow Circus worked with Fruit Fly for three months; the resulting show, *Red Alert* toured widely. In 1995, Fruit Fly had a training project with the Naingrada Clever Kids in Arnhem Land in the Northern Territory and in 1998 six people from Fruit Fly spent a week with Circus Ethiopia in Sydney and two trainers from Circus Eritrea were in residence for a year.

Despite this achievement, all has not been rosy financially. In 1996, facing extinction, Flying Fruit Fly mounted a public relations campaign that saved it. One of the results was a decision by the Arts Ministry to grant $30,000 for a business analysis of the circus and an examination of future funding options. An additional $50,000 was to be awarded from the

Department of Employment Education and Training to explore the situation, but when it became clear that such entry level programs would neither meet the needs of the circus nor be an appropriate use of those funds, "the Government has decided to increase the funding to the circus by a total of $600,000. The first payment was paid in 1995-1996 and equivalent amounts will be made in the next three financial years."[80]

Like professional circus schools in many nations that receive government aid directly or through education grants given students, the Flying Fruit Fly Circus has demonstrated how much can be achieved when there is official recognition of the value of Circus Learning.

Hiccup Circus

Graham Ellis, an English juggler and former teacher, created Hiccup Circus - the name is an acronym for Hawaii Island Community Circus Unity Program, in Pahoa, Hawaii. The Hiccup Circus is a component of Hawaii's Volcano Circus, a collective that has been teaching circus arts in Hawaii since 1981. Since 1983 Volcano has sponsored an annual international juggling festival that has grown from 60 to 200 participants. Volcano claims to be resurrecting traditional Hawaiian activities that included stilt walking, balancing games and magic. A Volcano brochure notes that Captain Cook's party wrote of seeing children juggling.

Ellis described the origins of the Hiccup Circus within Volcano:

> We started out about ten years ago as an afterschool program for kids and it was very popular and expanded. We got invited to do a couple shows and so we put a performing group together and before we knew it, we had a kids' circus and we were in big demand. Since then our afterschool programs have expanded to five different locations, three days a week and engage more than 180 students with a wide variety of ethnic backgrounds. We've been going into elementary schools and offering a program called Juggling for Success which is run by Dave Finnegan, the National Director of the Juggling Institute.

> We just concluded a two week tour of the Hiccup show Naturally High in the Bay Area in California. That was a big step for us, getting off the Islands. The performing troupe of six ranges in age from 12-17. In the show they juggle, do a lot of unicycling, stilt walk-

ing, some clowning, acrobatics and a lot of balancing with drama and singing thrown in. We have our own musical group, the five piece Sideshow Band, that accompanies the performance with original music. We don't do any aerial work; we don't use trampolines and we don't use animals.[81]

Ellis believes juggling has pedagogic value related to the discoveries of Educational Kineseology that physical activity can aid learning. A brochure for Juggling For Success sets forth "The Wonderful Benefits of Juggling" which could apply to circus arts in general:

- Develops and strengthens motor skills, eye-hand coordination and concentration.
- Integrates left and right sides of body and mind greatly improving learning abilities.
- Builds confidence and self esteem and provides a challenge to increase skill level.
- Enhances balance, rhythm and control.
- Focuses mind and relieves stress.
- Quick, easy and safe exercise involving minimal space and equipment.
- Non Contact, Non Competitive recreation.
- Develops teamwork.
- Males and females are equally adept.
- Enhances visual and auditory skills.
- Fantastic fun.[82]

Ellis and Finnegan conduct workshops in schools as part of Physical Education, Arts, and Science programs, the latter as part of a unit on force and movement. Working in an area that leads Hawaii in teenage pregnancies, domestic violence and drug abuse and has a high population of alienated students, Ellis found that mastering juggling and other circus skills provides students an opportunity to experience self-esteem as they learn success, coordination, cooperation and concentration.

The Hiccup show *Naturally High* plays indoors. In addition to its implicit message of the value of mastering circus skills, *Naturally High* offers explicit anti-tobacco and anti-drugs messages. Hiccup Circus also developed *Dr. Seuss in Words and Action*, a literacy program for libraries and schools. The messages the circus presents as well as the value of the skills it teaches have enabled Hiccup to gain funding from a variety of public and private agencies.

In recognition of its work, the Hiccup Circus was notified by the State Commission for National and Community Service in May, 1998 that it had been awarded the year's only new AmeriCorps program in Hawaii. The $140,000 grant would employ 13 AmeriCorps members and enable Hiccup to expand its educational services. There would be five elementary school self-esteem programs, three afterschool and five summer programs. The Hiccup Circus would be in schools, libraries and at community events and on at least two television shows to be broadcast on public access channels throughout the state.

However, the Federal Commission, which usually supports State Awards, rejected the proposal on the grounds that circus was not an appropriate activity for AmeriCorps. Ellis mounted a vigorous campaign to reverse the decision; many in the field wrote AmeriCorps to explain the values of Circus Learning. Still, the grant did not come through. Ellis was philosophical.

I decided that not getting the AmeriCorps grant was a good thing because it would only have made me more into a bureaucrat than I already am and I really want to be a teacher with a little directing as necessary. It turned out that the head office was just not ready to accept that circus offers a legitimate, credible education opportunity for youth. We have a lot of work to do in the US to catch up with Europe and Australia where circus education is well respected.

Apart from weekly classes, I'm rehearsing a new show with ten kids who have never performed before and it's a thrill. Every year the skill and enthusiasm level rises. Included in the new show is a six-person, five foot unicycle routine which is something I never dreamed of doing with 8-13 year old kids. And while I previously thought that a six year old unicyclist we had last year must have been a fluke, we now have another and even better.

So life in paradise is great. Our community of performers at Bellyacres had a wonderful winter and decided after ten years of discussion to go ahead with building a performance arts center on our land so now I'm fund raising for that, too. Never a dull moment in the circus education world.[83]

Ludvika Minicircus

Pictures from a Ludvika Minicircus brochure

The Ludvika Minicircus in Ludvika, Sweden is a circus club started by two professional bicyclists, Ola and Barbo Nordsrtom, in 1984 after they had been touring for twenty-five years. Like the Flying Fruit Fly Circus, the Ludvika Minicircus call itself "Ordinary kids doing extraordinary things." Unlike the Flying Fruit Fly, Ludvika is not integrated into a school system, but is an afterschool activity although it provides some free training in schools. The club has more than 190 members, 140 are children and young adults in active training. A group aged 11 to 22 tour as *The Ludvika Young Star Circus*. Ludvika also has a junior performing group of children 6-15 that performs for younger audiences.

The 1997 performance of the *Ludvika Young Star Circus* included The Wheelies, three 20 year old boys doing a sophisticated unicycle act; Jolly Roger, a solo unicycling act; the Goldies, four young girls balancing on a table; Four Dolls, four young girls doing acrobatics involving a tube; The Charleston Girls, two girl doing foot juggling; Cecilia, doing hand balancing on a table and on chairs; The Bellboys, eight boys on unicycles; Andre, doing the bicycle act he inherited from Ola Nordstrom; and the Acro Dancers, fifteen girls doing an acrobatic dance act. The acts in the Ludvika All Star Circus are either all-boy or all-girl although boys and girls do work together in the junior group. As Ludvika has no clowning instructors, there is no clowning in the performances. The *Young Star Circus* mostly performs indoors on stages; the show is usually 45-50 minutes long.

Ms. Nordstrom sees no conflict between tours and education. "Our kids are all very good at school so it is easy to get some weeks free every year. The teachers say that our kids learn more visiting all the countries than reading books, but they always have an academic plan with them on tours."[84]

Ms. Nordstrom described the company's finances:

We do get a small amount from the city ($4,000) plus a free training hall. The kids pay $30 a year for training as a member fee. There is no support from the government. We get money from our shows - even the young artists get paid.[85]

Suvelan Sircus

The Suvelan Sircus is an afterschool program in Espoo, Finland for 140 students ages four to twenty-two. The school specialties are acrobatics, trapeze, juggling and balance. The teachers are Lionel Lejeune (acrobatics, juggling), Maria Stenback (gymnastics) and Tatjana Litonius (acrobatics.) The Suvelan Sircus performs 50 and 60 times a year and participates in circus camps. Suvelan Sircus maintains contact with amateur circuses in Germany, Sweden, Russia and Estonia. The Russian amateur circus, Circus Grotesk, has performed with Suvelan Sirkus and coached its members. In 1999, members of Suvelan performed at the Jazz Festival in Aigullon, France and at the Circus Festival in Sylt, Germany. Suvelan Sirkus is a member of the Finnish Circus School Federation and sponsors an annual Circus Festival.

Wenatchee Youth Circus

The Wenatchee Youth Circus in Wenatchee, Washington was in its 46th season in the summer of 1998. Touring small towns and major cities - mostly in the northwest, it presented uninterrupted hour and fifteen or hour and twenty minute shows that featured highwire, flying and other traditional circus acts in the open air. A tent that could accommodate the 35 and 40 foot rigging for the high acts is beyond the Circus' financial means. The show's music is provided by a roll driven calliope and drums. The circus company is made up of 55 to 65 young people up to the age of 19 and 15-20 adults. The show equipment travels on two trucks; a forty-five foot flat bed carries five wagons - poles and stakes ride in the truck's possum belly, and a dining truck

The St. Leon High Wire troupe perform 30 feet up in a
Wenatchee Youth Circus performance. credit: April Boyce

that contains refrigerators, freezers, gas stoves and ovens. Personnel travel by cars mostly driven by parent chaperones. The usual stand is two days and the company lives on the lot in two 20 x 40 foot dressing tents.

The Wenatachee Youth Circus was created by Paul Pugh. It started as an afterschool tumbling program when Pugh began teaching Junior High English and Social Studies in Wenatchee. His annual pay was $3000 and he earned an extra $100 for the year for the tumbling program. In addition to the need for extra money, the circus came from Pugh's lifelong interest in circus. When he presented his tumblers, it was to the accompaniment of the recorded music of Ringling Brothers and Barnum & Bailey Bandmaster Merle Evans who later helped Pugh set up his own band and find music for it. The first performances included clowns and some juggling and later a tightwire. Looking back, Pugh sees that the goal of the program was always more than financial. He describes the mission of his circus:

"To have young people with unusual talent be able to share that talent with others and bring a little happiness into somebody else's life." I know it may sound hokey, but that is our mission statement. And to have the young people do it in a way where they can hold up their heads and say, "Hey, we did a good show. We brought some enjoyment or entertainment into somebody's life that didn't have it."

The number one thing the kids learn is responsibility. And they learn to get along with people - with each other. They realize they have something special, that not everybody can do what they do - juggling machetes or working a Chinese diablo or whatever. People look up to them and they realize they do have something[86]

The early shows entertained at the half-times of basketball and football games and at a children's Christmas party at the local theatre.

After two years teaching, I went into professional radio for a year and half and during that time we took the whole program to the local YMCA and our first show was called the Wenatchee YMCA Circus. We started in 1952-53 and gave our first public performance of 45-55 minutes in the spring of 1953. At the YMCA, we gradually started to get additional equipment. In 1954, we got a flying and return trapeze rigging and we all had to learn from scratch. I was the catcher the first four years. We learned by watching others. We didn't have professional coaches. We visited shows that came through the Northwest - Clyde Beatty and Ringling Brothers and various fairs that had acts. Those people gave us pointers. Over the years, professionals have been a great help to us.[87]

Pugh returned to teaching at the Junior High, became Boy's Counselor and then principal for eighteen years. At the school he stayed in touch with young people and was able to spot talent for the show.

Through the years we've developed fairly reputable trapeze acts and highwire acts and many of our young people have gone on to professional shows. I've furnished people to the Ashton's in Australia; we furnished people to several flying acts. I still have one girl with the Flying Valentines out of Houston, Texas. I've had five in that act. I have a girl who started on the Ashton show for a year and half and then got a job with another Australian circus that played Malaysia and Hong Kong. She came back to the United States and realized at this point, her life was in the air and she went to Circus Circus in Reno and then transferred to Las Vegas. Most of the kids who have gone professional do it from two to five years.[88]

While the majority of its performers are from the center of Washington, the Wenatchee Youth Circus also draws young people from around the state and the nation.

We've had African-Americans, Jewish kids, Islamic kids, Buddhists and Christians. Not all of them all the time, but this is a little community in Central Washington and we've been able to attract all these people at one time or another. I think that speaks well for what we're trying to do.[89]

Pugh has tried to get youngsters from China and Russia - he tried in Russia before Rob Mermin did, but was unable to come up with funding to underwrite such activities.

The trainers are Pugh, two assistants and Pugh's son who comes up from California for four weeks. The two assistants are preparing to take over when Pugh retires. At present, in addition to coaching, he books the shows and clowns in the performances.

The group practices Saturdays during the off-season – out-of-doors, while the weather permits; in the gym of the school where Pugh used to teach, during the winter. In spring, it takes three months to put the show together. The circus benefits from a good deal of continuity in its performers, but in 1993 the entire flying act graduated and Pugh had to start from scratch. There was a flying act in 1994 with flyers presenting they tricks they were capable of achieving. Over time, "the kids rise to the level of what they can do."[90]

The principal source of funding for The Wenatchee Youth Circus is money taken in at performances; the major expenses are food and transportation. Pugh and the other staff are unpaid; the performers contribute gas money. Costumes are built by mothers of the troupers; the only paid staff are the truck drivers. Without a tent, the Circus loses performances and income in bad weather, but over the years Pugh has become expert at picking locations and times where this is unlikely. Sometimes the show works out arrangements with sponsors and splits ticket income with them. Occasionally the Circus receives a fee for performances.

When the circus found it difficult keeping a band together, it substituted the calliope and drums which are sometimes supplemented by a trumpet. At one point, the calliope needed to be replaced, Two circus alumni organized a letter writing campaign that raised $10,000, including a $3,000 grant. The circus bought the new calliope that operates off player rolls. It can also operate manually when there is someone to play it.

The Greater Wenatchee Foundation has contributed about $8000 over the years. The gross income for the circus each year is between $50,000 and $80,000; that becomes the basis for the following year's budget. The show does concessions and sells souvenir programs to generate additional income.

The Wenatchee Youth Circus is an amateur entity that has developed a tradition of performing excellence that has enabled some graduates to make the transition to professional circuses. But the goal of the circus is to enrich the lives of its performers and its audiences by demonstrating the excitement of the American circus tradition.

Organizations

As the number of Youth Circuses and training programs in Circus Skills for young people grows, organizations have been established to set performance and safety standards. In Europe there are the **European Federation of Circus Schools** in Belgium, the **French and Rhones-Alpes Regional Federation of Circus Schools**, the **Finnish School Federation** and the **National Association of Youth Circus (NAYC)** in England that was established in 1994. The latter, in addition to providing advice and support, publishes a newsletter three times a year, arranges conferences and perhaps most importantly, publishes a Code of Practice.

Steve Ward, the NAYC secretary describes the organization:

The NAYC is an umbrella organization providing a support network for people working in the circus arts with young people. Its "mission statement" is to "develop the circus arts for, with and by young people" although the definition of what is a young person sometimes becomes very elastic! It would seem that the majority of young people falling into our work are mainly between six years and fourteen years, although again, obviously, there are groups working with older and younger as well. We estimate that the NAYC serves the needs of some 2500 young people around the UK.

Most member circus groups run their own training programmes, but the NAYC has attempted to provide training of a more general nature. To date we have run/organized the following:

First Aid training for circus work (Health & Safety Qualification)
BAGA Gymnastics training (level 5 qualification)

Working with Special Needs Youngsters
Directing for Circus Theatre
Workshop Leaders Training

We are also collaborating with a College of Further Education to devise a national award system in circus arts for young people. Hopefully these would be nationally recognized and become a platform for further vocational work in the field of circus arts for those young people wishing to develop a career.

You may be interested to note that I am just completing a Ph.D. research project into the use of circus within Education (being a qualified teacher myself) and some very interesting results are emerging as to the direct effects of circus activities upon child development.[91]

The NAYC Code of Practice establishes definitions for specialist areas of circus activity, lists training opportunities and establishes procedures for safe, systematic training within each specialty. It also considers access and equal opportunity, working with groups, indoor and outdoor venues, and equipment.

Although some youth circuses have been around a long time - the Circustheater Elleboog in Amsterdam is celebrating its fiftieth anniversary, youth circus is a phenomenon that has accompanied renewed interest in the west in Circus Arts. As Steve Ward said in a speech:

If we do not harness this energy then we jeopardize the place of Circus as cultural activity in the future. As Kristove Istvan, the Director of the Hungarian State Circus once said to me, 'The hope of the circus lies in the hands of the children.' The young of today are the tutors, performers, administrators, audiences and creative minds of tomorrow. What seeds are sown will be reaped in the future."[92]

In 1999, the **American Youth Circus Organization (AYCO)** was organized by Kevin O'Keefe of Circus Minimus. He and those who met with him – from Circus Smirkus, the Van Lodostov Circus, Carries Heller's Circus Camp, the Cascade Circus, the Pine Hill Waldorf Circus and the Berkshire Kids Circus saw a need to improve communication between the groups and to "encourage and support youth circus arts activities in America."

In a series of meetings at the Pompanuck Farm in Cambridge, New

York, the group focussed on the need to integrate circus arts into schools' core programs. Sue West, of Circus Sarasota, reported on her group's successful efforts to do this. An Education Committee began developing curricular guides. AYCO gives promise of helping to improve the situation of youth circus in the United States.

Aside from providing young people the opportunity to discover and develop talents that might lead to professional careers, youth circuses empower those involved by teaching discipline, focus and making clear to the participants that they are capable of achieving wonderful things alone and with others while maintaining a demanding performance schedule.

IV
Community Circuses

A number of communities have developed their own circuses. As the communities' children acquire Circus Learning from family and friends, the resulting performances become the source of community, as well as personal, pride.

The Belfast Community Circus School

There are few better examples of Circus Learning's healing potential than the Belfast Community Circus School in Northern Ireland. In the midst of sectarian, cross-community violence, the School has brought together Catholic and Protestant children to learn circus skills. The skills are demonstrated in performances given throughout Greater Belfast. The School, founded in 1985, was partially funded by the Arts Council of Northern Ireland. Co-founder Mike Moloney articulated his goal for the school as "the empowerment of human beings over their environment."[93] The School was the first Circus School in Great Britain to have its courses accredited by the educational system.

The School started a summer camp in 1988 that took youngsters from the School's Saturday classes in Belfast along with young people from elsewhere in Northern Ireland to the seaside resort of Newcastle. *Circus of Hope*, a one-hour film by Susan Rosenkrantz, documents the 1992 season. Anne McReynolds, the Belfast Community Circus School Development Director, described the goal of the camp in the film:

> This summer circus camp is a chance for all the children we have taught throughout the year and some children we've never met before to leave Belfast and the Greater Belfast area to come down to beautiful, sunny Newcastle to get a break from Belfast and learn circus skills with other children from other communities they wouldn't have met before in a lovely, safe environment.[94]

At the camp, the School staff was supplemented by circus specialists from around the world including Ringling's Peggy Williams and Graham Ellis of the HICCUP Circus in Hawaii.[95]   Williams met Australian Paul Woodhead while both were working with the Belfast Circus; she subsequently went to Australia to help him establish a school circus program in Dubbo, NSW.[96] The camp staff included international volunteers who took care of the catering and acted as counselors. The camp for about 40 youngsters ended each of its two 10 day sessions with a performance. Along the way, the camp had day programs for others youngsters. In 1992, the two sessions involved 605 people.

Things changed dramatically for the Belfast Community Circus School in 1999 when it moved into its own building and was able, for the first time, to offer programs all through the week. Will Chamberlain, the School's director, described the school's activities in January, 2000.

We have a full-time course for adults daytime and that's five days a week – Monday to Friday from nine until five. It's a one-off, but we are going to try to get funding to do it again. It's a course we're offering completely free to the students to train them in all aspects of circus and particularly in community circus. It's intended for people who are going to become circus teachers. Unfortunately, we're also turning them into highly skilled performers. We're expecting a fair amount of them to disappear around the world, but hopefully they'll come back at some point. In this eight-month intensive course, we have trainers from Canada, Australia, the United States, England, Scotland, Wales and, of course, Ireland.

We are no longer doing the accredited academic course although we still have links with the Performing Arts Course at the Belfast Institute of Further and Higher Education (BIFHE). That is where we were offering the accredited modules, but whilst they're still on the books, they haven't taken us up on that for a couple of years now.

Our fulltime course is funded by the Arts Council of Northern Ireland Lotteries Unit. Over the period of a year, we had put together a strategy for advancing the quality and quantity of circus teaching. That included the proposal for the course and it was through that that we got the building because we needed a full-time space.

We talked to a local development corporation which is government funded. It had just launched a scheme to turn this particular section of the city into an arts and cultural center. We had identified this space owned by the corporation and when they said, "We don't know if we have anything suitable," we said, "We know you own this building" and that kind of caught them out. We had already been through economic appraisal for the lottery so we were on the fast track. We pitched the board and convinced them so that this building, which is two small warehouses, was redeveloped to meet our needs. Our main training space and performance area is in the larger warehouse that is seventy-five feet long and twenty-five feet wide and there's a central section that is about thirty feet high. Prior to the refurbishment, it was about twelve feet, so, they totally rebuilt the building. We also have a small studio space where we have organized classes during the day where people can come in and train.

In addition to the full-time program, we have an extensive range of outreach projects. For example, this evening we have a group from the Probation Board. That is an ongoing project with them for teenagers who are on probation. The program is a means of enhancing self-esteem. They're here two hours a week and they can access our Saturday program as well. It opens the way for integration into normal, if you can call circus normal, activity. We have done work in that field for eight or nine years now and that is one of the big successes according to psychological evaluations of the impact of the work. That program is funded by the Probation Board. Over the years there have been a number of similar projects. About eight years ago we established one that became independent that was set in a residential home for "juvenile justice and care." That ran for six or seven years. Our funding is always a cocktail of things. We receive some funding for our core programs from the Arts Council of Northern Ireland.

We also have four evenings a week going out to work with young people in different communities in Belfast. We go once a week to Portadown to work with a cross-community group. We also go down on Saturday to a cross-border group. Most of that outreach work is funded by the City Council. We also receive money from the European Union Peace and Reconciliation Funds because much of our work is cross-community.

Although the situation in Belfast is changing, I don't think it has affected what we are doing. We have been pioneering this work for fifteen years so we're kind of ahead of the game. Ironically, the peace scenario means a reduction in funding from the European Union and we are looking for creative ways to replace it. There is still a demand for our work. People are still living where they were and the future for the peace process is in the young people. Working with them is paramount if we are going to broaden their experience and change their mindset.

Our staff is small. I'm the director. I have an Outreach Team Leader, a Program Manager for administration, and a Youth Circus Director. As teachers, we have a professional staff who also make their living from performance. They are self-employed people, freelancers.

Last year we didn't do the residential camp. We did a Summer School instead that took place here in Belfast. It was the same sort of idea – intensive circus work for a number of days. We divided it. One section was for 8-12 year olds and one for teenagers which reflects what we do during the year on Saturdays. We have three sessions on Saturday working with skills and bringing together different groups. This year we had some kids from the States from Fairfax, Virginia, because on our last summer project we took fourteen of our teenagers there. We also had kids up from Cork in the Republic. We wanted to broaden the experience of kids here and kids from the south as well.

We still do some parades through the community, but nowadays we find there are things like the cross-community Belfast Carnival that takes place every June. We play a big part in that and we still take part in community festivals. More and more nowadays with our outreach we link into particular areas and tie the circus workshops for local kids into participation by those kids in their own community festivals.

My background for this is that I was a professional clown for twelve years, but all the time I was clowning I was working on community circuses over in England. I founded two community circuses there and I have always been passionate about what circus can do for individuals. I've been here now three and a half years. My experience is that there is nothing that compares with we have going on here.

Last term, we ran nine outreach programs plus our three sessions on Saturday plus the full-time course plus evening rehearsals for our Christmas show. You get to these peaks of activity and think you can't do anything more, but we seem to somehow manage and keep growing.

After the full-time course ends, I'd like to see some more intensive training take place at some point in the future. I also think we could bring in groups from schools during the day or disabled groups or unemployed young people to work with them on circus in our space rather than always having to go to someone else's. I think we can now offer this space to other youth arts organizations and other community arts organizations. We could try and foster greater links with other groups. Dance would make sense. We have a wooden floor and a lot of space. Dance is part of our adult course. We haven't quite worked out what we're going to do afterwards. We hit the ground running with this place.

We had been looking for a building for a number of years and it was a very tight timetable last year. We got this program planned and funded by the Lotteries and we had set ourselves the time to start – the 20th of September. The building work didn't start until the beginning of May. It was completed and we were given the building on the 24th of September. Team building at the end of week one for the students was moving all our props and office stuff from one place to another.

I had thought the adult course was going to be a one-on, but now, when it looks like half the students will be taking off and doing their thing around the world, maybe we need to a do another course, but refocus it. Perhaps we should do something for people with kids so they're less likely to go away.

Here, some of our students have been with us for a long time. Our Outreach Leader started with us when she was 14. She's 25 now. She went away to University and came back to Belfast and was teaching and is now with us. One of our main tutors is 25. A very talented young man, he started with us in his teens. In our Teenage Circus we have kids who have been with us since the age of 7 or 8 who are now sixteen. I'd say on average, kids stick with us for three or four years. When we started the separate teenage circus, we had a lot of people joining up who when they'd got to 12 or 13 had stopped. They had a "career break" and came back.

We've always had a policy of letting our teenagers who wanted continued involvement assist the tutoring if they were that way inclined. They see there are possibilities of a career with us. I think it's important that kids can say, "Ah, if I work at it, I could be doing that. I could be teaching. I could be making some money from it." Some people, it takes them until they're eighteen and go off to university. For some people, it has replaced university. I think it's important that there is always that ladder of opportunity.

Our Teen Age circus now has thirty members. We're refocusing and thinking of it as a separate performance company. Our history is that our shows are inclusive so everybody gets a chance to perform. That's all right when you have thirty kids, but when you have a hundred, as we did in our Christmas show which went very well, that led us to look at how we can do more manageable smaller shows. I think the teenagers will form the backbone of any kind of performance company. It sounds good. It looks good on paper. We just need to get it into practice.[97]

Over fifteen years in a very difficult situation, The Belfast Community Circus School has demonstrated the special contribution Circus Learning can make within a community. The School has provided a venue that enabled youngsters to achieve a sense of their own capabilities while working cooperatively with those who come from both of Belfast's communities.

The YMCA, Bloomington, Illinois

The YMCA in Bloomington, Illinois gave its first circus performance in the spring of 1910. As the YMCA Circus included professional flying acts that trained in the area, young amateurs had the opportunity to observe and work with the professionals. In the 1920's, the YMCA Circus produced outstanding flying trapeze performers including Arthur Concello and Harold (Tuffy) Genders. Concello became the preeminent American flyer of his day; while performing with Ringling, he managed other flying acts. He and Genders became important figures in Ringling management. Except for a hiatus during World War I that extended until 1924, the YMCA Circus continued until World War II. Steve Gossard has described the the YMCA Circus in his fine history of trapeze performance.[98] Gossard also notes the way in which the YMCA Circus influenced the development of the Gamma Phi Circus at Illinois State University (see Chapter Nine.)

Circus Cabuwazi

Circus Cabuwazi was founded by a group of parents in Berlin, Germany in 1993 as a leisure time circus program for young people ten to seventeen. In 1994, Cabuwazi operated in the Berlin districts of Kreutzberg and Treptow teaching youngsters to develop acts based on traditional and *new* circus practices. "The art of circus and circus education is not to be understood as an end in itself, but as a means to develop and to realize creative ways of social engagement."[99]

Additional Cabuwazi programs were established in the district of Marzahn and in Altglienicke. Each of the four locations has its own circus tent. The four programs serve about 600 children, using a staff of 70. In 1998 the German Children's Relief organization honored Cabuwazi for its work. Cabuwazi students have won prizes at national and international festivals.

Children's Circus of Middletown

The Children's Circus of Middletown exists to provide all the kids of Middletown, CT with a safe, fun and challenging recreational summer program grounded in the circus arts, and to provide the city with a large-scale, high-quality, completely homegrown arts event which includes and reflects all segments of the community.[100]

"Cirque du Poulets," Children's Circus of Middletown.
credit: Eric Rich

The Children's Circus, directed by Dic Wheeler, provides a five-week, half-time program for youngsters 8-14. It operates under the Oddfellows Playhouse Youth Theater in conjunction with the Middletown Commission on the Arts' Kids Arts program. Funding comes from the city of Middletown, the Middlesex United Way, the Playhouse and modest student tuition which is on a sliding scale.

The program, started in 1988, originally accepted youngsters as young as five. The program expanded until 1993 when it involved 245 children and a staff of 38. After taking a year off in 1994, the program found its funding cut. Consequently, five- to seven-year olds were dropped. The reconfigured program involved 180 children, a size it has kept since.

During the first week, students experiment with all the circus disciplines, then choose two that are studied for the second and third week. All students are then cast into acts for the circus performance and the last two weeks are spent honing individual and group acts.

Fifteen to twenty adults and teenagers make up The Circus Band that rehearses three evenings a week before participating in dress rehearsals and the performances. About seventy more adults and youngsters participate in the twice weekly Tech Nights. Starting in 1998, performances were held on Andrus Field at Wesleyan University. Each year's show has a theme. The year the Circus moved to Wesleyan, it was *The Children's Circus Goes to College.* The previous year, the Circus presented *The Circus History of Middletown.* The 1999 show celebrated chickens with *Cirque du Poulets.* That year, The Children's Circus coordinated with another nonprofit arts organization, North End Rising. This allowed youngsters to participate in the Circus and North End Rising's Kids Art program for a full-day program.

Circus City Festival, Inc.

Peru, Indiana calls itself The Circus Capital of the World. Peru's involvement with circus began in 1884 when livery stable owner Ben Wallace and his partner, James Anderson, launched a traveling show. Wallace later became sole owner and went on to acquire other circuses including Hagenback which he transformed into the Hagenback-Wallace Circus that established a 500 acre home in Peru. The Hagenback-Wallace site later became the base of the American Circus Corporation that owned five circuses. In 1940, the quarters were turned into farms.

Circus City Festival brochure

Our great circus heritage was renewed in 1956 when the Circus Historical Society announced they were having their annual convention in Peru, Indiana. The local Jaycees took over the sponsorship and made arrangements for wagon tours, exhibits and a banquet. By 1958, the Peru Area Chamber of Commerce stepped in to promote an event that would revive Peru's circus past and many retired circus people offered their help as performers and trainers. . . .in 1960 they staged the first amateur circus in a rented tent with 36 performers and eleven clowns.

. . .our first three ring circus was held in a tent purchased from Carson & Barnes in 1962 and it was used for six years. . . The Board purchased the old lumber company building in 1967, no roof and luckily no rain. Robert Weaver, local artist and instructor, and architects designed a roof that gives the appearance of a huge tent and it was completed for the 1969 circus.[101]

In 1967 the CCFI board hired a head trainer from Florida State and had several until Bill Anderson, a product of our own circus, was hired. . .our circus would not be possible without the hundreds of Miami County youths ages 5 and 6 for kiddie clowns and 7 to 18 for performing in our circus. [College students who are circus alumni are allowed to return to the show while they are in college.] Over 300 sign up at our annual roundup and start practice in April. [About 200 appear in the show.] They are trained by former performers in our circus who learned their skills from those professionals who called Peru their home. After many hours of practice and the desire to be in the Circus, in July they put on a two and half hour spectacular show. This is an outstanding program for the young people who usually return until they graduate [high school] and the CCFI awards all who do [college] scholarships [$350 a year for four years if they continue to perform in the show, $350 the first year and $250 the other three years if they don't.]

. . .In addition to eleven performances in our arena, another successful part is the road shows. We have taken [a smaller version of] the show to every major city in Indiana and to surrounding states.[102]

The Greatest Amateur Show on Earth is a community effort. There are seven trainers, thirty to forty riggers, three ringmasters, one hundred and five band members, costumers, fifteen clowns, the eighteen member governing board, support personnel and enthusiastic audiences for the show. The two paid employees are the Circus City Festival Office Manager, Linda Cawood, and Head Trainer, Bill Anderson. When the hour long documentary film *Circus Town - USA* about the Peru Circus ran on NBC in 1970, the circus received requests from around the nation and abroad from young people who wanted to participate. The CCFI decided to keep the event local. The only requirement for participation is that one must be enrolled in one of the county's three schools. There is a hometown quality to the performances that begin with a parade that resembles a high school prom or homecoming as much as a circus spec as the audience is introduced to the Circus King and Queen who have been chosen by their peers, the runners up, and the performers.

The range of skill in the performance is as wide as the range in age. In the three ring tumbling act, one ring is filled with beginning tumblers doing basic somersaults, another with intermediate tumblers and a third with advanced tumblers flipping in the air. Performances have the excitement of a school athletic event, but the Peru Circus is different. Boys and girls work together; older and younger performers join forces in this noncompetitive celebration of skill and teamwork.

In 1996 the Young Americans highwire act presented a six-person pyramid; in 1997 they recreated the legendary seven-person pyramid. In 1998 the Young Americans presented an eight-person pyramid that won them a spot in the Guinness Book of Records - not as the first youth group to achieve this feat, but as the first group of any age to have done it. The Young Americans repeated their feat at the Monte Carlo Circus Festival although, due to a last minute illness, they presented a seven person pyramid. Trainer Randy Wallick is an alumnus of the Peru Amateur Circus who became a member of The White Angels highwire seven-person pyramid that won a silver medal in Monte Carlo in 1994. Two other White Angels were also graduates of the

Peru Circus. In Peru, Wallick has the Young Americans two feet off the ground in April, by July they are 25 feet in the air.

Adults appear in the show as ringmasters, riggers - at least thirty at a performance, trainers, and about fifteen adult clowns. Bruce Embrey, president of the Festival in 1997 and that year's ringmaster, is a local judge. One of the clowns appearing as a doctor is an actual MD. At a time when economics have forced professional circuses to cut back on musicians, fifty to fifty-five of the volunteer musicians participate in the band that accompanies the performances. There is a theme to each year's show; in 1997 it was *Mardi-Gras*, in 1998 it was *Broadway*. The main impact of the theme is on the music and the costuming. Essentially, the presentation is a traditional American three ring circus although newer equipment like Russian swings and bungees are used. More unifying than the theme is the sense of communal celebration

Katie Cohee, a member of the 1997 seven person pyramid, wrote of what her involvement with the circus meant to her.

When someone becomes involved in circus and does it for several years, it becomes something you can't get enough of. The most rewarding part of it is the performing part. The adrenaline rush you get after a performance is incredible. It's amazing to think all these people came to see you.

Circus will stick with you the rest of your life - it becomes a passion. Even though circus takes up so much time, once it's over for the year most of us wish that we could go in for one last show. Everyone involved makes up a big family that is part of something special.

Today there are not many organizations like this that involve volunteers from the community that donate enormous hours for free. The bond between performers and trainers is incredible, almost amazing. It comes to the point where you trust them so much that you just do what they tell you to without questioning safety.

Performers have so much trust in fellow performers as well as in trainers. Circus also gives performers confidence to do things outside the circus building. Many performers have more social skills and work better in team situations.

Circus allows kids in our town to be involved in something big, something people come from all over to see. When I go somewhere and mention that I am in a circus, people are in awe over it. They can't believe some of the things we do.

I only have a couple years left to be a performer and I know that I will greatly miss it when I am done. I have made so many friends, accomplished so many things through the circus and it has been part of my life since I was seven years old; it will be hard to leave.

I will definitely still be involved in other ways with the circus though. If my kids ever want to be part of the circus, I would encourage it 110%. I am not the only one that loves the circus this much; just wait until the last show and try to count the number of performers and trainers with tears in their eyes.[103]

The Peru Circus is the center for related community activities. Each year there is a Circus City Festival parade, the second largest in Indiana after the Indianapolis 500 parade. The Circus City Festival parade includes historic Circus Wagons, "bands, clowns, convertibles, calliopes, performers, dignitaries and much more will glide down the city street while on-lookers lace the sidewalks to get a glance and take in all the glitter."[104] The Peru Chapter of Sigma Phi Gamma sorority handles the circus concessions and the Xi Lambda chapter of Beta Sigma Phi sorority is responsible for each year's circus program. There is a road race, a midway, a crafts fair, bowling and basketball tournaments, calliope concerts. In the Circus building, there is a museum.

It's not real big, but it has an awful lot of history in it. It has articles, pictures, equipment, some costumes and head pieces that performers used to wear that go back to the 1920's and possibly earlier. We have a section that is set up for our youth circus and pictures of what the kids have done through the years.[105]

There is also the International Circus Hall of Fame located on the American Circus Corporation site and the Miami County Museum that has circus items on display.

The Peru Amateur Circus is an integral part of the community. The Circus allows young people who attend the schools in Miami county to participate in performances from the ages of 5 until they are in college. It allows them to do it with coaches and others who are their neighbors who themselves grew up performing in the circus. When the young people perform, their audience contains people who have known them all their lives. Encompassing both the community of performers and the community of audiences is the larger community of Peru, Indiana's shared circus past. The Peru Amateur Circus continues to evolve and develop its own traditions that contribute to its success.

Cirque du Monde

Cirque du Soleil, the most global circus entity functioning today, started in the streets. Its phenomenal success has not made it forget them. Approximately one percent of Cirque du Soleil's world wide ticket revenue is devoted to social action programs administered by its Department of Social Affairs and International Cooperation. These programs aid young people at risk, particularly street kids. While Cirque du Soleil supports organizations that work with these youths, its most unique contribution is through Cirque du Monde, an organization that brings Cirque du Soleil's circus expertise to local human service organizations that work with youths whose average age is 12 to 20. Together, Cirque du Monde and its local partners create circus skills training programs that enable young people to focus and develop the energies that have sustained them in difficult environments.

According to its brochure, *Cirque du Monde: A Cirque du Soleil Social Outreach Program*, Cirque du Monde does not claim to be a panacea for social ills, nor does it consider itself a diversion. The goal of Cirque du Monde is fostering the full development of youth who have not yet found meaningful places in society. "This may mean reconciliation with family, admission into a detox program, or even a dawning interest in an occupation or profession. But above all, the project provides a chance for participants to experience something positive that can act as a catalyst for growth in self-esteem and identity."[106]

Paul Laporte, director of the Department of Social Affairs and International Cooperation, explained Cirque du Monde's philosophy and financial approach. First, the program is partnership based. Cirque du Monde works with more than forty private and public sector organizations and with universities. Next, while the program operates in areas where Cirque du Soleil performs, it is also in Africa, Brazil, Chile, Columbia and Mongolia where Cirque du Soleil has no business interests. Third, Cirque du Monde is pro-active; it builds programs where none had existed. Fourth, Cirque du Soleil contributes to these programs what it does best – circus. "Cirque du Soleil is well known as a creative enterprise and we want to be creative when we work with kids at risk. We look for original, imaginative ways to work that reflect our nature."[107] Finally, the program is oriented towards supporting its partners by helping them generate financial leverage to develop their work. To this end, Cirque du Monde expects its partners to contribute facilities and other in-kind support that matches Cirque du Monde's contribution.

The idea that became Cirque du Monde began when Laporte was living in Brazil. At the end of the eighties, he was involved in a project for street kids, *Esse Rua Fosse Minha (If These Were My Streets)*. Circus Learning workshops proved to be an especially effective part of the program. In 1993, a Canadian based organization, Jeunesse du Monde, that had been working with youth internationally since 1959, created an alliance with other organizations to further this work. Cirque du Soleil was invited to become a partner. The next year the alliance received funding from Health and Welfare, a Canadian partnership fund. The alliance held two-week circus workshops in 1995 in South America in Recife and Rio de Janeiro, Brazil and Santiago, Chile; and in Canada in Montreal, Quebec City and Vancouver. Each workshop, presented in association with local groups, included two circus instructors from Cirque du Soleil. The Adobe Foundations documented the work in Rio de Janeiro and Montreal in a film, *When the Circus Comes to Town*.

The alliance became Cirque du Monde in 1996 and two-month workshops were held in Recife, Rio de Janeiro, Santiago, and Montreal. The same year, Cirque du Monde established a base in Amsterdam, the Netherlands, and researchers at McGill University and the Universite de Quebec a Montreal began to analyze Cirque du Monde's efforts. Their continuing research has been the basis for Cirque du Monde's self-evaluations. Oxfam-Quebec and Pueblito became Cirque du Monde partners in 1997 and discussions began which led to Oxfam-International becoming a partner. The following year, local partners were recruited to set up Cirque du Monde workshops in Abidjan, Ivory Coast; Dakar, Senegal; Douala, Cameroon; and Durban, South Africa. Participants from the Montreal workshops set up their own troupe, *Coralie* – the first of several such groups to be established in Montreal.

In 1999-2000, Cirque du Monde instituted a training program for Cirque du Monde instructors and helped establish training for social action through circus as part of the curriculum at the National Circus School in Montreal. Laporte reported that the first semester's course in September, 2000 would devote forty-five hours of study to exploring how artists can best work with youth and street kids. The second semester would expand the work with another forty-five hours of study. The goal of the program is to train people to work with Cirque du Monde or with other programs that do this work. Laporte was discussing with Belgian partners establishing a training program there; in the next few years he planned to do the same in South America, Africa and the Asia-Pacific region. "We would like to have five or six cities around the world that offer, more or less, the same training for working with street kids through circus."[108]

Cirque du Monde's continuously revised *Handbook for Instructors and Partners* sets forth the educational philosophy that animates training that contributes to physical, human and social development. The training enables students to integrate themselves more effectively into society while respecting each student's uniqueness. To make marginalized youngsters feel at home and important in the workshops, the Handbook advocates *pedagogie circulaire (circular learning).* This requires an atmosphere of "equality, equity, participation and mutual respect, both among the young people and between the trainers and the young people."[109] The Handbook notes that traditional hierarchical teaching methods do not suit marginalized young people. The Handbook goes on to urge trainers to prevent unhealthy competition from developing in the workshops. "Each young person is accepted at his or her own level and progress is measured against him or herself."[110]

Cirque du Monde workshops begin with the usual stretching and warm-ups. Here, more than elsewhere, these activities are important as a transition from the surrounding world to the work. The work itself consists of acrobatics, balancing and juggling which are pursued from rudimentary to sophisticated levels. Along the way, there are games, improvisations and team meetings. Safety is stressed and "the idea of having fun should be present."[111] Finally, acts are created.

The nature of a workshop depends on what coaches and equipment are available and on what the participants want. Students are encouraged to try everything. Ratios of coaches to students vary. Trapeze work requires a one-to-one ratio, while one coach to five or seven students is considered acceptable in acrobatics.

Coaches are seen as "social artists" who teach values, such as cooperation and perseverance, as well as skills. Coaches are expected to keep diversifying their own skills so they can adapt to the challenges they are presented.

To sustain the participants' motivation to master ever more difficult feats, many workshops present shows the nature of which depends on the circumstances that surround the workshop. In shows, one sees "the simple but primordial feeling of pride in yourself."[112]

Although some workshops produce students who create performing troupes, Laporte considers this a second level result. "It is much more important to develop self-esteem." As Cirque du Monde grows, aided by research based self-analysis, it refines its operation, but the goal is constant. Cirque du Monde works with local human service organizations to develop programs adapted to specific needs. These programs bring the life enhancing experience of circus training to youth who desperately need it.

The Great All American Youth Circus

The Great All American Youth Circus was founded in 1929 by Roy Coble, Director of the Redlands, California YMCA, who had been a performer with the Ringling show. The Great All American Youth Circus is now co-sponsored by the Community Arts Corporation, a nonprofit organization, The Circus teaches circus skills to over 100 children each year, September through May, at the YMCA.

The Youth Circus is funded through performances, fund-raisers, class fees and YMCA memberships. Unlike other youth activities, Circus is noncompetitive and focuses on individual and group skills presented in an entertaining and artistic theatrical performance with choreography, lighting. costumes and music.

The Great Y Circus emphasizes teamwork, dedication, trust, family, skill, showmanship, excitement and fun for both the participant and the observer. Circus teaches young people important values such as responsibility, commitment, self-confidence and self-discipline along with specialized skills.

Supported primarily by family, friends and volunteers, many alumni who have gone on to become professional return to help the next generation learn circus skills.

Young bodies are pushed to their maximum as they master new physical movements which equal or surpass feats of professional circus performers. Students work hard in their circus classes at the

YMCA throughout the year and follow in the YMCA philosophy of building body, mind and spirit.[113]

Acts taught at the Great Y Circus include unicycle, rings, handbalancing, acro-gymnasitics, spanish web, cradle, juggling, teeterboard, hanging perch, single and multiple bars, Roman ladders, pyramid bicycle, German gym wheel, low wire, clowns and dancing. The circus presents a Big Show each June and roadshows of various sizes. Performances and fund raising events support scholarships, costumes and equipment.

The Sailor Circus

Sailor Circus flying act.
credit: Sailor Circus

The Sailor Circus of Sarasota, Florida resembles the Peru Amateur Circus for good reason; both developed in communities that were homes to professional circus performers. Sarasota children were used to seeing performers practice in their yards and the performers' children attended Sarasota schools. It was not surprising when the Sarasota High School's gymnastics program developed into circus.

In the 1948-49 school year, while Bill Rutland was athletic director and head football coach at Sarasota High School, the ex-University of Georgia football star introduced tumbling and acrobatics into the physical education program as a means of conditioning his prospective athletes. This program became so popular and interested so many students that, before the year ended, Coach Rutland presented a program in the high school gymnasium, introducing the talent and skill of the high school youngsters in the field of acrobatics.

When more than 500 fans crowded into the small gym to see the program, Rutland recognized the fact that he had hit upon a popular program not only for the students themselves, but their parents and friends as well.

Whereupon, the next year, in 1950, the Sailor Circus made its formal debut as an outdoor spectacle on Ihrig Field. The origin and development of the Sailor Circus in Sarasota came as natural to this community as a 150-pound tarpon, a Rubens painting or a sunset in the Gulf. As the home of Ringling Bros. and Barnum & Bailey Circus, the Cristiani Brothers Circus, the Clyde Beatty Show and such, it was only natural that Sarasota youngster should gravitate to the little big top.[114]

It was *Sailor* Circus because that was the name given all Sarasota High teams when they traveled by ferry to St. Petersburg and Tampa in the 1920's. In 1952, Ringling Brothers and Barnum & Bailey management was so impressed by the Sailor Circus, it granted permission for Sailor Circus to call itself "The Greatest Little Show on Earth." The show acquired a 2,000 seat tent in 1958 that was used until a fund raising drive raised a quarter of a million dollars to erect a permanent building twenty-six years later which now includes a museum of Sailor Circus history.

Although the Sailor Circus had its origins in a curricular gymnastics program, the Sarasota County School Board sponsors the Sailor Circus as an extracurricular, afterschool program for students from grades 3 through 12. In 2000, Sailor Circus returned to its roots when it introduced a one-credit Circus Gymnastics class, taught by Sailor Circus director Susan Loeffler. (See Program Materials p. 247 for course objectives and grading procedure) The Circus Gymnastics class is separate from the extracurricular Sailor Circus.

The class is held in the Sailor Circus arena which is located on Sarasota High School property. Currently, students who attend SHS grades 9-12 may participate and earn a physical education credit. The course is a full school year and is held M-F 12:50-1:45 PM. It can only be taken once.[115]

The same high standards for behavior and effort apply to both the curricular and the extracurricular Sailor Circus activities. A 1995 flyer proclaims that the Sailor Circus "for the past 45 years has inspired over 5000 young people to stay out of trouble, away from drugs, and become a credit to their community." The same flyer notes, "Although sponsored by the Sarasota County School Board, Sailor Circus is completely funded by donations and gate receipts."[116]   Sailor Circus alumni were invited back to The Fiftieth Anniversary celebration in 1999.

Patricia Campbell, Sailor Circus Office manager, described the operation.

Our practice season runs from September through March, with performances in our arena in March and April. The school board provides us with the facility, two full-time staff members and two part-time staff members. We are self-funded through gate receipts, road shows, community functions and donations. We depend on our many volunteers to do a wide variety of things such as costumes, concessions, construction as well as training. Many of our trainers are retired circus professional performers and Sailor Circus alumni. Our amateur circus provides professional entertainment and has performed all over the world.[117]

Students rehearse about thirty hours a week. Training begins in September with rigging classes for middle and high school students and a mandatory Circus Introduction for all students. Training ends the first week in December and tryouts begin for the show. Band practice starts in January. At the end of February there is a full show practice followed by rehearsals of each half of the show and then of the full show. In mid-March performances begin at 7:15, each preceded by a 4:15 meeting/work call with selected acts practicing. At 5:30 there is a costume call, at 6:00 work stations and then the show. There were eleven performances in 1998 followed by an awards banquet. Since 1995, all performances have been sold out. College scholarships have been awarded to Sailor Circus graduates since 1998; they are now administered by the Sailor Circus Foundation, Inc. In 1996 the Sailor City Flying Trapeze participated in the Highland Festival in Minnesota where two Sailor Circus alumni were starting their own Circus of the Star.[118] The Sailor Circus has performed in more than half the states and overseas - including performances in Japan.

The 1997 Sailor Circus performance began with a concert by a band made up of members of Windjammers Unlimited, the circus music historical society. The band then accompanied the performance. Like the Peru band, the Sailor Circus band combines amateurs and professionals. As Sarasota is a retirement community, the Sailor Circus band includes former members of the New York Philharmonic and the Boston Symphony. A calliope is also used. The printed program listed 88 performers and 19 volunteer coaches and trainers that included former members of the circus, retired professionals and professionals still active such as aerialist Pedro Reis who was soon to start his own circus school.[119] Acts included tumbling, slide for life, web, perch pole, low casting, juggling, swinging trapeze, bicycle, cradle, giant wheel, ladder trap, shoot-through, adagio, risley, high wire that featured an all girl pyramid, ladders, rolling globes, hand balancing, Roman rings, low wire, teeterboard, unicycle and flying trapeze which has been a feature of the Sailor Circus since 1953.

The performances develop in a highly structured rehearsal period. The rules are demanding. (See Program Materials.) As Alla Youdina likes to point out, "Circus is hard and circus is dangerous." The rules governing the Sailor Circus remind young performers of these truths. Observing them makes possible the joy that comes from achieving difficult tasks and learning to do them with others. In the words of Julie Snyder, then the show's director,

The qualities that are stressed in Sailor Circus are Responsibility, Leadership, Dedication, Persistence, Self Confidence, Pride in a job well done, Being the best you can be, and above all - Laughter.[120]

Circus performance, like other theatrical forms, involves community. The performers prepare their presentation together. In circus, performers must also prepare their bodies for the rigors of performance for they are dependent on each other for their safety. Those who share these tasks are an interdependent community as long as the unknown of performance exists.

When a performance takes place, a new community is established that involves performers and audience. The audience may think it sits passively as it is entertained, but performers know how much the attitude and responsiveness of the audience contributes to the success of a performance. A run-through without an audience is not a performance. Audiences, whether they realize it or not, also establish community with the strangers seated beside them who share the same experience. As performers master difficulties, the audience - while not knowing the specific details - shares the mastery of those difficulties. When performers complete a feat and bow and the audience applauds, the community of performance is acknowledged.

Community circuses can bring audiences of young people a sense of their own possibilities to fulfill themselves as the performers have. The Hiccup performers also bring didactic messages about the dangers of drugs and tobacco that have special meaning when delivered by exemplary peers. The messages the Peru Circus and the Sailor Circus and Cirque du Monde deliver are less explicit as they demonstrate what dedicated young people can achieve.

This book is concerned with Circus Learning. As young people participate in circuses, they learn about their own strengths and about the values of work. Some discover that their developed skills permit them to pursue professional circus careers. Whether they do or not, and most do not and have no desire to do so, they learn what they are capable of achieving with hard work and dedication in community with others. In Peru and Sarasota and Belfast, they also learn that their world, with all the problems that exist, can be supportive.

V
Circus Camps

Many summer camps now include circus skills along with swimming, athletics, nature study and other traditional activities that provide healthy, recreational learning. This book looks at those camps where circus is a significant part of the program.

The Berkshire Circus Camp

The Berkshire Circus Camp, located on the campus of Berkshire Community College in Pittsfield, Massachusetts, opened in 1994. The three-week day camp has fifty to fifty-five participants, ages 8-13; there is a wait-

Campers practice clown makeup at the Berkshire Circus Camp, 1997.

ing list of others eager to attend. The camp is the brainchild of Dick Hamilton, a retired high school science teacher with a lifelong interest in circus. The late Rev. David Harris, who directed Circus Kingdom - a traveling youth circus, suggested that Hamilton start such a camp and recommended Jessica Hentoff and Mike Killian, of St. Louis, as circus professionals who could help him. Hamilton hired them. After Harris's death, his widow, Trudy, donated Circus Kingdom equipment and sheet music for the Circus Kingdom band which is now played by the local Eagles Band when it accompanies performances of the Berkshire Kids Circus.

The Berkshire Circus Camp has become a source of local pride; over one hundred community volunteers help each year. Proceeds from ticket and concession sales support scholarships for youngsters in the community who would otherwise not be able to attend. Hamilton prepares a Xeroxed hand-written newsletter, *The Circus Camp News,* each day to keep families connected to Camp activities. Volunteer carpenters built a marquee entrance to the gymnasium where the circus is held; they later built a second marquee that could be more easily stored. Alongside the entrance are circus wagons, also built by volunteers, that are used when the Camp participates in the Pittsfield Fourth of July parade. Large sideshow style banners made by the campers decorate the midway outside the entrance. A community volunteer made a calliope that first appeared in the 1998 performance.

When Hamilton wanted a base for the circus, he approached Alexandra Warshaw, the Berkshire Community College Director of Community Services. With no particular interest in circus and uncertain about having the campus invaded by children, she was dubious. Hamilton won her over. Warshaw became enthusiastic when she saw the program enrich the lives of its participants and the college's relationship with the community. As she wrote in the 1998 program

It takes a lot of people to put on a circus, and perhaps even more to put together a circus camp. We at BCC are impressed that all the right connections that a couple of enthusiastic, committed circus buffs can make to get things off the ground. A few more of us have, in the process, become circus buffs in our own work.

The Berkshire Circus Camp, by arousing local interest in circus, contributed to the establishment of a Tent (branch) of the Circus Fans Association in the area in 1998. People in Pittsfield and the surrounding area now see circus not just as performance, but as a process that enriches the lives of their children and the life of the community.

While Hamilton's enthusiasm started things, it was the expertise of Jessica Hentoff, her husband Mike Killian and their assistants that provided the Circus Learning. There is often a spiritual or ideological center to a circus or a Circus Learning operation; Jessica Hentoff has been that for the Berkshire Circus Camp even though she has not been on site since 1996.

Daughter of writer Nat Hentoff and painter Jessica Bernstein, Jessica Hentoff is described by her father as someone who always had "a paperback in the hip pocket of her jeans. I expected, as she did, that she would become a professor somewhere."[121] Her Senior thesis in Sociology at the State University of New York at Purchase was *With It and For It: Circus People as a Deviant Subculture.*

Hentoff's interest began at Purchase when she took an alternative course, offered between semesters, in Circus Arts. After learning juggling and clowning, she toured for a summer with David Harris' Circus Kingdom and was one of those wanting to become professional circus performers who established the Big Apple Circus. When Big Apple coaches Nina Krasavina and Gregory Fedin left to start their Circus Arts Center in Hoboken, New Jersey, Hentoff went with them. There, she developed a trapeze act with Kathy Hoyer that was the last professional act developed by Fedin and Krasavina before they closed their school.

While the act toured with Circus Flora, Hentoff was active in the outreach Circus Learning programs Flora developed in San Francisco and then in St. Louis where she became director of the Circus Flora School from 1988 to 1995. When Hentoff married Mike Killian, a clown and circus technical expert, the wedding took place in a tent. Hentoff entered on horseback; the officiating minister was David Harris.

Hentoff directed, and continues to direct, the St. Louis Arches, a tumbling troupe of youngsters age 10-17 that tours with Circus Flora. Donald Lee Hughes, a graduate of the Arches, now works with Hentoff and Killian in their own operation in St. Louis, *the everydaycircus,* that provides circus classes, residencies, entertainment and equipment.[122] Hughes is also Assistant Artistic Director of the Berkshire Circus Camp.

A promotional flyer from *the everydaycircus* also describes the work Hentoff and Killian do at the Berkshire Circus Camp.

Ladies and gentlemen, may we present to you a most entertaining and wonderful new program. It is designed to develop self-confidence, hand-eye coordination, trust in others and respect for one's self. By turning you upside down, we teach you to stand on your own two feet. By dropping objects, we teach you to catch them. By having you walk all over someone, we teach you to take care of them. By having you clown around, we teach you to take yourself seriously. All this and you'll have fun doing it in a circus skills class from everyday-circus. Real circus performers teach you tumbling, juggling, partner acrobatics, balancing, pyramids trapeze and clowning.

In 1997, the first year the Hentoff was not in attendance, Killian was asked if there was a difference in the program without her.

She's tougher than I am. She first learned circus from the Russian who was with Big Apple at the beginning and he'd have them start everyday by climbing ropes twenty times. When she'd wilt after about sixteen, he'd blame it on her weak Jewish blood so she'd do the twenty. She's tougher than I am. Maybe I emphasize the camp more than the show.[123]

There was still rigorous work involved as the campers sought to master difficult circus skills. The camp also includes traditional camp activities. After roll call, announcements, warm-ups and some free play on the equipment at 9:00, the group broke into three units, each led by a counselor. Most days, the 10-12 period was divided in three and each group took turns at non-competitive games, swimming in the college pool, and arts and crafts. In the afternoon, the group broke into four units that take turns at circus skills. By Tuesday of the second week, campers filled out Show Choice Questionnaires indicating first, second and third choices for the show. The acts were single trapeze, double trapeze, triple trapeze, Spanish web, juggling, plate spinning, diablo, devil sticks, rolla bolla, gym wheel, ladders, partner acrobatics, wire (high and low), bicycle, unicycle, rolling globe, ringmaster, clowning, stilt walking and pyramids. Along the way, circus makeup was taught. The Circus Learning was supplemented by demonstrations by visiting performers and circus videos. The camp equipment grows each year, much of it built by Killian.

The organizing principle for the Berkshire Kids Circus show is one Jessica Hentoff offered this author in a letter when he began gathering material for this book. She assured him that creating the book was "Like putting a circus together: order the skills into individual acts (chapters) and acts into the show (book.)"[124] That is how the impressive performances of the Berkshire Circus Camp are organized. All fifty-five youngsters participate and the Eagles Band - of about twenty pieces, provides spirited accompaniment.

There are reminders that the performance is part of a camp program. The performances seen by the author in 1997, 1998, and 1999 began with a speech by the Artistic Director thanking the college, the community and all those already acknowledged in the program. There was little attempt to theatricalize the performance by giving it uninterrupted momentum or by integrating it with a theme; it was a presentation of skills. There were traditional clown acts. What animated the performance was the exuberance of the participants. Their enthusiastic unicycling, juggling, trapeze, web, clowning, high and low wire walking was infectious.

The 2000 performance was different. That year Killian stepped back from full-time direction of the program, and Carlo Gentile, the Assistant Artistic Director, took over. In 2001, Gentile was to become Artistic Director. The 2000 performance displayed the same skill level as previous years. There was less clowning - Killian's specialty, but there was a new sense of urgency and theatricality. The student ringmasters' with their lengthy introductions were replaced by Gentile identifying performers from an off stage microphone without interrupting the action. Entrances and exits became dynamic parts of the acts with the performers tumbling into position.

Watching all the performances one realizes that no matter what the orientation of a Circus Learning situation, - whether to *new* or traditional circus, or what strategies are used to train students, the most significant factors affecting success are the individual student's coordination, body strength, body type and willingness to work. Circus Learning presents opportunities youngsters respond to according to their abilities and the agendas they set themselves. Just as some students are more comfortable in traditional academic situations than others, the same range of learning skill and will is present in Circus Learning. However, Circus Learning allows each student with the will to achieve, an opportunity to do so. The justified self-esteem experienced when accomplishments are made is a treasure for young people.

Camp Imagin-Ere

Circus Learning was half the focus of Camp Imagin-Ere in Canada; the other half was computer learning. Parents were urged to "vacation in the Gaspé or the Maritimes for a week or two this summer and leave the kids at Camp Imagine-Ere."[125] It was both day camp and stay-over camp for youngsters who enrolled for one, two or three weeks. There was a weekly show in which students demonstrated what they had learned on trapeze, in acrobatics, juggling, clowning and mime. Campers promoted the show with computer generated posters and used spread sheets and word processing in planning the show.

The Camp was cancelled before the 2000 season. Perhaps its cancellation provides insight into the difficulties faced by those creating circus camps.

Camp imagine-Ere, an independent small business, is unable to continue functioning given the conditions arising from the economic policies of Quebec. In specific, the camp can't go on without investing financially much more than its revenues permit, meaning that it would be necessary to expand in order to continue. And we can't expand while offering the same high quality of instruction without further major investment. How can we justify such investment for a business that draws revenue during only seven weeks of the year? We believe it's time to face facts and step aside for government or other non-profit organizations who are subsidized for such investments. We intend to forge ahead with other projects.

This prospect pains us, because we've spent many exciting summers with the kids who attended. All of us developed our know-how, our wisdom and our creativity while at the camp, thanks to one of the best reputations for quality in the North American market. So all was not in vain; the kids who benefited won't forget and won't have gone unchanged, because Camp Imagine-Ere really touched everyone who participated.[126]

Camp Winnarainbow

Camp Winnarainbow, situated on the Hog Farm Collective ranch in Northern California, is different. While Camp Imagine-Ere integrated circus skills with the latest computer technology, Camp Winnarainbow integrates them with the counter-culture idealism of the 1960's and 1970's in which its founder, Wavy Gravy, was deeply involved.

Campers sleep in tepees, awakening to the sound of a conch shell horn signaling the beginning of camp activities. After breakfast they gather for Wavy's morning reading which might include a passage from Walt Whitman, the Tao Te Ching, Robert Fulgham, or something Wavy has authored himself. Singing and exercise follow, then it's off to classes in juggling, mime, trapeze work, magic, African dance, mask making, Native American studies or martial arts. Free time may be spent swimming in a lake or careening down its waterslide, playing volleyball or exploring the woods.

Camp Winnarainbow is aggressive in its commitment to racial, cultural and economic diversity. Tuition ranges from $465 to $1,200 for one-, two-, or three-weeks sessions. Last year, Winnarainbow provided scholarship money to one third of its campers, some of whom were homeless. Camp literature stresses health and safety, indicating the circus classes are taught by experienced instructors and that a registered nurse is on duty at all times.[127]

The camp is rooted in Wavy Gravy's commitment to the alternate life style he has lived. He was Master of Ceremonies at the original Woodstock where he proposed, "What we have in mind is breakfast in bed for 400,000." In 1994 he was Master of Ceremonies at Woodstock 2. The two activities in which he continues to be involved are Camp Winnarainbow and Seva, an international medical aid organization. Wavy Gravy's background includes study at the Neighborhood Playhouse in New York. During the sixties he journeyed to Northern Arizona to live with the Hopi Indians. Along the way, he changed his name from Hugh Romney. His wife Bonnie, who later took the Sufi name Jahanara, is co-director of the camp. For a while Wavy owned land in Northern Vermont as part of a project of deeding land back to itself. He is also known as the inspiration for a flavor of Ben and Jerry's ice cream.

He founded Camp Winnarainbow in 1974 in the Mendocino woodlands; in 1984 the camp moved to Laytonville, California where it now attracts about 400 youngsters between 7 and 14 each year.

Different as the ideology is between Camp Winnarainbow and Camp Imagin-Ere or Peru's Circus City Festival or the Sailor Circus discussed in the last chapter, there is a commonality among them. All appreciate how Circus Learning enables young people to focus their creativity and work cooperatively. Camp Winnarainbow seeks to "create a living environment of love, safety and harmony. Camp teaches responsibility for one's own inner behavior and develops confidence, inner security and appropriate self expression."[128] This is not so different from the Redlands circus that sees circus skills fitting with the YMCA philosophy of building body, mind and spirit.[129]

Not surprisingly, there is much interaction between Circus Learning organizations. Peru Amateur Circus has hired head trainers from the Wenatchee Youth Circus in Washington and Florida's Flying High Circus.[130]

Carrie Heller, a social worker in Atlanta, Georgia was influenced by her work with Wavy Gravy to develop the Carrie Heller Circus Camp[131] as a way to foster mental health.

CircusCamp '98: A Spectacle From Scratch

This nine day workshop retreat in the state of Washington was

dedicated to the sharing and revitalization of circus and circus skills, culminating in a performance open to the public. CircusCamp '98 is envisioned as a gathering place where people new to circus can gain skills and those with experience can share and network in a non-hierarchical, community based context. Our vision is to begin a process of reclaiming circus not only as entertainment to be consumed, but as an accessible and active model for personal transformation, community empowerment and social change.

Circus and circus skills are endemic to the cultural fabric worldwide. The recent outcropping and revitalization of circus and circus related arts in the United States is no coincidence. As people become disillusioned by the cultural bankruptcy of the TV age, we dig deep into the roots of folk and popular culture seeking meaning and magic. Circus has the potential for both. It is a place where we can come together to share our wonder, laughter and delight. At the same time it stretches our abilities and offers discipline to our play.

Circus has suffered the same ills as many other arts in our country, its development often determined by capital and profit. In instigating this nine day retreat, it is our intention to bring circus back to the people, realizing it as something human and authentic that can be shared by all. Thus, we look forward toward the roots and traditions of circus, while incorporating contemporary themes, addressing vital issues of concern to our community with humor and compassion.[132]

Skills to be taught included clowning and physical theatre, juggling and object manipulation, stiltwalking, tumbling and acrobatics, pageantry, fire swinging, trapeze, balancing skills and performance collaboration. One of the the sponsors of CircusCamp '98 was WAIL (Where Art is Living), a collective at Prag Tree Farm in Arlington, Washington which was the site of the camp. WAIL's mission is to create a place where art and agriculture coexist.

The other sponsor was Wise Fools Community Arts, a nonprofit arts organization dedicated to creative action, celebration and change.

The following December, K. Ruby of Wise Fool, one of the staff, looked back at the program with satisfaction.

CircusCamp was a great success. There were forty participants and eleven staff. The teachers were Jennifer Miller of Circus Amok (NY), Daniel Gulko of Cirque Pocheros (France), Nathan Scott of Cry of the Rooster (Seattle), myself, Linet Andrea, a trapezist (Britain) and Ted Dzielak, musical director of Dell' Arte School (Seattle). We did a lot of skills sharing and training - Trapeze, Ropes (slack and tight), Acrobatics, Juggling, Fire Work, Unicycle, Puppetry, Stiltwalking and more. We created a two hour circus in six days that was well attended by about 250 people.

Prior to the circus we had sideshows and workshops for the audience to participate in as well as concessions - great food by our fabulous cook and an organic fruits and veggie stand. The whole retreat was held on a farm. At this time there is no plan to do it again.[133]

The New Age rhetoric of Circus Camp '98 recalls the ideas that animated The Big Apple Circus when it was created in 1976. Circuscamp also reminds us again how Circus Learning finds supporters across the ideological spectrum.

Circus Minimus - The Circus Kids Create

This summer circus day camp usually has two week sessions in five or six different locations. During the winter, its director, Kevin O'Keefe, conducts school residencies and after-school programs, continues his own circus studies and performs his one-man circus show.

Circus Minimus operated in the early summer in Bennington, Vermont from 1994 to 1999. It created a core of devoted parents and returning youngsters who built on the previous years' skills which many practiced over the winter. Circus Minimus also developed local additions to the training staff. Bennington is typical of the places where *The Circus Kids Create* operates. As O'Keefe wrote in a newsletter,

Kevin O'Keefe teaches a Circus Minimus performer to "style and smile," 1998

There is a core of dedicated kids, staff and energy wherever we go. Our creative juices are replenished by the wonderful energy the kids bring to every circus.[134]

Circus Minimus was sponsored in Bennington by the Bennington College Early Childhood Center and was situated in the Greenwall Auditorium of the College's Visual and Performing Arts building. In 1998, thirty-one children participated. In addition to O'Keefe, there were five instructors, four interns and four junior interns. Sean-Marie Oller, whose two children participated in the program - one moved on to Circus Smirkus, was the local producer. Later in the summer, Minimus returned to the area with a program in Cambridge, New York; the two programs shared staff. Lisa Carrino, the producer in Cambridge, was in charge of the arts component of the program in both venues. Under her leadership, the participants produced original decorations and costume elements for the show that concluded each session. Carrino also did choreography.

Circus Minimus comes to town the way a professional circus comes to town; it is guaranteed a place to perform by a local presenter who benefits from having brought an activity that is valuable in itself and shares in whatever profits are generated. In this case, the sources of income are the students' tuition and ticket sales for the performance. The difference between Circus Minimus and a traveling show is that local children are the performers, some of the staff is local and the performance is adapted to the community. When Minimus set up shop for the first time at the Bardavon Opera House, the longest continuously operating theatre in New York state, O'Keefe saw to it that the "historical/theatrical ghosts came out of retirement and joined a group of local kids."[135]

O'Keefe, who was co-director of the Big Apple schools residencies for five years, has adapted the Big Apple process for bringing Circus Learning to children in East Harlem to other venues. Those who produce Circus

Minimus are often middle-class parents who find it a non-competitive physical activity that helps their children develop skills and self-esteem. O'Keefe, a charismatic teacher and showman, and his staff, take his six to 13 year old charges through an intense two weeks. At the end, their show, often built around a theme, integrates circus skills with mime and dance. The show is enhanced by the art work the participants created. The bright recorded music supports the exuberant tone of the performance which is set by O'Keefe who participates as ringmaster and performer.

The show is preceded by a sideshow in an adjoining space and concludes with the performers dancing with the audience. Sometimes there is an act in which parents participate with their children. *The Circus Kids Create* has style and theatrical coherence; it is not a collection of unrelated acts. The single performance is the culmination of intense, but relaxed rehearsals that go Monday through Friday, 9:00 A.M. until 2:30. At one point during rehearsals in Bennington in 1997, O'Keefe cautioned his staff that they were taking the performance too seriously. He reminded them the goal of the program is to enable the kids to have a good time, but substantial demands are made on the participants.

Each day's rehearsal starts with a thorough warm-up conducted by O'Keefe in a way that is interactive and fun. During the first week the participants sample as many skills as they wish, but by Friday afternoon they choose those they are serious about. O'Keefe explained this to the children before warm-ups on the Thursday of the first week in 1997 in Bennington.

> At a buffet restaurant you get to eat a little bit of everything. At a regular restaurant you have to settle on one dish. OK? The first week here is like eating at a buffet restaurant. You get to try everything - walking the tightwire, juggling - everything. The second week is more like eating at a regular restaurant. There's only so much time, you only have so big a stomach and you realize, "There's only so much I can put in there and I'm going to put in juggling and wire walking or clowning and tumbling or tumbling and roller blading." You see what I'm saying? You're going to have to start making choices. So try everything now, but by tomorrow afternoon you should have a choice made. Not everybody is going to be in every routine. We talked about this the other day, remember?

He concluded his pre-warm-up talk:

I want to remind you again, this a no put-down zone. That includes talking about people to your friends. Talk about it when you leave here if you absolutely have to, but don't talk about it while you're here.

We're moving along. It's only Thursday.

During the day, the youngsters moved from station to station working at different disciplines and on visual elements for the show. Traditional skills were adapted to particular problems as they arose. O'Keefe brought in a long corrugated tube; he and the youngsters tried to figure out how to use it in performance. They found that two performers could stand on it and make it roll; further exploration showed that two more could ride inside, their heads showing from the open ends. Upended, the tube could transform into a cannon. The first day did not resolve the problem of how to get a person to eject as a projectile from the cannon, but exploration had begun. A scenario started to evolve that O'Keefe, with his ever present felt pen, jotted on a piece of paper. Girls would stand on the tube and roll it with their feet. Others would somersault over the moving tube. A magician would appear who would conjure the two heads to appear in the ends of the tube. Then the transformation of the tube into a cannon would begin.

When working with clowns, O'Keefe develops routines through improvisation. In Bennington, he started by explaining that everything clowns encounter is new to them so their responses, as their costumes, are extreme. He had the neophyte clowns list descriptive words for clowns and for what clowns do. He put pieces of paper in a hat; each bore the name of an emotional attribute the group had ascribed to clowns. O'Keefe split the group in half. Each person in the group drew a piece of paper and studied it. One at a time, they stood, closed their eyes and imagined they were in a bubble filled with that emotion. When they opened their eyes, O'Keefe encouraged them to find a gesture that embodied the emotion. He then froze them into pieces of sculpture and the other half of the group visited the "museum" and tried to to determine what the qualities were. In many cases, the performers' efforts were correctly identified.

Students who had been with Bennington Circus Minimus in the three previous years came to the 1997 session with impressive skills. One seven year old could run across the gym mats, do two one-hand supported flips and end with an unsupported flip. She and some others could already make it to the end of the portable tightwire that stood about eighteen inches off the floor.

Demonstrating the tightwire apparatus, O'Keefe made clear it was not for everyone. Although close to the floor, falls from the wire could "bite." "It looks like a tightwire, but it's an alligator," he told them. Tightwire walkers were accompanied by spotters. To dance on the wire, one must walk first. To do this, one must focus on a spot - the "X" O'Keefe had marked on the tower towards which the walkers headed. Walkers learned to counterbalance their weight to keep it centered over the wire. O'Keefe demonstrated the preferred way to center the foot over the wire, sliding each foot forward from the other. At whatever point one left the wire, whether at the tower or along the way, the students were reminded, "Style and smile!"

Each day ended with all participants demonstrating what they had learned. O'Keefe's guidelines for the presentations were, "One turn, three chances and style." At the end of each demonstration, successful or not, the students styled with a circus bow for the rest of the company, assembled parents and friends. After the demonstration, the students, each with a hand on O'Keefe, shared in an improvised rhyming prayer to the Circus Gods.

This is how the 1997 Cambridge session concluded just before the performance. After admonishing the youngsters not to touch their faces - they all wore whiteface clown makeup and matching T-shirts, O'Keefe said:

Whatever happens, you worked real hard for two weeks. You had a lot of fun, and we've accomplished something. OK? Remember when we met two weeks ago I said, "You won't believe in two weeks how quickly the time will have gone by and how much you'll get accomplished and how much fun you'll have." Was that right?

Kids: Yes, yes, yes.

Kevin: So you'll have to take that into consideration when you're styling and smiling at the end of whatever it is you're doing. What we should be doing now - aside from listening to me, is keeping your sequence straight in every routine.

So don't touch your faces and everybody take a deep breath.

Kids: Ahhh.

Kevin: If you want to think about something, think about the sequence of the show and what you're doing as you go through the show.

Put your hands on mine, dudes. Take a deep breath.

Hold your circus high!

Kids: Hold your circus high!

Kevin : Use your puffy red shoes

Kids: Use your puffy red shoes

Kevin: And your funny pink wig

Kids: And your funny pink wig

Kevin: And your big fat nose.

Kids: And your big fat nose.

Kevin: Look down on us and smile on us.

Kids: Look down on us and smile on us.

Kevin: Look at our big fat toes.

Kids: Look at our big fat toes.

Kevin: Watch our curly straight hair.

Kids: Watch our curly straight hair.

Kevin: Make us be funny.

Kids: Make us be funny.

Kevin: Be sure we're having a good time.

Kids: Be sure we're having a good time.

Kevin: Make sure we're having fun.

Kids: Make sure we're having fun.

Kevin: Make sure that next year -

Kids: Make sure that next year -

Kevin: We'll come back with no fear,

Kids: We'll come back with no fear,

Kevin: Without any beer,

Kids: Without any beer,

Kevin: Or a single tear!

Kids: Or a single tear!

Kevin: Have a good year fellahs!

Circus Minimus teaches youngsters circus skills and helps them share in the creation of a joyous theatrical undertaking that is rooted in their community.

Circus Smirkus Camp

The Circus Smirkus Camp, like other circus camps, is open to students with all levels of expertise who wish to learn new skills or develop existing skills. The camp's sessions - usually two weeks, are open to campers 8 to 16. The camp is held at the 240 acre White Mountain School in New Hampshire. According to its 1997 brochure

Success is guaranteed: each camper masters a new trick at his/her own level. There is no competition in the circus, only helping hands to do our personal best. Each session ends with a final Circus Show for parents and friends. . . .Our overall staff/camper ratio is 1:3 and includes both a coaching staff and counselors. . . .A typical day begins with group warm-up exercises followed by three hours of 45 minute classes. Children are divided into four groups and rotate between four stations: juggling, aerials, equlibristics (tightwire, stilts, rolling globe, unicycle, etc.), and acrobatics. Afternoon classes include clowning and special classes: (The Ancient Art of Pie Throwing, Techniques of Falling Down, The Science of Silliness, Madcap Mime, Magic Tricks Made Easy), and rehearsals for the Big Show. All classes emphasize working at your own pace, safety and serious FUN. By the end of the first week, campers tend to gravitate to specific skills and have the option to focus on them during the second week. Coaches are available during rec time to offer additional individualized training to campers.

Afternoon recreational activities (swimming, hikes, basketball, tennis, hanging out) are all supervised. Evening activities include a faculty show, circus films, games, storytelling, music, campfires, etc.

As noted earlier, Circus Smirkus coaches join the staff of the camp which opens after Circus Smirkus goes on the road. In 1998, the camp added a special session for advanced students. According to Rob Mermin, director of the Circus and the camp

We gets kids from overseas and all over the States. We've developed an effective Counselor-in-Training program. A lot of them start as assistants to coaches and a couple have moved on to become coaches.

The usual maximum number of kids for each session is 60, but for one session we went to 75. We're looking for a new site for the camp so we can grow. Where we are, we're limited in the time we can use that place. We have enough interest to have more than three sessions. We're hoping to build our own facility in the future.

There are scholarships for the kids in the circus, but not in the camp which helps fund the circus. Not only does it feed the show with money, it feeds the show with new talent.[136]

Recreation Department in Vero Beach Florida
In addition to gymnastics, this program offers

the Aerial Circus Class, which includes instruction in trapeze, Spanish Web, cloud swing, ladder and revolving trapeze. In addition, an eight week Aerial Antics Circus Camp for serious performing arts students is conducted each spring in preparation for the Annual Aerial Antics Circus.[137]

The Sports & Arts Center at Island Lake
This high powered summer camp in Northern Pennsylvania offers young people 7-17 Team and Individual Sports, Tennis, Gymnastics, Horsemanship (English, Western Dressage, Jumping), Theatre (Musicals, Drama, Cabaret, Voice Lessons, Improvisation, Commercial Technique, Audition Technique), Dance (Tap, Ballet, Broadway Jazz, Lyrical Jazz, Modern, Pointe, Choreography, Movement Improvisation, Aerobics), Magic (Close-Up, Stage, Illusion, Card, Coin), Pioneering (Challenge Course, Backpacking, Shelter Building, Outdoor Cooking, Orienteering, Rapelling, Mountain Climbing, Whitewater Tubing), Waterfront (Swimming, Sailing, Windsurfing, Waterskiing, Kayaking, Snorkeling, Whitewater Boating), Science (Biology, Chemistry, Mechanical Science, Astronomy, Electronics, Earth Sciences, Ecology, Physics, Radio Station, Video, Rocketry, Computer), Arts & Crafts, Mountain Biking (Single Track, Double Track, *and* Circus (5 types of Trapeze, Flying Trapeze, Juggling, Rolling Globe, Clowning, Handbalancing, Mini-Trampoline, Acrobatics, Circus Bike, Tightwire, Unicycle, Aerial ladder, Slack Rope, Tumbling.)

Triple trapeze at the Sports & Arts Center at Island Lake.
credit: Sports & Arts Center at Island Lake

Start with the basics and let your imagination run free. Learn at your own pace; practice and advance at your own speed. Once you get started, there is no limit to what you can accomplish. . . .The skills you learn and the techniques involved encourage personal and physical strength, promote coordination, cooperation, team work, agility, flexibility, concentration, and self esteem.

Best of all, you can perform your new circus skills for your friends, counselors and parents in our fully costumed circus shows each session. Whether you are an aerialist, acrobat, clown, or ringmaster, you can try things you have only dreamed of and discover that dreams can come true at Island Lake.[138]

Circus Learning at the Sports & Arts Center at Island Lake may be one element in a rich recreational and learning environment, but it does demonstrate how pervasive an appreciation of Circus Learning's value has become.

Van Lodostov Family Circus
The Van Lodostov Family Circus, a summer circus day camp in Norwich, Vermont, is operated by Ted Lawrence. Lawrence is a Clown College graduate, a former Ringling clown and a former faculty member of Clown College. Before beginning his clown career, he was a physics teacher. He now teaches physics as a clown in school programs of Slapstick Science that he presents four days a week during the school year throughout the Northeast. His performance often ends with a back flip from a teeterboard over a seven foot cutout of basketball star Shaquille O'Neill as Lawrence demonstrates physical principles.

After a school performance, Lawrence described the camp.

Van Lodostov is a side line for the summers only. It's a hobby with real deep roots. I've always loved doing the circus stuff. I've always been a rambunctious, crash-around, walk-on-the-wire kind of kid and the summers are where I get my circus fix. I bring in those folks from all over that I used to tour with or taught with somewhere, and we get together and share what we had once with the next generation. That's really what it's all about.[139]

The camp sessions are two weeks. They are preceded by one-week in-school residencies in June when Lawrence finds it too hot to conduct his Dr, Quark programs.

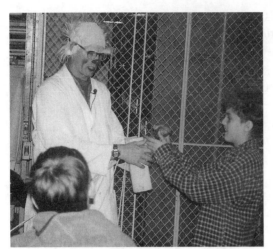

Ted Lawrence as Dr. Quintan Quark presents a Slapstick Science lesson, April 5, 2000 in Greenwich, New York.

The camp programs I run are not performance based and they are not show biz. At the end we do a recital. It's different than what Kevin [O'Keefe] does. He goes in to do a show. In the camp, our kids pick out what they want to do in the show. If they want to do tightwire, they have to be able to walk across it five times before they fall off which makes it more interesting for the audiences. More or less, kids get to do what they want to do. To juggle, you have to be able to keep your things up in the air. We lay down the standards and the kids always find something they want to do within two weeks.

I'm really excited about Norwich this year because it's our third year and that's usually where you see kids take off. So far we haven't put acts together. It's been real basic, but this year I want to get the kids ready for solo stuff. I'll tell them, "Work with diablo for three hours and come back when you have an act for me that goes from here to here." You can't do that until they have something to work with. We planted the seeds three years ago.[140]

The program is paid for by the participants through the Norwich Recreation Department. The 1999 staff included Barry Lubin (Grandma) who taught clowning and circus history; Ray Grins, who had taught with the National Circus Project, had been Ringmaster with The Circus Jaeger and had worked with Cirk Riga in Latvia, taught juggling, hand skills, unicycle, teeterboard, stilts and clowning; Lawrence's wife, Letty Miller, taught Spanish web, static trapeze, contortion, tight wire and acted as Resident Mom.

Although seasonal, circus camps introduce students to Circus Learning. When camps are a recurring part of a young person's experience, they permit campers to move beyond introduction to circus skills to mastery of them and, such is the nature of Circus Learning, the more one masters, the more it become possible to master.

VI
Circus Residencies

In circus residencies, visiting trainers enrich school curriculums with Circus Learning. As in circus camps, the training usually ends with a demonstration performance. Residencies impact the schools' physical education programs - sometimes supplying a program where none exists. In some residencies, Art, English and other teachers adapt their work to the circus activity. Some residencies are annual, others happen once with no follow-up. Some have related after-school programs that allow interested students to continue their Circus Learning after the residency ends. Some Physical Education teachers incorporate the Circus Skills they have learned along with the students into their curriculum.

The Big Apple Circus – Beyond the Ring™

When The Big Apple Circus was founded, it hoped to establish a school that would produce performers for the show. As a first step, the Circus started a pre-professional program in the Harbor School for the Performing Arts in East Harlem. One performing group, The Backstreet Flyers, emerged from this training program and joined the Circus. That program ended and no other groups have moved from the training programs to the circus. Acrobat Carlos Guity, the last product of the original program to perform with the Big Apple Circus, left the show at the end of the 1998 season.

The Big Apple Circus' current training is confined to the two or three, three or four week circus residencies held each year in East Harlem and to an afterschool program at the Alternative Education Complex 117 where interested students can continue their Circus Learning. November 20, 1997, the Big Apple Circus Arts in Education program (later renamed Beyond the Ring™) presented an afternoon performance at PS 155 in East Harlem, a mainly Hispanic area with many families newly arrived. Earlier in the day, the 155 participant fifth and sixth graders had done another show for the rest of the school. The residency that led to the program began three weeks earlier with a demonstration of circus skills by the instructors

Acrobats perform at the end of the Big Apple residency at PS 155 in New York City, November 20, 1997.

For the performances at PS 155, the walls and stage of the school auditorium were decorated with brightly painted pictures of clowns and large cutout tigers, monkeys and bears. The cutouts were identical suggesting the teacher controlled pumpkins that appear in school windows at Halloween and the turkeys of Thanksgiving. Students may have painted the figures; they did not design them, but the effect was cheery and circuslike.

The school's principal welcomed the guests, mostly families of the performers, in English and Spanish. She was followed by the head of the Parent Teachers Association who encouraged parents to join the Association. She explained what a parent teacher organization was and how the parents' participation could support their children's learning.

Greg De Santo, who has clowned for Big Apple and Ringling, was the top hatted Ringmaster-interlocutor who introduced the acts much as Kevin O'Keefe does with Circus Minimus. While O'Keefe is involved with the acts as well as introducing them, DeSanto did not participate in the presentation. Viveca Gardiner, the Big Apple Circus Director of Special Projects, worked the large boombox that provided contemporary and circus music that accompanied the acts.

The participants' achievements in juggling and tumbling were on an introductory level although several demonstrated talent and a strong affinity for the work. The show was a joyous experience for the participants who smiled with pride at their achievements; the joy was shared by their parents.

DeSanto's wife, Karen, also a clown, had led the children to create original clown act on "Beauty School Drop Outs", a clown mirror skit and traditional acts like "The Enlarging Machine" and "The World's Strongest Man". Frank Sellito, who is in charge of the Big Apple afterschool program, taught acrobatics; Russell Davis was the juggling instructor. Instruction had taken place during regular class hours. There had been a total of ten, forty-minute meetings with each group and each act was done by a class. All but one of the six participating classes appeared in a juggling act, an acrobatic act and a clown act; this meant there was little more than three classes to prepare each act. One sixth grade class only did a juggling act. The clown acts had rehearsed in the auditorium; acrobatic and juggling acts had rehearsed in the school's gymnasium. All performing students wore Big Apple T-Shirts; clowns also wore red noses.

Ms. Gardiner states that a goal of the residencies is to stimulate work in other arts and in writing. The Circus provides guide lines

and not just for art, but for circus math and circus reading and circus history. We give them materials and projections. We do require that there be some writing exercises that are generally pretty simple. We leave it up to the teachers - if they're working on poetry, they can do circus poetry. Some teachers will have them write about "How do you feel about the circus?", "What do you want to be in the circus" and the final one will be, "How did it feel to be on stage?" Just anything to get them writing.[141]

In 1999 it became possible to download the fifty-three page *Big Apple Circus Study Guide* from the Big Apple Circus Web site.

Leslie Moore, principal of Junior High 99, who oversees the project for the Board of Education, has been involved with the Big Apple schools program from the beginning. According to Gardiner, Moore "is the consultant to the program who advises us on educational issues and school issues and Board of Ed issues. She helps make our contacts with schools; she oversees the teaching staff. Anytime you work in the schools you have to be licensed by the Board of Ed."[142]

According to Moore, "I'm here because I started this program and I want to be sure it maintains its integrity and its quality of teaching and the level of expectation and its focus and the vision which changes as the education changes."[143]   Later in the day at the after school program, Moore expressed disappointment that PS 155 had provided no art component for the residency. The clown pictures and the animal cutouts had been created during the previous year's residency.

We'll evaluate, do we go back or go to a new school? I think we should go to a different school each time. The teachers didn't come through for us; they did last year. There was a lot of excitement. If they're not going to follow through on what we request, then why go back? It's not an expensive program. It costs the school $1500. It's cheap compared to other programs and it integrates art into the curriculum.[144]

According to Gardiner, the $1500. the school pays, which comes from a Board of Education arts grant, is about 15% of the cost of the program. The New York State Council on the Arts requires a 15% contribution from recipient schools before it provides assistance. The New York State Council contributed 35% and Big Apple fund raised for the rest.

Anyone attending a performance like the one at PS 155 can see its value for the students, the school and the community. Gardiner believes there is a great need for the program.

In another school we worked in, the kids had never been to their own gym. We're talking about 10 to 12 year olds who have no performing arts program, no visual arts program, no physical education program, no music. They have never been on the stage. They have never performed. The stage was just for showing them movies; it was like a holding room. Physical education is particularly frustrating because it doesn't cost anything. It's not a question of the budget being cut. You turn kids loose in a gym; you give them a rubber ball. Kids need to run around. They have so much energy.

In our first program, I had a ton of kids who wanted to do art. We changed the program, now kids do both. At that time, they were either onstage or backstage and I had a lot of kids who wanted to do backstage. I asked a girl, a fifth grader, maybe eleven years old, whether she liked art. She said, "I don't know, our teacher says we're too old for art." I don't mean to be on a soap box about this, but I honestly think that you can't learn to think and form an opinion and understand where your emotions come from without arts education. So we do try and it's just so clear how much it means to the kids and how much pride they take in performing and showing off what they're doing to their parents.[145]

Students in the lower grades at PS 155 who saw the program probably did not have one of their own when they reached fifth grade. In a city where the need is great and the resources limited such inequities may be inevitable, but they are unfortunate. Students who develop an interest in circus skills during residencies can continue in the Big Apple afterschool program that is conducted two afternoons a week for children from third grade up. There the skill level moves beyond the rudimentary and is demonstrated in a Spring show. Students in the afterschool program work on parallel bars, trapeze, unicycles, stilts, Spanish web, rolling globes and mini-tramps. Clowning is taught later in the year. There is a staff of seven instructors and four paid interns who graduated from the program. Leslie Moore, who is always in attendance, noted values the program fostered.

They do compete in their own way - in terms of doing better in their skills. And there is cooperation. You see, they're helping each other with the bikes and that's what we try to foster - kids working with each other instead of against each other.[146]

Moore established ground rules for the program which is funded entirely by Big Apple. Each participant signs a contract that must be adhered to; each must attend on a regular basis. In Moore's words, "The rules are very consistent. In everything that you want to be good, you must be consistent. We got it down to a science."[147]

At the Spring Show of the afterschool program held on the morning of June 11, 1998, bleachers had been set up at one end of the gymnasium where the program is held. Large Big Apple Circus posters decorated the walls. The printed program indicated that the participants were drawn from twelve schools. The 10:00 AM show, one of several, was for school children.

Most participants were costumed in Big Apple T-shirts; some aerial performers wore leotards with decorative tops. The trainers acted as spotters and support people. Hilary Chaplain, the Clowning Instructor, was the ringmaster. A few youngsters wore clown makeup and clowned throughout the presentation; in large clown acts, other clowns wore red noses. The recorded music reflected Sellito's background as an acrobat at the Metropolitan Opera; it often seemed unrelated to the performance.

Performers in the Big Apple Arts in Education Spring Show, July 11, 1998.

Chaplain kept things moving, but the presentation was more a demonstration of untheatricalized skills than a show. One exception was an act in which girls on stilts dressed as angels and boys on the floor, as devils. Unicycle and juggling skills were good - a few performers outstanding. The most advanced were the male tumblers. While the majority of performers appeared to be elementary and middle school students, the tumblers were older. One wonders if tumbling is more appealing to inner city teenage boys than other circus arts. One thinks of the Backstreet Flyers that came out of the early years of the Big Apple schools program and of the St. Louis Arches produced by Circus Flora's school. The Big Apple Spring Show 1998 would have been enhanced if someone had Kevin O'Keefe's ability to transform skills into a "show," not just for the audience, but for the participants. However, the performers' spirit was infectious; their pride in their achievements palpable. The audience response suggested how exciting it was for the youngsters to witness their peers' achievements.

The Big Apple Beyond the Ring™ program is important for bringing Circus Learning to students who have limited opportunities to discover their strengths and capabilities. The program points up the unmet need for such learning.

Join the Circus . . . Become a Star!

Circus of the Kids logo

Circus of the Kids

Bruce Pfeffer's Circus of the Kids in Tallahassee, Florida offers a menu of programs to sponsoring organizations. (See Program Materials.) Pfeffer, a graduate of the Florida State University circus program, started The Circus of the Kids in 1982 after being one of four FSU graduates who set up circus programs at Club Med. Circus of the Kids programs have operated at schools in Florida, Massachusetts, Ontario, Tennessee and Maryland; at resorts in Florida and New York; on cruise ships; at camps in New York, Connecticut and Pennsylvania; for recreation departments in Florida and New Hampshire.

Skills taught include acrobatics, juggling, clowning, teeterboard, bicycle, highwire and flying trapeze. The eight- to twelve-person staff figures importantly in the performances. Safety lines are used in the high acts and in teeterboard. Circus of the Kids supplies all apparatus, liability insurance, props, ring curbs, costumes and makeup, music, *Circus Across the Curriculum* - an interdisciplinary academic package developed especially for circus, organizing and fund raising materials, press releases, video equipment for instructional use. Circus of the Kids encourages sponsors to use the performances as the focus for fundraising.

Circus of the Kids teaches responsibility, exercises muscles, develops motor skills, builds self-esteem, enhances stage presence, creates community support and good will, generates positive media attention and most important: benefits all youngsters.

There's no such thing as being unable to make the team in Circus of the Kids. All students can participate whether large, small, quick, slow, short, tall, or even physically or mentally challenged.

Circus of the Kids puts all your students in the spotlight![148]

Circus Smirkus Residency

The context for the Circus Smirkus Residency at Sudbury's Country School in Vermont in December, 1997 was so different from the context for the Big Apple Residency at PS 155 in East Harlem the previous month, that comparisons are impossible. Sudbury is a small town in a rural area; its elementary school, almost hidden from the road, is built into the side of a hill. Sudbury's Country School is not an island surrounded by the kinds of social problems that surround PS 155. Vermont does have its own poverty - often hidden in the hills and Vermont's children are not exempt from social ills, but the pressure is less. At Sudbury, the all-white student body does not have its learning complicated by the need to master English as a second language as do many at P.S. 155.

Sudbury's Country School is open classroom. The classes are Primary Unit (first and second grade), Intermediate Unit (third and fourth grade), and the Fifth and Sixth Grade Unit. The modern school building is mostly one room; the groups separated by walls that do not reach the ceiling. Rather than dealing with 155 fifth and sixth graders as the Big Apple residency had at PS 155, the Smirkus Residency at Sudbury involved all sixty or so students in the school, including one who is autistic, as well as the teachers and the principal.

The residency was conducted by Troy Wunderle, who had toured with

Troy Wunderle teaches plate spinning during the Circus Smirkus residency in the Sudbury, Vermont Country School, 1997.

Ringling for a year and a half as a clown, and his wife Sara, a recent University of Vermont graduate in physical therapy who learned juggling, stilt walking and other circus skills. Troy earned a degree in Graphic Design before going to Ringling's Clown College where he met Rob Mermin who was then its co-director. Until 1996, Mermin conducted the Smirkus residencies himself; he hired Wunderle to join him and by the end of the year Wunderle was doing them himself and with Sara.

During the two week residency, the Wunderles worked with the older Units two hours a day; with the younger Unit, one hour. The first day the Wunderles demonstrated circus skills. Because the entire school was studying pre-history, the final presentation at nearby Otter Valley High School was *A Prehistoric Circus*. While the skills of the student were rudimentary, they were put together into a coherent, well-paced show. The stage was decorated as if prehistoric; the magic act involved a floating, irregularly shaped, rock. The primary class was divided into turtles whose heads poked through cardboard shells, and dinosaurs who wore costumes of garbage bags and cardboard spines. Cecilia Dixon, a grandmother-volunteer, created the costumes. In the performance, the turtles were slow moving on all fours; the dinosaurs loud, aggressive and mischievous. They performed in what was essentially a clown act in which they sat up and took poses on cue from Troy Wunderle whose clown sensibility infused everything. Each act was set up as a gag with a payoff - in circus terms, a "blow off".

Troy Wunderle, costumed in striped tights and a striped long sleeved shirt that stuck out from his cave man costume, was the onstage cheerleader. His face smeared with earth-colored makeup, he wore black eyeglass frames. Sara, also costumed as a cave person, was at the side of the stage operating the taped music while she did a narration about a group of cave people who had a Vermont style town meeting and decided to invent the circus.

The Intermediate Unit did acrobatics - somersaults and diving somersaults over one, two, three and four prone children. Then, the smallest member of the group was selected to leap over all of the others. Aghast at being chosen, he refused, but finally agreed. The others lay down. After a long warmup, rather than jump, he ran over them.

The Fifth and Sixth Grade Unit did acrobatics and the magic levitation act with a rock. They also did a routine where four people sat on chairs and linked arms which held them up when the chairs were removed. It was the routine Molly Pelley, a Smirkus graduate clowning with Ringling that year, was doing on the Greatest Show on Earth.

Faculty participated in the training sessions and in the performance demonstrating new found skills. The autistic child, in full makeup and costume and accompanied by a tutor, carried a sign across the stage in the opening parade. The teachers did a routine while seated with crossed legs, on a row of chairs, the principal at the end. After a while, the teacher at the other end from the principal asked the person next to her, "Now?" The question was passed along the row to the principal who said, "No" and passed the answer back. After several attempts the principal said, "Yes," and all crossed their legs simultaneously in the other direction.

The training and the show gave participants and audience a sense that circus skills are fun and impressive when they are mastered. There was community involvement and Troy Wunderle's humor, mastery of skills and his ability to adapt them to the time available and abilities of his students made it successful.

As the printed program said :

This program was made possible through a generous contribution of the William Center Trust Fund. Thanks to Rob Mermin for the inspiration from Circus Smirkus. We would like to thank the many volunteers who helped with the circus. We especially appreciate the efforts of the students of Sudbury who invested their time and energy to make this show a success. Thank you Troy and Sara for this wonderful experience. The students and staff have learned from you, enjoyed working with you, and above all, had fun with you.

Not all Smirkus Residencies residencies are in schools as small as Sudbury. Residencies in Burlington, Vermont can involve over 300 students. Smirkus offers two options for residencies: Option I is a skills workshop, Option II includes a show. The weekly fees for either option depend on the number of students involved: under 75, 75-250 and over 250. Most Option I residencies are for one week; Option II for two. In November 1998, Smirkus had already booked ten residencies for the year and by the end would have more.

Schools in Vermont and New Hampshire may apply to the State Arts Councils for assistance in paying for Smirkus residencies. Smirkus residencies are at the middle to upper end of Vermont and New Hampshire residencies in terms of expense, but in the words of Smirkus Adminstrator Beth LeCours,

> We're probably one of the only residencies that reaches all the kids. Dance residencies start to do that, but there are always boys who don't want to dance. Or there are kids who don't want to be involved if the residencies do things in the visual arts saying, "I can't draw." With circus everybody finds something to do.[149]

Schools also apply for other grants, some of them local. If grants figure importantly in funding a residence, it is difficult to get a grant for a second year. However, Le Cours tells of a school in New Hampshire where a residency

> worked out so fabulously that they are going to use it again for their last two weeks of school when the kids are hyped up and the teachers are kind of at their low. It was a great way to finish the year. It kept everybody interested and they could tie up what they'd been doing in Science and Gym and Art so they didn't lose momentum. They took on the commitment in their school to fund raise so they could do it again this year.[150]

In 1999, Jesse Dryden, another graduate of Clown College, assisted Troy Wunderle before assuming responsibility for his own Smirkus residencies. During the 1999-2000 year Wunderle and Dryden conducted residencies in 21 schools. The Smirkus residencies embody the Circus Smirkus Philosophy of Education: "Circus Smirkus is a nonprofit organization founded in Vermont to provide a format for kids and adults to collaborate as colleagues in life enhancing artistic adventures through the circus."[151]

Great Youth Circus
Tim Tegge, who grew up on his family's small circus and for a while headed Clown Alley on the Clyde Beatty-Cole Brothers Circus, created The Great Youth Circus in 1998. Its first residence was at the Wilson Middle School in Appleton, Wisconsin. The staff included Tegge; his wife Gigi who has worked as clown and illusionist with her husband; Russian aerialist Gulnara Salakhova; Robert Goode, a juggler, hand balancer and magician; and Ukrainian Oleg Gapon, acrobat and teeterboard artist. The four-week residency culminated in public performances.

Tim Tegge coaches a young aerialist during the first residency of his Great Youth Circus at the Appleton, Wisconsin Middle School, 1998.
Credit: Great Youth Circus

Tegge described his intentions for the program on the second day of the residency:

This is the first attempt for me doing a full-fledged youth circus program. I'm using professional circus performers as instructors. The first week and a half we are invading the standard physical education classes. We're giving everybody a chance to try their hands at swinging on the trapeze, doing the web, juggling and tumbling. We're up against certain restrictions. For example, we have a former Ukrainian trampoline champion, Oleg Gapon, but there's a Wisconsin law that prohibits the use of trampolines on school premises. So we're trying to dance around that.

We're working on a lot of the basics. Single trapeze work, various kinds of aerial work, rolla bolla, balancing and things like that. We'll be doing magic and illusions, professional style circus clowning. We're having regular theatrical makeup classes. What we're trying to do is take the best of traditional circus things and the more advanced type of circus things that seem to be so successful today.

This is a trial thing for us to see what is possible. You have to find your own niche and everyone has a different way of going about things. At the end of this month-long program, we will present five public performances. The show will have about 100 students participating in it. We're professional performers looking at what we can do with kids. We can't look at the word impossible, because we couldn't even think of being here then. We're not going to be able to get kids doing triple somersaults, but what they are going to do they'll be able to be proud of. They will be dressed in professional wardrobe. We have assembled a collection from performers. I've purchased things, had performers loan or give things to me and a lot of that stems from the fact that I've been in the business professionally; I have these contacts. So we're ahead on that standpoint, but at this point it's sort of let's just take a deep breath and away we go.[152]

Publicity photographs show students in traditional clown makeup. Specially designed printed posters and newspaper ads were prepared for the show. After the show, Tegge said,

It was a great success all the way around. The four public performances all received standing ovations. We jam packed 'em. It was really just a great project.

The trampoline was all set, but we couldn't do anything with fire. That was the only snag. A friend of mine who was on the steering committee is a circus fan and he videotaped all our rehearsals; the PE classes and all the performances. We are going to start tomorrow putting together a tape of the show - actually a couple different tapes. We're going to put together a promotional tape as well as a tape we can offer to the kids. I did a magazine program.

A school in the Upper Peninsula of Michigan is interested in us. They came to see the show with some people from the school district and expressed interest in doing something up there.

We only lost five kids over the month period. Two were so bogged down with overloaded schedules that they just couldn't participate. One was kind of a problem child and ended up getting himself in enough trouble that he excused himself and there were two that registered that never showed up for practices. We had 101 participating students.

They handed out questionnaires to all the students and all the parents involved and one of the questions was, "Would you be interested in seeing this project return next year?" There was not one single negative response so we will be back.

I had a couple of dates on Friday and Saturday this past week for fund raisers I did with a couple of the instructors I had used for the school project. I also took two of the kids who were jugglers and used them on the show; they did a great job. I think we got them brainwashed to think of this as a career. We hear that one of the girls that was doing lyra - it's a round trapeze - has told her folks that's what she wants for Christmas.

It turned out being a lot more than we expected it to be all around. It was a great amount of work, but it was so much more rewarding in every way than we could have possibly anticipated.[153]

Green Fools - Bricks and Earth Circus

A recurring theme in this book is the use of Circus Learning to address the needs of disadvantaged youth. Xstine P. Cook and Kathleen "Mooky" Cornish created The Bricks and Earth Circus in 2000 to serve First Nation youngsters in Western Canada. Cook wrote of the venture,

It was created by the founders and Dean Bareham and Jennifer Esdale of Green Fools Theatre, a physical theatre company in Calgary, Canada, with the collaboration of Birddancer, a Cree per-former. It's the Sex Pistols meets Cirque du Soleil bringing kick-butt theatre to small Canadian towns.

The Bricks and Earth Circus toured to remote communities in Alberta, including towns and First Nation villages in the summer of 2000. It also played in Calgary, Edmonton and Lethbridge. A work-shop component was put into practice in every location except Edmonton. The compa-ny worked with children up to four hours a day for four days teaching stilt walking, juggling, tum-bling, banner painting and clowning. The chil-dren had opportunities to perform in the shows in their own segments. It was a wonderful experi-ence and plenty of hard work. Our open air venue, the St. Louis Double Tipi Big Top (named for the

Buffalo Guards, Brick and Earth Circus.
Credit:Xpandora

Western/rebel/outlaw/hero Louis Riel) was very vulnerable to weather and required hours to set up and tear down. Due to it being our first year, we had a minimal crew and found that the intensive labour of running a circus was very hard on our artists. We made mistakes, but we learned a lot. In the coming seasons we aim to return to the communities in which we have begun building future circus stars and to head overseas.[154]

Cook amplified her thoughts about Bricks and Earth Circus's first season in a phone interview.

Much of the development work was paid for by government grants. The Canada Council's Millenium Fund provided $75,000. There were additional grants from the Canada Council and the Alberta Foundation for the Arts. When we were on the road, we relied on fees by the various First Nation organizations that brought us in to teach circus skills to their kids. At the Whitefish Lake Reservation, the kids were about 10 to 15 and at others they were younger, five to 12. In addition to teaching circus skills, we also did workshops about how to have stage presence and hold a stage.

The circus enclosure was two tipis that were a lobby. A fence ran around the area with a big scaffolding backdrop and a circus ring on the ground. It was quite beautiful. At the end of the four days, we had our own Green Fools show that ran about two hours and within that was a part where the community kids performed. The show was a play that had circus skills involved in it. We had hoped to have a tightrope walker and a trampoline group, but couldn't afford it this year so we worked with the skills the troupe had.

The tour was about five months. We started in mid May and were done by mid September, but we weren't gone the whole time. We imagined that we would be, but we had about five weeks off here and there. We would come home and then go back out again.

When we do it again, we're deemphasizing the play part, adding more circus and making it shorter - an hour. The show was about the treatment of the natives in Calgary and more specifically the loss of the buffalo which were wiped out when the trains came out west. The second half was very dramatic. We changed it half way through the season and made it lighter, but retained that content. We had a massive buffalo head carved out of styrofoam that was balanced in a balancing act and got knocked down when a big Iron Horse puppet came in. The revised show will retain some elements of that.

Green Fools is a mask and puppet company so we thought we'd have a puppet menagerie with a bear and owls and coyotes and all the different North American creatures, but we only had the buffalo and the coyote. We'll do more of that next year as well as some smaller scale things so we can do an aerial act.

The kids totally loved it. On the reserves there is really nothing else going on. At the first reserve we didn't set time and space parameters for the kids and they were around 24 hours a day. All over everything, all the time. But they were pretty amazing. A couple of them had a trampoline in their yard so they could do standing flips off the fence posts and on the ground, too. We had them do that in the circus.

The proposal we made to Millenium Fund was totally monstrous and we pulled it off somehow, but just barely. We haven't had enough punishment. We'll take it out again next year. [155]

National Circus Project

The National Circus Project, in Westbury, New York, is a nonprofit educational corporation that provides a variety of Circus Learning residence options. JeanPaul Jenack, the founder and director, began developing a circus arts program on Long Island in the 1970's and incorporated the National Circus Project in 1984. At a time when school budgets, especially in the area of enrichment, are strained, Jenack's programs, which integrate smoothly into school schedules, have proven attractive. They are their cost-effective, exciting, and provide learning.

National Circus Project flyer

They also help schools meet mandates for Physical Education activities that include all students. The National Circus Project has also developed circus related materials for academic courses. The various National Circus Project programs are described in Program Literature (p. 247).

National Circus Project also provides *The Greatest Show in Schools* in which larger groups of instructors help students prepare a circus performance; *The One-Man Circus,* a solo circus performance; *The Center-Ring Mini-Circus,* a two person performance; *The Big Top Stage Circus* a 75-90 minute performance by a troupe of circus artists; and *Estrada – Walk-around Entertainment* that includes stilt-walking, unicycling, clowning, face painting, magic, balloon sculpture, object manipulation and "character" or interactive performing for events.

National Circus Project is the largest Circus Learning residency program encountered in preparing this study. Each year it meets between 275,000 and 375,000 students in schools and camps. Its twelve core employees work forty-eight weeks a year and receive health insurance, retirement benefits and a pension plan. About twenty-two other instructors work part-time.

About ten percent of National Circus Project's work is in Senior High Schools. This is the only residency program the author encountered that had entered High Schools. In an interview, Benack told how this happened and how the National Circus Project evolved.

We wound up with a Senior High program as a result of having presented programs in elementary schools over the years, having that follow into middle school and then into high schools. We have kids in some school districts we have been collaborating with for twelve to fifteen years.

An aspect of our program that has made it successful is the way many schools use the culminating event of our residence program as their fund raiser. The schools often find that if they take a chance with us the first year, and then have a fund raiser the second year, they can generate the entire cost of the program. Some schools discover they can not afford to not have us because the program pays for itself.

It all started in the early 70's when I taught Circus Arts through the Department of Health, Physical Education, Recreation and Dance at Nassau Community College on Long Island. I taught a series of tumbling and circus arts courses for theatre majors. This was about the time Hovey Burgess was teaching in colleges and Nina Krasavina and Gregory Fedin were working in New York City and then in Hoboken. There was a lot of hype then about creating a top-level, professional circus school. I had been to the Moscow Circus School and various Chinese acrobatic centers and they did not have professional schools at first. They had established feeder mechanisms. Acrobatics and circus skills were taught at the youngest levels of education and then up through the lines. All kids received this training and the best could move to excel. That appeared to me to be the model that had succeeded in every country that had an effective circus education system. Most people want to go up in education; I thought it would be interesting to go down.

I wrote a grant to National Endowment for the Arts. I redefined circus for them by saying it was an oral tradition art that was usually passed down from masters to apprentices; that it was usually a family, or sub-community, oriented activity that had its own language, code, conduct and other things that classify it as a folk art. They funded me for two years to work in a school district in New York where I created a K-12 Circus Education Program.

The program, a regular part of Physical Education, was successful and continued for twenty years. I was asked about setting up similar programs at other schools. I began, not running residences, but as a consultant for the Physical Education or Athletics Departments helping them set up their programs. Then I realized that wasn't working because the teachers were afraid they would have to master all the skills. I decided the best thing to do was to get into their classes and run a model activity and show them everything that was necessary for them to run it. I set up the stations, the commands, the safety procedures, and provided the educational language they would need to justify it as a curricular activity.

I set up a workshop residency program in 1979-1980. In the first year, I did about 240 schools and I thought something here is meeting the kids' needs. At that time there was a push towards lifetime and leisure sports activity. The schools were being given mandates to provide individual, self-directed, non-contact or low-contact, isotonic, aerobic activities, but the mandates were not funded. Teachers saw that circus classes met their needs and provided motivation for students. Kids who were non-verbal or in racial, social or economic minorities, could fit in an expressive activity and experience heightened self-esteem.

I believe the reason our program has become so widespread is that I designed it to fit into the average school day. When we come into a school, there is a presentation during the regularly scheduled morning assembly. Subsequent to that, we teach for five periods as part of the physical education program the way teachers teach. Teachers say to us, "You don't disrupt the program, you become part of the school."

We work with gifted and talented kids; we work with kids who are in the adaptive Phys Ed program. As a result, schools feel justified bringing in our program because it's not a program for the few, it's a program for the many. Some other programs immediately try to get to the next level of performance. They have all the kids in a basic workshop and then audition and take twelve or fifteen or twenty kids and work with them. We do a culminating event with eighty or hundred – sometimes a hundred and sixty kids. They may not perform at an extremely high level the first year, but all those kids will have gone through the essential rite of passage of learning a basic series of skills, refining one of more of them so they have a beginning a middle and end to their trick. They interact with others who will be in that act. They understand their function in context of a performance which is followed by the validation of the community. Even at an elementary level, the kids understand what they have done. They haven't watched an elite group do things they can't do.

The National Circus Project and other groups that work from the bottom up are thriving while many of the "professional" programs that started when we did are gone. If we could get a partnership and work hand in hand, our work could take off across the country. We could have our circus schools radiating off a national facility that was fed by a variety of feeder mechanisms with a variety of approaches. It would give us some of the best talent in the world. [156]

Circus residencies, like circus camps, enrich the lives of young people by introducing them to Circus Learning. The best possible situations permit students to continue their learning after the residences end.

VII
Inschool Programs

Preparing this study, the author encountered three primary schools, one in Australia, the others in the United States, that integrate Circus Learning into their curriculums. Public school teachers started two of the programs by teaching circus skills before and after school. The other program, at a private school, began when a parent with circus skills was asked to do a circus activity. One wonders how many such programs, first marginal and then integral to a school, have been created by determined individuals. One hopes that as more skilled performers emerge from the new Circus Learning programs, more people will be available to combine circus and teaching.

Cascade Elementary School

When interviewed, Jerry Burkhalter had been Physical Education Specialist at the 550 student Cascade Elementary School in Renton, Washington ten years. During that time, his Circus Arts program became the centerpiece of the school's Physical Education.

Cascade Elementary School unicyclists in the 1999 Renton River Days Parade. credit: Cascade Elementary School

I encourage kids to experiment with unique activities. There is a balance program that includes unicycles – the tall ones, all kinds, walking balls and balance beams; juggling; and acro-tumbling. The kids use a punch trampoline and perform aerials all the way from front-tucks, half-flips, straddle-mounts, 360's - the basic things. The most impressive trick is the front tuck over people. When you have a program like this, you get lots of publicity. We've had newspapers and television involved and we participate in community activities. That keeps the kids pumped up.

It began with a zero-hour class – before school starts, and an after-school program. Last year, I made some changes when I became involved in a Masters of Education program and needed the time before and after school to work on papers. As a result, I made Circus Arts part of the Physical Education program.

The first month I give instruction in the circus skills. Then I give the students choice-based activities. There are probably twelve including acro-tumbling, trapeze, rings, climbing ropes, unicycling, walking ball, and juggling. Stations are set up and the kids can move from one to another.

Circus Arts has become the core of my PE program. If I were to draw a curriculum template, in the center it would say, "Circus Arts: unicycling, juggling, walking balls, acro-tumbling and more." From there it would branch out to basketball, volleyball and so on. We can get a line soccer game going for twenty minutes and stop it and go into a program where the circus equipment comes out and the kids have ten minutes of choice time on it. Then we put it away and do three minutes of jumping rope and then play a game of dodgeball or something. Once we've done with basketball, we come right back to Circus Arts for a week. Then we go to volleyball and we come back. The kids are constantly getting the interval work they need to learn those skills starting in the first grade.

That's when I start them juggling scarves and doing forward rolls – lots of forward rolls and a lot of punching off the ramp and landing on two feet. The first graders walk on walking balls; they are a kick on them. I have five little unicycles. I set them out at a station and have the kids walk over, take them, wheel them in front of them and go through little patterns and around corners. They're not even sitting on them, but they're feeling the wheel. Then I teach them to put them away properly with the seat down. They have a ball with them and some of them sit against the wall on them and learn the basic mounts and dismounts. A few ride; more do in the second grade. Lots in the third grade and lots and lots in the fourth grade. It becomes a fourth grade thing. The fifth graders have been doing it for four years – they're off playing football, but they come back when we do programs. They're still the best in the school.

We've done a full blown circus for our school and others as fund raisers. That was fun. We did it with the sixth graders back when we had sixth graders. Now they're off at the Middle School. Losing the sixth grade took away a year of development, especially in juggling. I used to have sixth graders juggling torches and passing clubs. We haven't had too much of that in the fifth grade. We have also done assemblies for other schools, performed at senior citizen centers, and have been a major attraction at the annual Renton River Days parade. We've done half-time performances for professional, college and highschool basketball games. We've probably done thirty perfor-mances over the last ten years.

I've always enjoyed playing. That's why I got into Physical Education. When you're at play, even the work becomes fun. When I turned forty, I decided to try to ride a unicycle. I had come across five of them in the district in the boiler room of the Maplewood Elementary School. They hadn't been used in ten years. I fixed them up and started with the five and went from there. First, I taught myself to ride. That was brutal; you don't want to hear about that. After I could ride, I thought, wouldn't juggling be neat with this? You think of a unicycle, you think of a juggler. So I taught myself that, too. Then I used books and went to clinics. I perform a lot myself. I've done assemblies and classroom performances. I teach a poetry class while I juggle.

Now that I'm in the Masters program, I've taken a step back and see that I've given back a lot of the control I once worked to get. Right now, if a first grade kid comes in and bangs off five back hand-springs, I'll say, "Do it again. Keep doing it, but put some mats down and make it safe." I've seen so many teachers who'd say to a kid like that, "Sit down. We don't do those in gym," because they think it's dangerous. It's a matter of giving the kids something. If it wasn't a unicycle, it would be a volleyball or something. If they have the work ethic and the patience and the determination to learn to ride a unicy-cle, they are good at just about everything they choose to do.[157]

Dubbo West Public School

The year after Jerry Burkhalter started his program, Paul Woodhead started a circus program at the Dubbo West Public School in New South Wales, Australia. By 1998, the program had become so successful that he and another teacher, Deborah Duffy, published a detailed account of what they had achieved to encourage others to follow suit.[158]

Woodhead and Duffy believe Circus Learning offers what traditional sports fail to offer - fitness training, participation and skill development for *all* children. Since students follow their own agendas in Circus Learning, failure is not possible; students decide when and how to participate as individuals or as parts of groups. Circus Learning also provides a way for children to play out roles they create in their imaginations. The program developed by Woodhead and Duffy has a strong theatrical element; as students develop skills, acts emerge that comment on the contemporary world. To achieve this, Woodhead and Duffy propose two rules - share your equipment and knowledge; respect the equipment and return it to its rightful place when you are done.

The authors see competition in Circus Learning as different than that which occurs in traditional physical education. In Circus Learning, competition is goal centered. Children are not afraid of trying because there is no judgment on drops or falls, there is no failure, just an opportunity to try again. Even when a child is asking to pass a skill level, the emphasis is not on the failure to pass, but the need to retry, to persevere until the skill is mastered.[159]

The Dubbo Circus Learning program began as a response to the needs of children with behavioral problems. It offered isolated children an opportunity to participate in group activities; it was also an opportunity for outsiders to abandon the social roles in which they were trapped as bullies, victims or the unusual.

There is certainly an impact (major in our case) on the culture of a school when Circus is integrated into the school's curriculum. This is especially so if it is more than just a PE program. We initiated ours purely as a welfare program and that is still essentially what it is, although it amounts to up to 30% of the sports program in any one term and caters for up to 25% of children during lunchtime.[160]

Circus Learning *Physical Education* classes focus on techniques for mastering one piece of apparatus per lesson. Circus Learning, as *School Sport*, is more concerned with participation and peer teaching. *Lunchtime Circus*, which has had greatest impact at Dubbo, allows children to come and go and use the equipment freely. There are also performances that permit students to present their work in a theatrical setting. Dubbo added a weekly afterschool class to permit graduates to continue to develop their skills and prepare acts to audition for the performing unit. *Circus in Schools* notes an additional value of Circus Learning in a school context; it permits teachers and students to know each other better and for all to become acquainted with members of the school community with whom they are not otherwise involved.

At the center of Circus Learning at Dubbo are six clearly defined skill levels assigned to each circus activity. As students move from level to level, their accomplishments are acknowledged in school assemblies. The level system provides children an opportunity to set goals and to progress safely. *Circus in Schools* provides levels of achievement for diablo, juggling, stilts, tumbling, devil stick, rola bola, unicycle, clowning, acrobatics, and balance and spin.

Woodhead and Duffy offer suggestions for developing performances that showcase students' circus skills. *Parades* can be part of local festivals; *Busking,* in which students integrate skills into short routines, become more sophisticated as the skill levels increase. The Busking routines can be presented informally in a variety of settings and as part of *Full Circus Performances.*

Circus West is the name of the Dubbo West circus performance. In addition to providing students an opportunity to transform skills into performance, *Circus West* helps other schools develop circus programs by demonstrating the advantages of Circus Learning in education. Circus West adapted rules from the Sailor Circus in Sarasota, Florida. While Sailor Circus participants are required to maintain good grades, at Dubbo West "It is possible that insistence on academic standards will be eased to give children with less academic ability a chance to stay in as members."[161]

Woodhead and Duffy note the salutary effects the Dubbo West program has had not only on participants, but on the school that is now known for its innovative programs; Circus being the most notable. The benefits extend to the larger community which uses Circus West in Festivals in place of bringing in outside entertainment. Circus West has also been paid to teach and perform at other schools, some quite distant. Circus West, and the program of which it is part, have been recognized by the State Governor and the Minister of Education on a number of occasions.

Circus Learning has become part of the curriculum at several other schools in New South Wales. **Campbelltown Performing Arts High School** started an extra-curricular circus activity in 1993; it soon became an elective subject for years seven-ten and a performing group developed. **Plumpton High School** makes tumbling and clowning part of its Sports Coaching course for years nine and ten; there is additional work in years eleven and twelve in Drama, Health and Physical Education. **Condobolin High School** started offering Circus in 1996 and made it a sports option in 1997. The **Acrobatic Arts Community School** in Wodonga, Victoria, Australia, which changed its name to the **Flying Fruit Fly School**, was discussed in Chapter Three.

The Pine Hill Waldorf School

Waldorf Schools, based on the teaching of German educator Rudolf Steiner, believe learning must be physical and creative as well as intellectual if a child is to achieve "wholeness." All students learn to knit, crochet and do carpentry as part of their classroom work; studies are introduced when they are considered most appropriate to children's development. Circus Arts are placed in the Middle School curriculum. In Waldorf Schools, art is not something done when the

Unicyclists perform in the 1998 Pine Hill Waldorf School Hilltop Circus. The act concluded with 10 unicyclists.

"real" work is over and gymnastics are not an interruption of learning. Spatial Dynamics, the Waldorf term for gymnastics, aims at "the gradually unfolding spatial awareness and movement capacities of the human being."[162]

The presentation of Circus Skills varies in Waldorf schools; some do

none. The program at the Pine Hill Waldorf School in Wilton, New Hampshire began when Jackie Davis, a student's parent who is a mime married to a former Ringling clown, was asked by teachers to bring circus skills to the school. A parent couple who were circus fans gave Davis $1,000 seed money. She bought two unicycles, juggling clubs and other basic equipment. As students developed skills, it seemed a logical next step to Davis to put together The Hill Top Circus "presented by the Incredibly Amazing Middle School Students of the Pine Hill Waldorf School".[163]

The 1998 Third Annual Hilltop Circus, presented on the school's stage February 6, 7 and 8, honored the school's 25th anniversary.   Davis directed the show from a drum set at the side of the stage; she was joined by the local seven piece Hollis Dixieland Band and a keyboardist. The show featured Davis, joined by three students doing club juggling; other jugglers; gymnasts; tightwire performers; magicians; clowns; dancers; and a mime act - The Acme Do-It-Yourself Mime Kit, in which would-be mimes were presented with an empty package that contained equipment around which they built their act. The climax of that year's Hilltop Circus was a ten-student unicycle act. The circus allowed the students to transform their skills into a joyous performance that was exciting for the community. It also raised money for the Pine Hill Physical Education program.

Between performances, Davis reflected on her Pine Hill experience.

It's taken me three circuses to really get my feet wet. This year something happened; something clicked in the kids and they took it up. There is a skill level in many of them that is extraordinary. I have one boy who went to the Smirkus Camp last summer who's juggling five balls. He says, "I can only keep them going for a while." I told him I didn't care how long he can keep them in the air. There are also kids who just started in the fall in the Circus Arts block that meets twice a week for two months. I teach them pyramids, balancing, juggling, tumbling - club twirling. I don't have a club twirling act this year, but I will next.[164]

When asked if Middle School adolescents weren't uncomfortable using their bodies in the ways required in circus, Davis said,

They *are* uncomfortable; that's why this is so important. They are at an age when they start piercing their bodies and painting their hair green, but you put them up here in a socially condoned context where they can paint their hair green and it's ok. We don't have any green hair, but they could put on wigs or whatever[165]

The following year Davis was advanced from adjunct faculty to half-time Movement Educator.

They created a position for me. Last year I had it pretty cushy. I just did circus and was sort of an exalted outsider and could do what I wanted. Now I have to play more by the rules. I have a meeting coming up because the school, as a Waldorf School with its philosophy, wants to make sure that the circus is pedagogically correct.

There was no Physical Education program in the school up until now so I'm trying to create a curriculum and learn how to teach and pull in the philosophy of the school on movement which is different than the average. I have my ideas and I have to adapt anything that's in books. Stuff that some books say is appropriate for second grade, I don't think it is[166]

Davis was then in the third year of a five year training program in Spatial Dynamics attended by Waldorf movement teachers and others.

There are circus components in it. Juggling, diablo, tumbling, acrobatics, pyramids and club twirling. We also do javelin, discus, jump rope, and some good old fashioned folk lore children's games and something called Bothmer Gymnastics named for Fritz von Bothmer who created a movement regime with Rudolph Steiner. These are contemplative movement exercises that work with the planes of space and gravity and levity. Putting the human being as a place between the above and the below. [167]

The training sessions were conducted by Jaimen McMillan, the international director of Spatial Dynamics, who encouraged Davis to share her circus experience with the other American Waldorf teachers. Davis discovered that although Circus Skills are suggested for Waldorf Middle Schools, most of the schools did little with them.

I brought a pyramid to my Spatial Dynamics colleagues and they had a blast. The people who are training are very excited about circus arts and that's where I feel I can multiply my work because these are people going back to schools. Guess what? Most Waldorf Schools don't have gyms. There are Waldorf teachers that would love to do circus, but they say they have to do snow shoeing because they don't have space. The first thing a public school builds is a gymnasium. Of course they put their competitive sports there, but they also do gymnastics.

It is different in Europe. Waldorf Schools in Germany and France are big on circus so to say Waldorf is not big on circus is not true. It is more there than here because circus is more a part of their culture. Jaimen created Circus Calibastra at our mother school in Stuttgart.

My feeling is that there is a lot of support in American Waldorf Schools for the idea of circus, but not a lot of knowledge of how to go about it. Colleagues in Spatial Dynamics say, "I would love to do that, but where do I start? I don't have any money." They are stuck on step one. I tell them, "Step one is easy. Just get tennis balls, fill them with bird seed, get your mats out." They answer that they don't have gymnasiums.

The other thing about Waldorf is that people are not coming from a circus experience. I just happened to marry a clown; I just happen to be a mime who had studied with Marcel Marceau. [168]

As she worked at Pine Hill Waldorf school, Davis became interested in the possibility of circus in public schools.

There was a statewide meeting of all the New Hampshire physical educators funded by the New Hampshire Association of Health, Physical Education, Recreation and Dance to which I now belong. It was a two-day conference and I spoke on Circus Arts in the Middle School curriculum. I found people in the public sector who have a Circus Arts Block, but they don't necessarily see how to develop juggling or gymnastics from a theatrical point of view. I told them they could do it and it would be good for their program, good for their kids and good for getting media attention. I realize that most people are not as committed to making a big circus as I am. I met with some terrific enthusiasm from a few public school people. There is a principal who wants to do a circus in his lower school so we will be talking about that.[169]

As she was preparing her fourth Hilltop circus, Davis hoped she had started something at the school that

would continue to thrive even if I job myself out and start some seeds in other schools. Pine Hill has been a fertile ground for me. Now I feel called almost. I was never on a circus, but I feel there is so much that can happen to these kids. With video games and things like that, kids aren't going out to play and they don't know how to make teams anymore.[170]

Interviewed again after her fifth Hilltop Circus, Davis reexamined her Circus Skills work at Pine Hill.

I was full time this year because another teacher was on sabbatical. Next year they wanted to cut me back to three-quarter time. I counterproposed that I cut back to half-time, teaching in the grades, and then do the circus block. They would pay me to direct the circus as if I were an artist-in-residence and they would get money from outside for that. That is not as good for me from a financial point of view, but it frees a lot of my time. Many of my movement colleagues in Waldorf schools do not have full-time positions. Instead of being a team player, I'll be doing my own thing and outside work.

I have become involved with the American Youth Circus Organization(AYCO) and expect I'll do more work bringing circus to schools. I have a small troupe of graduates from Hilltop Circus, The Flying Gravity Circus, that performs and does Skills Workshops for children and Education Workshops for teachers.

Pine Hill is very committed to having circus. The parents, the students, the teachers rally around it and this year they came forward and supported me in getting everything done. We are at a point now where circus is embraced. When we first started, I was the only one who had a picture of how it would look. Over the five years, I have been able to step back and the circus has developed a life of its own. I happen to be at the helm, but I have been educating the faculty as I have been educated about what other Waldorf schools are doing and now there is the AYCO movement. This isn't just a Waldorf phenomenon; this is something happening in our culture.[171]

Asked about how Circus Skills fit in with the Waldorf philosophy of age appropriate curriculum, Davis commented,

I'm more of a believer in it than when I started. Even though you can, as I have done, introduce three ball juggling in the fifth grade, there is the question of when children possess the eye-hand coordination to juggle successfully and the maturity level to pursue it and not be frustrated and throw down the balls and walk away. I think there are windows of opportunity where certain things meet the child better than at other times.

Other Waldorf schools have circuses that involve the whole school They have end-of-the-year performances that include 3rd through 12th grade classes. It is different than what you might see in Circus Smirkus where you get kids throwing themselves forward, "Here I am!" With the Waldorf schools, it is more reserved. The kids are more likely to do group than solo acts. They might pretend that they are trained butterflies. There is something a little softer because of the philosophical belief that children don't really land in themselves until about 14. Until then they are still unfolding. About the age of nine you see a preview of adolescence coming where the children are stepping into themselves, but the philosophy is that by the time they are in the middle school, they are beginning to form into the adults they are going to be. And I can see that.

The whole thing of teendom – acting out, going for thrills and risks, experimenting with sex and drugs; circus arts can channel that energy in healthy ways. Balancing on a tight wire or standing on a globe or riding a unicycle are things you really have to do in order to be successful. There is nothing phony. You get up in front of 300 people and there's a rush. Also, this is the time when the body and mind are undergoing all these changes – the hormonal things. They're lengthening and they don't know where to place themselves. When you put them on a tightrope or have them focus for juggling, they have to be balanced and coordinated and self-controlled. There is a great range of benefits that is possible at this time more than any other. This is the window where if they can do this, they are going to have an easier time going through puberty.[172]

The Pine Hill Waldorf School provided an environment where Jackie Davis demonstrated that an ongoing curricular circus program can enrich a school. Hopefully, private and public schools in New Hampshire will benefit from her determination to offer children Circus Learning and the opportunity to perform as part of a circus.

Circus Learning's holistic approach to the development of all children can be more than a temporary infusion of excitement in the life of a school. As demonstrated by the schools discussed in this chapter, Circus Learning can be a continuing part of the curriculum. What is needed is not vast expenditures, but knowledgeable and determined leaders and sympathetic administrations.

VIII
Year-Round Independent Circus Programs

As with Community Circuses, Year-Round Independent Circus Programs make it possible for Circus Learning to be a continuing part of people's lives. As skills improve, students can move to greater challenges. The programs examined in this chapter are associated with schools, rather than a community based circus. However, most schools do present performances so perhaps the distinction is arbitrary. The Belfast Community Circus might just as well be included here, but, "Year-Round Independent Circus Programs" is, in Pooh's immortal words, a "useful pot to put things in."

Albuquerque School for Circus Arts

Rosalind Rojas described her Albuquerque School for Circus Arts two months after it opened. She also discussed her background in circus and as a circus teacher.

Our program is both recreational and pre-professional. The recreational program is for kids from six to 16. Our pre-professional program, for people 18-25, is for theatre people from the Albuquerque area who want to improve their theatre skills. We do basic tumbling, partner acrobatics, static and swinging trapeze, Spanish web, cloud swing, aerial perch and are in the process of building a teeterboard. Eventually, I will do flying. My background is also strong in dance so there is a dance component, too.

Last year I started the camp and this year, March 26, the full time school officially opened. Right now we have a registration of 50. I rent space in Duke City, a gymnastics facility, but there is a big space in the back where I'm starting to build a structure that will be exclusively mine. I'm funding it with the camp which is booked for this

year. I have 25 kids each week. Last year I did two weeks; this year
I'm doing three and people are asking me to do more. Next year I
will.

I started with a couple thousand dollars of my own money and
began to build up my equipment. I'm going for nonprofit status soon
so I can fund raise. I learned about that when I was the director for
ten years of the Big Apple Circus education program, the Arts
Connection. Once I get nonprofit status, I will contact schools about
doing residencies.

Beside me, my staff is Kate Enright who teaches basic mime and
principles of clowning; I use one of the tumbling staff of Duke City
Gymnastics; and I'm interviewing for a full time staff member. Some
ex-Ringling people have retired here.

At the end of the circus camp, we put on performances and have
been asked to do shows in SummerFest. Right now I am trying to get
the kids to understand that a commitment to circus training means
personal responsibility and responsibility for the equipment. There is
a recreational aspect to this, but there is also a part that is competitive
and professional They have to understand professional circus life so
we teach circus history, run videos, and have lecture demonstrations.
They have to understand how circus functions in different places; how
it was in the Soviet Union.

As for me, I'm a native New Yorker. I went to the High School
for Performing Arts. Then I was principal dancer with the Puerto
Rican Ballet Company, was in the Dance Theatre of Harlem, trained
with Alvin Ailey and was in his third company. I retired from dance
because I wanted to eat.

In college I learned some tumbling and got involved in competitive gymnastics. I went to Moscow the year before the 1980 Olympics
and then retired when President Carter boycotted the Olympics. I was
invited to compete on Puerto Rico's national team. I ended up teaching trampoline and tumbling and circus. That's how I got started with
New York School for Circus Arts of the Big Apple Circus. I was the
school director of the Arts Connection that was done in conjunction
with the New York City Public Schools. I took several of our kids to
the Monte Carlo International Circus School Competition in 1989. I

also became a Big Apple Circus company member when the company was still small and they were performing in the green tent. I was stand-in wire walker, aerialist – company swing. I guess they created that for me. I can do Roman Rings, web, a lot of things. I ended up being the liaison between the School and the Circus.

I went to the Pickle Family Circus for a year. They asked me to come back and do a triple somersault off the teeterboard. I said not at my age and four years ago I came to New Mexico. I had been home-schooling my daughter all these years and I guess I did a good job because she got a scholarship to a fine private school here. I was home doing dishes thinking, what am I doing? Then I realized there was no big circus school here. Now I am able to make a living. I'm happy here.[173]

Carrie Heller Circus Arts, LLC

Carrie Heller began her circus studies at age eight at a summer camp. Her teachers were members of the Flying High Circus from Florida State University. At fourteen, she took over responsibility for the camp's program and began writing the training manual now used by her teachers at Carrie Heller's Circus Camp, a year round operation in Atlanta, Georgia. Each Spring, Heller, whose specialty is trapeze, and her students present a show that raises scholarship money for the program and for youth projects with which Heller is involved. Having made circus part of the life of Atlanta, she and her students also per-

Carrie Heller's performing class, 1997, in The Web of Life. Credit: Richard Lubrant

form at community functions.

Ms. Heller's continuing work as a clinical social worker gives her program a unique orientation.

When I first did psychotherapy in Atlanta, I set up a trapeze so I could do my own workout and do some shows and the director of an exercise studio asked me to teach a class. Some of my clients came in because I started specializing in play therapy. I expanded that and did what people two or three years later called Rope Courses when they took groups of people into settings where there were all kinds of challenging physical things. Teams had to work together - for example, to climb over a fence without touching the ground. I did it with trapezes and Spanish webs and that kind of thing.

It is now known as Experiential Therapy; I was just doing my own thing and throwing my skills into it. I ended up directing the clinical services at the Bridge Family Center of Atlanta that worked with families and children and then it became a runaway shelter. I became director of their clinical services for a year or two, then I went into a small private practice and taught more circus classes. When I had others teaching for me, I gave them some background on how to do reflective listening and speak to people from a positive perspective. If I heard somebody say something in class that sounded negative, I'd go to them after class and say, "Let me tell you another way that you can say this." Then they started thinking differently.

I'd say to some of the clients in my private practice, "Let's go in the studio for one session and just play on the equipment. If you'd like to try that out." They were really into it so we'd go into the studio. As they walked across the tightwire, I'd talk to them about feeling their center. When they got off, I'd say, "How do you feel about walking across that tightwire?"

Normally you don't ask people that, but when I was working in therapy I would, so doing circus skills I did and got responses like "Wow, I didn't know I could do that. I'm a victim of abuse and I never thought that my body could do anything like that." I got them to start expanding upon their bodies in a different way. It's not the answer to sexual or physical abuse, but it's another perspective to use with someone. Some of these people wanted to continue in the studio. People who might be a little bit overweight - instead of thinking, "OK, I'm going to lose weight now because I'm progressing so much in my therapy I don't need to have all this weight any more," might think, "I'll be able to pull myself up on the trapeze easier if I lose a bit of weight." And they received out of it what everyone receives - the self-esteem.

I was being a therapist the whole time. I was doing reflective listening: "I noticed that you can pull yourself up on the trapeze much easier than last week." Or I'd say, "I notice you're getting really strong." These are things that teachers say sometimes, but I do it constantly. I teach my teachers to do the same thing. It's amazing the shifts you see in people when you say simple things like that. I'm not giving them advice, I'm just feeding back things they said to me and combining it with what I observed.

I have parents say to me, "Since Johnny has taken circus class, for the first time he is now willing to try out for softball. I think the confidence he gained from your class has transferred."

When I went to the US Virgin Islands with Wavy Gravy, we worked with kids who came from violent, chaotic backgrounds. They were the most challenged intellectually in school - the teachers knew they were smart, but they weren't doing well. They learned some of our stuff; some of them mastered juggling. After we left, the teachers told us those children were doing better in school

I like to integrate kids from all kinds of backgrounds and in my summer camp we do that. There are kids from all walks of life in Atlanta that come to Circus Camp. The directors of the youth organizations that sponsor scholarship children at the Camp know I have a therapy degree and that I utilize this in my work with the children as well as in training the staff at Circus Camp.

I have spent years using my circus training in my therapy with individuals, families and groups. I have developed what I call Circus Arts Therapy. This is a form of experiential play therapy that is, among other things, a direct way to build trust through physical interaction. Circus Arts Therapy is also an effective way to shift one's personal body image and develop a sense of self-esteem as individuals express themselves creatively in new ways. I will be doing a presentation/workshop in April, 1999 for the World Congress on Child and Play Therapy in Toronto, Canada on my Circus Arts Therapy. For years I have been developing specific techniques utilizing circus equipment and activities in a therapeutic milieu to assist individuals, families and groups in the process of healing as well as in encouraging personal growth.

During the year, I work with some private schools; I've been doing it for five years. Word has spread through the homeschooling community and a number of those parents make work with me part of their children's program.

At Wavy Gravy's Camp Winnarainbow in California where I was aerial supervisor and experiential play therapist, they integrate scholarship kids with wealthy children. They have the same philosophy I do except that they're a sleepaway camp so a lot more intense stuff goes down there. We had little sessions where we would talk with kids together because issues would come up and I think it's a great environment when you have people who know what they're doing. Being able to do the circus stuff is icing on the cake

I create an environment every Monday morning at my camp to make the children feel safe. I follow the Tribes Program. Some of its principles are - No Put Downs, Attentive Listening, No Hitting, that kind of thing. I get the kids to do skits on these things. They're the things you hear at most camps, but I make a big deal out of them. We talk about - why don't you put anyone down? Because it really hurts their feelings. If there's ever anything that goes on like that, it is immediately attended to. We create an atmosphere that is a little different than other places. Camp Winnarainbow is the one other place I'm aware of that has the same kind of atmosphere. It's like creating a cocoon of peace and safety for the children; they know not only are they going to have fun, but if anyone is mean to them, it's going to be handled appropriately.

I do this training every summer in addition to the training for the counselors who are going to use the equipment. I give information on how to deal with kids with Attention Deficit Disorder, how to do problem solving. Each counselor knows about using "I" language instead of saying "You." I think they're armed with more information than most counselors. We're not just teaching kids circus skills, we're teaching them about respecting themselves, other people and the environment.

The work I do on the triple trapeze is an example of a group experience around creating together. I put families up on a trapeze so they can hold each other. There might be a father and son who are not very physical with each other; I can tell when they come. Or they can be from a family therapy session I did. I'll make the dad do a catcher's hang and hold his child while the child does a trick. When they come down, their relationship is changed. I could have done hours of therapy with them and then, in those two minutes, their relationship changed. It's a magical thing to watch.

Based on the same premise, I'll take a bunch of kids that don't get along together or kids that do or kids that don't know each other or have judgments against each other and I'll put them all on the triple trapeze. I'll say. "OK, create a trick. Pick a trick and do it together. Who wants to be the leader? Who's going to count to three?" I'll make them make all these decisions themselves and when they come down, they're one step closer to being bonded.

You can take that one step further with kids and adults who've been in the performance class for years. In our shows every year, the creation of the performance is, for the most part, a group experience. I see myself mostly as a facilitator. Sometimes I'm stronger on the choreography and tell them what to do, but for the most part, they do the creating themselves. They have to work things out with each other, right down to what costumes they're going to wear. I have to approve it, but I don't remember ever not approving anything. It's more important to me that they make the decisions than that they look good.[174]

But they do look good. One need not be privy to the creative process to be impressed by the product that results. Heller is not only an effective therapist, but an effective performer and choreographer. Heller refers to herself as *aerial dancer* - not acrobat. Her performances and those of her camp reflect this orientation. While most circus acts are built around a series of tricks of increasing complexity that conclude with a climax or "blow-off, " Heller's are dances involving a series of choreographed movements and poses on and off circus equipment. The tempo is slow and the acts end quietly with a strong pose. It is as if "tricks" would disrupt the meditative flow of the work. Heller's solo called "Enerchi" in the 1997 show *The Web of Life, an aerial dance extravaganza* was described in the program:

This dance form combines the arts of Chi Kung and Tai Chi. Both of these ancient Chinese arts are internal energy exercises - a type of moving meditation to help move energy in and through the body.[175]

The act begins as Heller bows to a large drum and drummer. She then mounts a low, static trapeze to Cirque du Soleil style music. After a series of movements and poses on the bar and the supporting ropes, she dismounts to do an extended series of slow, rhythmic, floor movements. The music ends; she returns to the drummer who starts drumming. She mounts the trapeze which now swings and she does another series of choreographed movements and poses. The act ends as she returns to the ground and huddles down.

The 1997 show was a benefit for two Atlanta youth foundations. Each act had a theme relating to Heller's belief that "There is a Web, an almost invisible thread, that joins us all."[176] The opening act was "Weaving the Web"; the show ended with "Receiving the Web," and "Interweaving." Four girls in black costumes performing on a triple trapeze were called "Life and Death." Some acts were preceded by poems, others were accompanied by girls dancing with flowing cloths, one was accompanied by a girl on a trapeze playing a flute. Only one male performed in the regular acts; three adult males appeared as clowns. Given the gentle nature of the performance, the clowns seemed to have difficulty finding an appropriate tone. Vince Tororici, wearing a clown nose and no other makeup, did an interactive act with the audience involving a can that sprayed things and concluded with a devil stick routine. Two men, one in drag, did a travesty trapeze act. Heller and Cindy Alana, who shared responsibility with Heller for the show's concept, did a whimsical commercial, "The Ecstasy of Chocolate."

The 1998 "Aerial Dance and Acrobatics Extravaganza" was called *The Magic Bus* "It's funky fun from the start as tie-died performers swing down out of a bus parked in midair and get down to the rhythms of Smash Mouth."[177]

Carrie Heller's training program demonstrates how a psychological orientation can enhance Circus Learning. Her philosophy is set forth on the first page of the Training Manual she prepared for her instructors. (See Program Literature, p. 248.)

Cascade Youth Circus (CYC)

The Cascade Youth Circus is located in Maple Valley, Washington, about 40 minutes southeast of Seattle. Debbie Johnson, the director, founded the Circus in 1985. Johnson also operates a dance program and gymnastics program in the same facility. The CYC mission is to provide youth with an opportunity to participate in a positive social environment that promotes individual achievement, artistic expression, teamwork and community service. (CYC) provides instruction in basic circus skills including tumbling, acrosports, tight-wire walking, juggling and clowning.

Families of youth circus participants are expected to work hand in hand with coaches towards the fulfillment of our mission. The role of the parent includes attending parent meetings, helping with fundraisers, encouraging their own child as well as other troupe members, and helping with performances.

A primary goal of youth circus coaches is to encourage students to take increasing responsibility for their own learning and for their parents to be actively engaged in the process. During regular practice sessions, students learn exercises and behaviors which can be practiced at home. As students become more diligent about continuing their training at home, their skills increase more rapidly and they begin to take on a leadership role in the troupe. As students take increasing responsibility for their own learning, they become an inspiration to their peers, thereby strengthening the troupe as a whole.[177a]

Johnson described the program,

We have beginner, intermediate and advanced circus classes – 101, 201 301. If students are off the street they're in beginning class until they show us that they can do a certain number of skills on everything. When they have five skills on all the things we offer, they can move up to intermediate and when they have ten they can move up to advanced. Once they get into intermediate, they can study a specialty. When the kids take specialty classes they still have to be part of one of the core classes. We teach versatility. They may not be great at everything. I have an advanced kid who hates unicycle, but she does it while she loves her specialties - web and corde lisse and trapeze.

The circus program, which has four teachers, is a separate corporation that rents space in our gym. Students join our performing troupe – which is a class, by audition which is kind of funny because we take everyone who auditions. We do it because we have found if they are willing to be put on the spot to audition, they'll be willing to get in front of an audience which means we don't have to go through the stage fright thing which was a problem in the past. Also, if they audition there is more dedication. Anybody at any of the levels can audition. We take beginners into the troupe, but most don't try out because they feel they want to learn more first. The beginners who join the troupe just don't have as big a role as the other kids.

Our circus program is as expensive as our gymnastics program. Beginners pay forty-two dollars for four weeks. The more hours students study, the greater the discount. By the time they add specialty classes it's really cheap per hour, but by then they are basically paying $100 a month because they are taking two or three specialty classes and their core class. The performance class costs $35 a month if we're not performing, but when we have paid gigs, that money becomes a credit against their payment. If we're performing a lot, they don't pay anything.

We offer scholarships at all three levels. When one of our students graduates high school, if the student has been in circus the last three years, we give a small college scholarship and some equipment that's been donated.

Not all of our performance gigs are paid. We do interactive visits for scouting and other community groups so they can try out circus things. We go to a foster care situation that's like a small campus. We teach them to juggle and unicycle and walk on the tightwire . None of them join our school because they are in a transition situation and they are almost an hour a way. Going there for our kids is like being part of a Big Brother or Big Sister group. Probably half of our performances or our interactive work is free. We just call it community service. It's neat for our kids because they get to share something that they love with somebody who just doesn't have that opportunity.[177b]

Johnson also does circus residencies in area public and private schools. "I do units on circus arts coordinating them with the school's teachers. I've also worked with homeschoolers at a satellite school."[177c]

Circus of the Star

Betty and Dan Butler started their circus training at Sarasota's Sailor Circus and continued at Florida State University. They established Circus of the Star at a recreational facility in St. Paul, Minnesota in the fall of 1994. Unlike Southern Florida, St. Paul has no circus tradition. One of the problems facing the Butlers in St. Paul was explaining what they were doing. The year-round training program for children 5-18 started with 30 participants and minimal equipment. Betty Butler explains what came next.

Circus of the Star aerial act. credit: Mike Long

After nine months of rehearsal getting the kids initiated into circus skills, we wanted to have a recital or exhibition to show off to the neighborhood. The Highland Fest is the big annual arts and crafts festival in our neighborhood, probably 10,000 visitors come to it and we thought it would be a good time to exhibit our first round of skills.

Our show just exploded. People came to see it and had no idea that's what we had been doing. They didn't know we were teaching actual circus skills. They'd never heard of that so we just took the community by surprise. Since then, Highland Fest has evolved into our annual time to show the community what we do. Now we try to do it with more fanfare and we do other things to get more exposure to the Twin Cities at large.[178]

Circus of the Star met the larger community when it performed at the 1996 Winter Carnival. Circus of the Star quickly became such a popular member of the community, it was serving one hundred children, as many as its shared facility could accommodate. There was a waiting list of 350. This, in spite of the occasional harassment some participating boys received as "Circus Boys" from peers unfamiliar with circus.

The fourth annual Circus of the Star at the 1998 Highland Fest included the youngest performers on side-by-side and star trapeze, unicycle, swinging trapeze, adagio, double trapeze, clowning, acrobatics done by a troupe of six to 14 year olds, Spanish web, high wire, cloud swing, comedy vaulting, an aerial ladder ballet, hand balancing, juggling, Russian and Roman rings, bike, teeterboard and skypole. There were 76 performers.

The 1998 coaches were Directors Betty and Dan Butler; Bert Harrison who studied clowning with Carlo Mazzone Clementi of the Dell'Arte School, Dominque Serand of the Theatre de la Jeune Lune, and Bill Irwin; Mike Lumnzer who won the World Juggling Championship at competitions held in 1996; Pat Schoonover, a Sister of St. Joseph of Carondelet, who is a member of Twin City unicycle club; Meg Emery, a former Ringling show girl and aerialist who then studied with Russian circus artists Nina Krasavina and Gregory Fedin; Alison Harrington, a gymnastics coach; and Lili Rancone, a dancer who choreographed the bicycle-for-five act, juggling, adagio and teeterboard.

The philosophy of Circus of the Star - and the basis for its name, is the belief that "Every kid can be a star."

At Circus of the Star, no child is ever disappointed by "not making the team" or not being allowed to perform. Every child is given the opportunity to grow and challenge themselves, to learn who they are, to develop relationships with adult mentors, with their peers and with the community, and to learn the value of discipline and hard work.

In a framework unusual by today's standards of sports and competitiveness, circus participants bring themselves to a new levels of performance with the understanding that, even when trying their hardest, they may fall, drop their juggling clubs, or miss a trick. "We smile, bow, style and move on!"[179]

Endorsed by St. Paul's Mayor, Norm Coleman, who had been won over after seeing the program, Circus of the Star began a $1,600,000 fund raiser, "Raising the Big Top" five years after it had begun. While the Twin Cities does not have a circus tradition, it does have a tradition of philanthropy and Circus of the Star tapped into it. The City of St. Paul awarded a $200,000 "Star" grant to launch the fund drive. By the spring of 2000, more than $1,500,000 had been raised and the groundbreaking took place. Plans called for the building to open the following September. Dan Butler described the structure.

It is 130 feet wide, ninety feet long and forty-fix feet high. Every fifteen feet, steel trusses go from one end all the way over the top to the other end. They support the thick, fire-resistant material over it and every ten years or so, depending on the elements, we'll have a capital improvement campaign to replace the roof. It's relatively inexpensive – about $75,000. The insulated building will be air conditioned.[180]

Circus of the Star involves more members of the community than its performers. Riggers and other support people are community volunteers. Parents raise money for costumes and for the circus by selling ads in the circus program. Although a private school that charges tuition, Circus of the Star reaches out to all parts of the community. Its mission statement announces that it will "use the circus arts as an alternative teaching method and intervention program for youth at risk, serving as a signature cultural attraction which strengthens and integrates the St. Paul community." The Salvation Army provides transportation for children in disadvantaged areas who participate with scholarships. In the new facility, Circus of the Star intends to serve youth and families throughout the Twin Cities as it develops a program for more than 500 students, including seventy-five scholarship students. All students will participate in the Home Show which, as with the Sailor Circus and the Florida State's Flying High Circus, will be the annual signature attraction and a major source of revenue.

In 1997, Circus of the Star established a successful satellite project at the Salvation Army that offered free workshops. In the words of Michael G. Frederickson, Salvation Army Community Center Director, "Circus of the Star is a program which fosters the most positive experiences for everyone involved which enhances and works towards a positive change in people's lives." Also projected as part of the expanded work at the new center is a Circus Care unit that will bring clowning and juggling to terminally ill children; Circus of the Star has started a pilot project with Shriners Hospital.

Plans call for a free ticket program for economically disadvantaged and physically disabled residents of the area to attend Circus performances; educational programs for studying the history of circus arts; and pre-school and adult circus skills classes for people with special needs. There will be opportunities for Circus of the Star performers to meet other performing children from around the world by participating in international competitions.

Circus of the Star is committed to the idea that all children make the team and perform. At the same time, a high degree of excellence is achieved by many of the performers although the rules are not as demanding as those the Butlers knew when they performed at Sailor Circus. Students at Circus of the Star need not forswear other extracurricular activities while participating in the Circus. As a result, the Circus has a large population of boys who have the freedom to do other sports. Betty Butler notes that

> We don't like absenteeism; it hurts the kids if they want to progress. As we get closer to the shows, we do say, "Don't miss more than three practices or it could jeopardize your position in the show." That's about as hard as we take it. We want them there and they know if they want to perform, they have to be there and for the most part they are.[181]

Dan Butler summarized what has happened at Circus of the Star.

> We started it to do something we love, to give something to the community. Thanks to what Cirque du Soleil and the *new* circus have done in the last fifteen years, there's a whole new performing arts element in circus along with a healthy view of what circus is. We happened to hit a wave we knew nothing about. Ten years from today, we could see circus schools in the United States very similar to gymnastics schools. The bottom line, no matter how much spectacle you create, is how can you help young people in different ways than all the traditional activities.[182]

CIRKIDS

The program for CirKids In Vancouver, British Columbia, Canada is described on the CirKids Web site:

> CirKids was founded in 1984 by a group of parents in the arts community who wanted to give their kids the once-in-a-lifetime chance to perform in a circus troupe. It was inspired by the Australian Fruit Fly Circus which came to the Vancouver International Children's Festival in 1982 and returned for Expo '86

> The school is fully equipped with trampolines, aerial trapezes, *corde lisse*, tightwires, gymnastics mats, juggling equipment, unicycles and all aerial and ground safety devices. Equipment is tested regularly for safety.

Students are instructed in all circus skills and are encouraged to develop routines in their favorite areas. They are never pressured to continue something with which they feel uncomfortable or unsafe.

There are many different activities, everyone can be good at something. From that comes confidence and self-esteem. With that confidence, kids can go where they never dreamed to go: walking a tight wire, juggling fire, or taking a flip off a trapeze.

Classes are under supervision of our experienced coaches who have NCCP [National Coaches Certification Program] level 2 training, as well as their skill in circus arts. Guest artists and specialty workshops are a frequent part of the yearly program. The coach to CirKid ratio is 1 to 7 or better. [1:3 in aerial work and artistic bike.]

Circus may involve gymnastics, but it isn't gymanstics. It's all about personal and cooperative achievement. There are no points to be scored and no losers. There's only the thrill of seeing the audiences' jaws drop. CirKids provides physical and personal challenges – a place where people can discover themselves and learn to work with others.

In December we have a showcase for parents to see what everyone has been learning; parents can try out the equipment themselves, too! In June, every program puts on a show. In addition, kids appear at such places as the Vancouver International Children's Festival, the Vancouver Art Gallery, Science World, the Dragon Boat Festival, and more.

In the summer we also run a summer camp at Bayview Community School. Each one-week camp gets a kid underway in more than one circus skill; the week ends in a circus performance with trapezes, tightwires, balancing and juggling.[183]

Between eighty and 100 youngsters are involved in CirKids. Classes take place Tuesdays and Wednesday, 5:00-8:30 PM; Saturdays, 9:00AM to 3:15PM; and Sundays, 10:00AM to 2:00 PM. Children are grouped by approximate age and ability. The five to seven year old *Lions* focus on mastering motor skills. They juggle scarves, do low wire and globe walking. *Development* is for seven to 11 year olds. Progress is marked as students move through Red, White and Blue levels of achievement. *Development* children move on to *Apprentice* where they develop one or two specialties. *Fast-track* is for strongly motivated youngsters with no circus arts background. Finally, *Performance* youngsters participate in professional performance. The group of about twenty ranges in age from 10 to 16. Its members learn to choreograph themselves and others.

Mischa Sandberg, Managing Director of CirKids, discussed the program:

We're not organized around classes, though we do use rotations, like in a gymnastics program. Every performer has to have a certain set of skills so that we can build shows on short notice to match unique situations. So, everyone juggles, rides unicycles, tumbles and does some kind of aerial work. As kids reach about age 12, they get a stronger notion of what they enjoy and what they're good at and they tend to do extra work in such areas.

Our primary emphasis is performing; our second is a rounded set of skills and strengths for kids who are aiming for the Ecole nationale de cirque [National Circus School in Montreal]; our third is on good fun and motor skill development for younger kids for whom tightwire walking, static trapeze and human pyramids are a non-competitive way to figure out what they are good at and what they enjoy. We figure that a competitive gymnastics "career" only lasts a few years; people will juggle at parties and ride mountain unicycles long enough that they'll be teaching their own kids how.

All kids not ready for public performing, track themselves on their own skill charts. Once they can competently juggle, unicycle and whatever, they work in groups on routines or individually on particular skills.

There are four senior coaches. One is specialized in tumbling, one is world class at trampoline coaching and teaches cradle routines, and two who grew up as CirKids and became both professional coaches and circus trainers. On and off we have coaches who are ex-Cirque du Soleil. Working for them are five junior coaches. They include a non-circus professional gymnastics and dance instructor and four ex-CirKids who can intruct in juggling, unicycling, aerials, tumbling, tightwire, etc.

We rent hours in a gymnasium. This is a sore point for us. It is too low for us to rig a flying trapeze and we are constantly moving our equipment in and out of storage.

A small number of the kids who have trained with us have gone on to the Ecole nationale de cirque. Three of them are currently professional circus people. Others still keep up their skills. We've lost a fair number of boys over the years who suddenly discovered that if you can juggle or spin a diablo and walk on stilts, you can get a busker's license and make money.

We have a board of directors. We are a nonprofit society. At different times we've had either an office manager or a general manager. Currently the parent body has been rather active and all non-coaching positions are staffed by parents of kids who have been in the program three years or more.[184]

CirKids provides scholarships, although not enough to satisfy the need. Like other community based programs, CirKids makes Circus Learning a respected and valued resource that provides opportunities for children to develop their skills and their sense of self over time.

everydaycircus

Jessica Hentoff and Mike Killian's *everydaycircus* in St. Louis was mentioned in Chapter Five's discussion of the Berkshire Circus Camp. *everydaycircus* is a year-round entity that provides circus skills training, performances, equipment and expertise. (See Program Literature, p. 248.) The philosophy of everydaycircus is set forth in its residency flyer:

This program will not only teach children about circus skills, it will also teach them more about themselves! The course is designed to develop physical

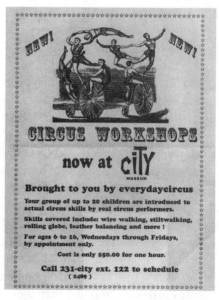

CIRCUS WORKSHOPS
now at CITY
MUSEUM
Brought to you by everydaycircus
Your group of up to 20 children are introduced to actual circus skills by real circus performers.
Skills covered include: wire walking, stiltwalking, rolling globe, feather balancing and more !
For ages 6 to 16, Wednesdays through Fridays, by appointment only.
Cost is only $50.00 for one hour.
Call 231-city ext. 122 to schedule
(2489)

Flyer for an everyday circus program at City Museum.

coordination, mental concentration, trust, responsibility, fear control and self confidence.[185]

Hentoff continues to coach the St. Louis Arches, a tumbling group she started when she headed the Circus Flora school, but the focus for everyday circus shifted when it moved into City Museum - an eclectic operation located in a former shoe factory in the city's downtown loft area. City Museum has been called a Discovery Zone with hard edges. Hentoff described the impact of the move.

The Museum is now the site for everydaycircus. Our motto used to be "We bring the excitement of circus to you," but we had to change it because now, though we still go out to people, we expect people to come to us. I homeschool my kids and I'm in a homeschool group; we offer co-op classes so I teach a homeschool circus class at the Museum and I teach the Arches down there. We're talking about doing more teaching at the Museum.

I do some residencies through a group here called School Partnership that brings people into the public schools. I also run a program at the Cimloch Community Center. The people who run it are wonderful and they give the Arches a home. Kathy Hoyer, who was my performing partner for five years, will be teaching a class for me at the Center of Contemporary Arts.

Mostly, I'm down at the Museum. We do birthday parties there and have a souvenir stand and a concessions booth. I still book out acts and rent our moon bounces, but we've permanantly put our popcorn and cotton candy machines in the Museum. The big thing there is our shows that we do every weekend, every hour on the hour. Mike and I do most of them and Donald Hughes, who is now on salary with us. It's a half-hour show and we book other people in. Long term, I'd love to have circus people come through and book them. Short term, I'm using local people. I have a woman with a petting zoo who does Talk with the Animals, a mime, different clowns, magicians. One of the clowns does accordian and juggling on a giraffe unicycle. And the Arches, of course. The Museum subsidizes the Arches shows and they're starting to help with our shows. The shows get people to our part of the museum and then they buy our concessions.[186]

The Arches still tour with Circus Flora. That is Hentoff's only connection with Circus Flora although Circus Flora is talking about using her if they develop their school. Meanwhile, everydaycircus continues to enrich the life of St. Louis.

Fern Street Circus

The Fern Street Circus in San Diego, California draws inspiration from West African music, Italian circus, the *new* circus and street performance. Fern Street Circus is a year-round adult performing group that operates an after-school program in a Recreation Center and integrates graduates from the afterschool program into its performances. John Highkin, director of Fern Street Circus, describes it.

We are a single-ring theatrical circus that has been in existence since 1991. We have always stayed within San Diego county although

Juggler in the Fern Street Circus production Hamar (The Big City), 1999. credit: Fern Street Circus

I'm hoping we will be able to get out of the county next year. We perform outdoors with a set we have developed over the years. We have aerial rigging and a series of colorfully painted backdrops. Each year the centerpiece of what we do is a show in Balboa Park - the main park in San Diego. We do varying degrees of narrative telling a story, but at this point I am skeptical about how much narrative you can do in a circus.

We utilize people who live around San Diego who are, in one way or another, circus or variety artists. We have a longtime affiliation with the Canestrelli family. They landed in San Diego in 1987 to work at Sea World. They came on a three or six week contract and never left. They put down roots in San Diego which none of them had ever done. Pietro Canistrelli has six kids and four of them have performed with us at one time or another; he and his wife still do. Pietro calls himself "Pop." He is 73 and has been in circus since he was twenty minutes old. Ottavio is the only one of the children who stayed in circus. In 1997 we brought the Flying Wallendas to perform in our annual show.

We started an afterschool program in 1993 at a local rec center. We are in a center city area called Golden Hill - a mixed neighborhood economically and culturally. There are relatively well-off people and there are a lot of poor people and they all sort of mish mash in the neighborhood. The people who use the rec center are disproportionately African American or Latino and mostly poor kids.

I always wanted to mix adults and kids. The first couple years we did that informally with two, three or four kids and when we started the afterschool program I said, "Any kid who's in our afterschool program can be in the annual show." The first year was just lunacy; we had no guidelines developed for behavior. We were unprepared for twenty-five or thirty kids running around backstage. After '96, we said this is getting out of hand; we could never get enough parents to participate. We now have fewer kids in the show. The first criterion for selecting them is what the show needs; the second is the kids' skill; the third is attitude.

We've had three brothers who have been in the program since '94. They are fundamentalist Christian homeschoolers whose mom wanted them to have contact with other cultures. They've been at it for four and a half years. They worked with Pop on their own and developed a three person knockabout comedy routine in the Italian tradition. Those three brothers we've always put in the show.

Our afterschool program has always been free. Initially it was a program of the City of San Diego. That switched over to the California Arts Council, Artists in Residence program. It's a matching grant. We get two or three foundations who give money so we can double the amount.

At the beginning of the year, we are just one day a week, then two days depending on the season. In the gymnasium we have a couple trapezes, a web, a mechanic and underneath it we have a full-sized trampoline. We have a couple of mini-tramps. We do juggling, clowning and we have a low wire set up outside and Pop does that. We have a couple rolling globes and if we can free up staff, we use them.

We start with a fifteen minute group warmup at 4:00, then the kids go off in different directions. We have a person who stays at each station and a supervisor who floats around and another supervisor at a table. The most similar program I've seen is the afterschool program Big Apple does in East Harlem. In the new year, we're hoping to start a program on Fridays to serve advanced kids.

In our annual show in 1998, we had about twenty kids and about fifteen adults. More kids, but the central roles are always adults. The kids provide resonance for them. We do a big spectacle in each show and there are a lot of kids in that. I think it helps having people of all ages just as it helps having people of different cultures. I think that's one of the things that has endeared us to people locally. I want to replicate that when we tour. I hope to go to Pasadena next June and I want to hook up with local schools and arts organizations doing physical theatre of some form and gather a pool of kids to be in spectacles and if there are kids with special skills, we would put them in the show in some featured away.

We have a couple of teenagers who will definitely tour with us. There's a young woman who has been a gymnast since she was six or seven. She's now fifteen and an important part of our shows.

In our performances, we have live music. Our first couple years we had a guy playing accordion and another guy who played guitar and percussion instruments and sang in Spanish. They left after the second year and the accordionist got us a young guy who had done a lot of theatre composition. He was a keyboard player with a BA in ethnomusicology from UCLA. He performed with us for five years. We had him and a drummer. The keyboard player layered everything and had it sequenced in the keyboard. All he had to do was trigger it and he could play on top. When he left, he downloaded all this material and our main juggler, who plays keyboards, uses it and we play live a lot - keyboard and drums. There was need for a bass player and I thought I'd like to do that and now I do. We're planning on having new music composed for us next year.

We perform throughout the year. I'm trying to put together six consecutive weeks in May and June with the centerpiece being our

Balboa Park show. In a couple years I'd like to be able to get a small tent. Right now I'm trying to chase down some bleachers.[187]

The open ended eclecticism of the Fern Street Circus means that the Circus Learning takes place in a context of children learning from adults and then performing with them. The ethnic, cultural, racial, economic and age diversity of Fern Street in an ongoing year-round situation means that Circus Learning offers students not just the satisfaction that comes from mastering skills and learning to work cooperatively, but an opportunity to learn about the larger world.

Flying Trapeze Programs

Flying Trapeze has gained favor as a recreational activity independent of its relationship to circus. It has become a popular program at many Camp Meds. Sam Keen's book *Learning to Fly: Trapeze – Reflections on Fear, Trust and the Joy of Letting Go* extols the pleasures of flying "for anyone needing to confront deeply rooted fears. An unprecedented adventure of the soul and psyche."[188] The book, published by a subsidiary of Random House, appeared on the Psychology/Self Help shelves of bookstores and was promoted in the Spring of 1999 with a $100,000 national marketing campaign.

We will look at a few of the many flying schools that have emerged in which recreational activity and professional training coexist.

Flyer **Tito Gaona**, for years a headline flyer with Ringling Brothers and Barnum and Bailey, Big Apple, and other circuses, opened a trapeze school in 1998 at The Sports Complex, the former Ringling quarters in Venice, Florida. **Trapeze Arts, Inc**. in Sonoma County, California, is run by flyer Stephen Gaudreau who developed the Flying Trapeze program at the San Francisco School of Circus. Another recreational Flying Trapeze program is **Circus Arts Workshop** in McLean, Virginia. One of the oldest is the **Imperial Flyers** of Denver, Colorado which has been in operation since 1928.

Like Maria Carillo of **Circus Arts & Acrobatics**, Jonathan Conant, has a varied background that does not include circus. Also like her, after becoming an amateur flyer, he invested his savings in a school, **Trapezeschool.com.**

It is pretty much a full scale athletic training center where people come and learn, not only trapeze, but all sorts of arts that are normally related with circus. We are also starting to transition more into aerial dance and athletics

It's a 350 acre farm in New Paltz, New York. On it we have some of the best rock climbing in the region and a couple of the best climbers in the area who live and work on the farm. The farm leads on to mountains so you can walk from our farm for weeks and weeks and never have to meet civilization. We have a horseback riding facility as well. My board members include Maria Carrillo, Sam Keen, Tito Gaona, and we work together. I am training other staff to do the work on the trapeze and I have people coming through internationally to do professional training.

People come for short-term courses and longer-term training. Some days people just show up. Last summer we had a couple show up on their honeymoon and they just wanted to try something exciting and they came for the day.

I have people coming this summer who will camp and work for me on the farm all summer in trade for being on the trapeze. I've just got back from Costa Rica and I'm opening up another site in Monetzuma to try to get that crowd going down there.

The funding is very creative on my part. I'm a money person. I'm more a business person than anything else. I've had to train myself. I don't consider myself circus. I consider myself someone who wants to teach people how to move in space more gracefully and sort of move us into the next evolution of what I believe we're going to be doing as a race and also help people move through fear and just do a lot of processing around the feelings that come up around dealing with something like flying.

I have a varied background. I have done psychology work, I had a marriage and family counseling service, I've worked with schizophrenics, I've done a lot of Outward Bound type of programs and worked in a lot of kids' camps. I also have done a lot of music. I presently own a music recording studio in New York and I do film scoring for National Public Television. I was a professional dancer when I was younger. I just love to do a lot of different things. A few years ago I fell in love with the trapeze and decided it was something I wanted to do.

Our classes are about an hour and forty-five minutes long and this year we're starting out at $35. for that class period so we're definitely right in there with everybody else in the country. And then things will get more expensive as we have higher level teachers to do workshops.

Right now in February, we're waiting for it not to be so desperately cold. I expect we'll be working in April or May.[189]

The Trapezeschool.com Web Site adds:

We are a family of Flyers; acrobats, dancers, artists and forward thinkers dedicated to the advancement of body, mind and spirit. The courses we produce are extremely fun, challenging and supportive. Every one of you has a dream. Something you wish you could do. The flying arts are a playground for dreams. A place to challenge your fears, do unimagined feats, be inspired by others and encouraged by their cheers.

We offer a safe and magical environment. A place where anything is possible and everything is worth a try. We will guide and teach you how to do more you have ever done before! Great people, big fun and adventure, a place to bound past your limitations. It's all here at TRAPEZESCHOOL.COM. [190]

In addition to the flying programs at some of the circus camps discussed in Chapter Five, many summer camps that do not focus on circus have added recreational flying programs. Bernandette Pace, who directs three of them, provides insight into the burgeoning interest in flying.

At the camps I work at, the kids are there for four to eight weeks and they can become very accomplished flyers. They have elective programs where they can take the trapeze class one, two or three times a day – each class is about an hour. I restrict the class to twelve people so everybody gets at least three turns an hour. Some of these kids have been coming back to camp for years and come in knowing the basics. The way we run the program, everyone gets one or two turns and then they get a chance to fly. That is to be caught by the catcher. Some of the kids will be doing eight to ten different tricks by the end of the training program.

I own two trapezes. Two of the camps I work with have their own, I bring the trapeze to the third. The youngest kids in my programs are six. Occasionally you get a five year old and that's fine, too, as long as they want to go up. I used to have cable ladders to climb to the pedestal and that was a big challenge in itself so to expedite things, I started using extension ladders and now anyone can scamper up. It makes a tougher decision for them when they get up there whether they want to go.

The kids are strong enough to fly. My granddaughter went off before she was two years old. In my yard, I have two single trapeze units and she had her own little swing three feet off the ground. She was standing on the chair and swinging; her little hands didn't even go all the way around the trapeze bar and she'd swing and swing. She wanted to go on the trapeze so she did. She did one for three swings. Of course she was wearing a spotting belt. She's now six and wants to go without the belt and I say, "No." But she swings on the trapeze as if she had no belt. She does splits and knee hangs. She does a back flip. When you spot somebody you can hold them up in the air and assist them a lot, but I tell her spotter - I'm usually on the pedestal letting her off, "Don't hold her up in the air. I want her to know what it feels like to fall in the net." So long as she's falling right, they let her free fall. She also has very little fear which is why she is not ready to go without the belt.

There's another trapeze I set up at Club Getaway in Kent, Connecticut each summer that has both child and adult programs. Two groups of children come in for a week and it's not so much a training program as just an experience. The kids usually just get to swing on the trapeze one time because they're only there for two days. The adults come weekends. It can be a one-time experience, but they also have a group of "Frequent Flyers" that come every weekend. They have extensive training and some of them are very accomplished.

At the camps, my teaching is done by various people. Some have been trained the way I was at the Denver Center YMCA and at similar places around the country, but most come out of the Club Med system. People do not have official degrees. It's just through on the job training that they learn to do it.

I am only involved with teaching high flying trapeze, but I do have a rainy day program of teaching hula hoops just because I can do that inside.[191]

Ms. Pace's background includes recreational flying and professional work in circuses.

I do other things. I have a single trapeze act and other acts and Spanish Web and Lyre. I've traveled with the Royal Hanneford Circus and Circus Gatti; I did a couple shows with Circus Corona. For most shows I did high flying trapeze and Spanish Web. I did a Christmas circus in Puerto Rico where I did high flying trapeze, single trapeze and a slide for life - you hook your foot to a trolley and slide down inverted on an inclined wire. When I was traveling with Royal Hanneford, I did single trapeze under the motorcyle on an inclined wire. That was a big rush because in some of the arenas you're a hundred feet in the air. I also rode the elephants with that show

I started flying approximately 1970 at The Denver Central YMCA. I built a trapeze and became associated with various gymnasts and met people on circuses. I have a small circus myself, The Highflyers Family Circus. It is a group of people from Bloomington, Indiana. They are gymnasts, divers, whatever, who have families here and are interested in circus arts. Our first shows in '86 were quite amateurish, but over the years they became more professional. Many of the people who trained with me went on to become professional circus people and traveled for three, four, five, six, eight years and then returned to Bloomington to live and are part of the circus group while they are raising families. They have the circus enthusiasm in the blood.

Unlike some people, I do not feel religious about the trapeze experience. However, I must say that I have an intense emotional involvement with trapeze. If I were to write a book, I would have a chapter called, "Through Sickness and Health." Once I started, I never quit. I absolutely love it. Mostly I'm in it for the recreation, but if you're under any emotional stress, you really don't have time for it when you're on a pedestal flying. I went through a divorce in '93 after being married for twenty-eight years and I must say that flying was the only time I could forget my situation. I flew a lot then just to escape.[192]

Main Space Circus

Marsha Kennington grew up doing gymnastics and diving in California. As an adult, she turned these skills to trapeze and toured with circuses for twenty years before settling in 1986 in Toronto where she established the Main Space Circus Corporation.

Main Space logo

We run the two Harbourfront summer camps - circus arts and flying trapeze, as well as their March Break camp. But now there's more. An important part of the Main Space Circus Corp. is its own School of Circus Arts. Currently working out of two Toronto locations from September to June, the school offers a Youth Troupe program for children ages seven and up, an Apprentice Program (toward our Performance Troupe), an adult Circus Arts program, a Flying Trapeze program (for all ages) and a Bungee Acrobatics program. The school is also contracted to run both the March Break and the Summer Camp programs for the Bloor Jewish Community Center.

In the summer months our whole operation moves to the outdoor Toronto waterfront location. In addition to the 10 weeks of children's camps that run during the day, we run outdoors flying trapeze lessons every evening and on weekends from June to September. Between the school and the camps, Main Space teaches almost 700 students yearly.

Main Space is often asked to arrange for performers to appear at outdoor events, nightclubs, private functions and in film, television and advertising. The creation of the Main Space Performance Troupe was a direct response to these requests. Members of the Troupe include athletes and actors, established circus artists and professional instructors as well as graduates of our own School of Circus Arts.

Our talented instructors are also in demand for their valuable behind-the-scenes expertise in a variety of circus and athletic disci-

plines. Main Space also builds and/or provides consultation on other
professional trapeze rigs.[193]

Kennington described the Main Space philosophy:

Having been both a diver and a gymnast myself, I know that most
training programs are geared towards competition. But circus is not
about trying to win something. Oh, sure, there's competition between
performers; that happens in every field and it's just human nature.
But in the culture of the circus, we try to turn that edge into teamwork.
Everyone has to work together to make the circus happen.

When you watch circus artists perform, they make it seem so
easy; they make you think, "I can do that." Do they fly through the
air with the greatest of ease? No way, but making it look easy is the
trick! It's hard work, to be sure, but getting there can be, and should
be, an enjoyable process. It takes personal drive, self-discipline and
self-motivation. With the guidance of a good coach, by learning to
listen and applying the skills you've learned, you will earn that self-
esteem, that feeling of achievement.

At Main Space, our primary job is to have fun. We want children
to be children. We want our performers to apply the skills they've
learned creatively; we want them to play, too, but within a structure.
In the circus world, play without structure just doesn't work. Through
experimentation, the performers use these tools to develop their own
style. From this, they will eventually create art and, perhaps, magic.[194]

In 1991, Main Space moved into and renovated The Main Space
Theatre, formerly a silent movie house, but soon outgrew it. Kennington
wanted to have her own space, but

I've pretty much given up looking for a building here because the
loft and condominium situation has been exploding; what used to be
a dollar a square foot is now twenty. I know I could go north or into
Mississaugua and get a building, but the core people and staff that I
have are not interested in that. So as long as I can have the buildings
I have now, we're fine.[195]

The high ceilings at Variety Village on Danforth Avenue in
Scarborough allow Main Space to operate its indoor Flying Trapeze and

Bungee Acrobatics programs. The Bloor Jewish Community Center on Spadina Avenue is the site of the Saturday Youth Troupe for children seven and up that offers beginner and intermediate acrobatics, tightwire, trampoline, mini-tramp, stilts, swinging and static trapeze, cylinder balancing, juggling, gymwheel and unicycle. The Bloor Center also provides space for the Sunday Apprentice Program; adult recreational circus classes and the Performance Troupe whose members are chosen by audition or invitation.

The influence of Cirque du Soleil extends from Quebec to Ontario. As Kennington notes, "the focus up here is the Cirque du Soleil style and when people call us for gigs, that's what they want."[196] Photographs of the Main Space Performing Troupe show costuming and make up that reflect Cirque du Soleil influence.

At one time, Montreal's National Circus School considered establishing five circus schools across Canada. Kennington was approached about heading a school in Toronto, but nothing came of the plan. One reason may be that the Province of Ontario does not support circus the way the Province of Quebec does. As was noted in the discussion of the National Circus School in Chapter Two, students can apply their Quebec education grants towards study for a degree at the National Circus School. Main Space is an after-school program; it operates outside the educational system.

Marsha Kennington started the school because it seemed appropriate to her that after twenty years of performing, she should pass on what she had learned

for the purpose of a full circle. You learn these things and to apply your lessons to life; not just lessons for lessons' sake. It is not necessary to run away and join a circus to get them. People say to me, "Why do people take circus lessons?" Well, why play hockey? Because you want to, because you like it. Isn't that enough reason? We don't give diplomas but for the kids who stick with this, there are life lessons. They have to commit. If they screw up, I let them know.[197]

Marsha Kennington echoes Alla Youdina in noting that circus is dangerous. Through human error or mechanical failure, accidents occur. Kennington's daughter, Ginger, was injured in a fall from a trapeze while touring with Circus Chimera in 1998.

When that happened to my daughter, I went through Hell with the whole thing. I wondered if I wanted to continue doing this and putting people's lives at risk because, with all of our safety precautions, that's what we do.

One of my roommates, a woman in her thirties, has a rare blood disease and she's not going to live. She just looked at me and said, "Some people call having a life taking a risk." That hit home. There's risk in everything. All we can do is the best we can and know that there is risk.198

In October, 1999, Kennington sold the Main Space corporation. The new owners opened a new indoor space. Kennington continued her relationship with Main Space as an independent contractor.

New Way Circus Center

The Russian American Kids Circus in Brooklyn, New York is a performing group of children all of whom spoke Russian as their first language. The Circus evolved from the year round work of the New Way Circus Center, Inc., housed in the Newman Jewish Community Center in the heart of the immigrant Russian community. When visited in 1998, the program, not yet four years old, had made impressive strides; especially when one considers it

Rehearsal, Russian American Kids Circus. credit: Maike Schulz

was created by people new to the American way of doing things. The Center had recently opened a year round Circus Preschool in addition to its after-school program, vacation day camps, and the Russian American Kids Circus. There were plans for an adult circus as the youngsters mature.

As the program is new to Brooklyn, its performers are new to circus. They are not children who would have taken to acrobatics, aerial work, uni-cycling and clowning if the circus had not been there. The goal of the New Way Circus Center is not just producing performers, but getting all youngsters to discover their talents.

We do not select children who are talented. We are accepting every single child proving that every child is talented. When the chil-dren come, they are physically weak so we have to prepare them physically. They have to become strong. At the end of their lessons, we have a fifteen minute free time to do what they want. As we watch, Alex can produce something that will fit them perfectly.[199]

Regina and Alex Berenchtein and Regina's mother are the founders of the New Way Circus Center. Alex Berenchtein, an honors graduate of the Moscow Circus School, has performed in twenty-nine countries. He taught and performed extensively in the United States before settling in Brooklyn. According to Regina,

Alex cannot live without circus so I thought to myself, what can I do? I have to support him and that's the way it works in a Jewish family. When someone wants something, the whole family has to support it - physically, emotionally, financially. So we started by our-selves. Nobody believed in us. They said, "Oh, no, it is impossible. We believe in your talent and your energy, but it is not easy to make it." We thought, nothing is easy, but we will make it.[200]

Alex Berenchtein, the chief trainer, sets the tone for the performances which are disciplined, skilled, filled with a clown's exuberance and accompa-nied by recorded Russian music. Regina Berenchtein, whose background is in music, is the chief administrator who has mastered the complexities of building an arts program in a capitalist economy.

I learned a lot of things. We came as immigrants and had to prove to ourselves that we can make it. Financially we lost everything in Russia. In order to be successful in this country, number one - you have to have a real family. Besides the family, you have to have real friends. You have it - you can make it. It takes time. It's quite difficult.[201]

   She learned about nonprofit status, courting influential public figures, pursuing grants and garnering good public relations as the organization's outside person. Her mother, Olga Patigul, in Russia a nurse, takes care of the internal administrative work, scheduling classes, meeting the needs of students and parents and is available for medical emergencies. The New Way Circus Center operates five days a week; the host establishment is closed for Friday and Saturday *shabbos*. In what other circus program do you see a bespectacled boy with a *yamalka* doing flips and juggling?

   The New Way Circus Center occupies the gym of the Community Center and has refurbished rooms for its preschool. It also has offices, a kitchen and communal eating area which reinforces the family ambiance of the operation. The three directors are a literal family; the students members of an extended family.

   The New Way Circus Center is unique in its plan to create a lifelong program for its participants. Children move from the Circus Preschool into the other programs; as they get sufficiently proficient they move into the Russian American Kids Circus. Having invested so much time and effort into training them, the New Way Circus Center hopes that student performers will graduate into the proposed adult circus as performers, trainers or support personnel.

   The New Way Circus Center reminds one of New York grocery stores operated by immigrant Korean families. Regina Berenchtein routinely puts in 18 hour days. Alex Berenchtein starts his day snacking with the preschoolers, accompanying them to the playground and leading them in circus activities after the schooling is over. He then oversees the afterschool programs, residencies and performances assisted by another Moscow Circus veteran, Igor Loktev. The New Way Circus Center team also includes a German photographer, a Greek graphic designer (from Russia), a Puerto Rican consultant and an American lawyer.

   Regina Berenchtein believes the organization will eventually have to move to a seven day a week facility if it is to serve the community as it wants to. As it is, many children who are free on Saturday, but attend church on Sunday, are deprived of weekend participation. Although the performing group is now the *Russian* American Kids Circus, that title might change as the program engages a more diverse population. Students beyond the Russian community already encounter the New Way Circus Center through school residencies it conducts in the five boroughs, on Long Island and in New Jersey.

Its first four years suggests that The New Way Circus Center encapsulates the historic experience of immigrants in the United States. When the Berenchteins decided to start a circus training program, they were unable to provide collateral for bank loans. They turned to Russian immigrant friends who knew Alex's reputation and understood the family's determination. "New York New York; If You Can Make it here, You Can Make it Anywhere," became the family mantra. When they found space in the community that had supported them, they opened Alex's Center for the Performing Arts, Inc. and their first students were Russian American children. They started with juggling and some mats for tumbling. Since then, Alex Berenchtein has designed equipment including an elaborate portable tightwire with rotating end units that permit climbing on an incline.

Alex's Center for the Performing Arts transformed into the New Way Circus Center as it pursued nonprofit status. Its first grant came from Consolidated Edison. Meanwhile, income generated by performances and appearances of the Russian American Kids Circus went to support the nonprofit organization, especially in the form of scholarships.

The progress The New Way Circus Center has made is impressive. Whether the skilled graduates of the Kids Circus will choose to stay within the institution remains to be seen. Immigrant history suggests that as the New Way Circus Center is moving from an immigrant community into the mainstream, some of its graduates might leave the extended family the Berenchteins have created.

Commenting on the New Way Circus Center, Regina Berenchtein says,

I have never been in a circus and I so regret it because you grow up healthier, plus you get a lot of art work. You can create yourself; you can complete yourself.[202]

Providence Circus School

The Providence Circus School was founded in the Fall of 1998 by the What Cheer Art Company, a nonprofit Rhode Island Arts Corporation. The School offers weekend classes for youngsters 10-18 in basic circus skills - balance, tumbling, juggling, clowning, unicycling and others. The primary Providence Circus School class meets Sunday afternoons for eight week sessions in the Fall, Winter and Spring. Three scholarships are offered at each session. Classes are held in the All Childrens Theater (ACT) and performances are given in the Providence Children's Museum and other community venues. Director Judith Plotz taught balance at the Circus Smirkus Camp.

Tumbling class, Providence Circus School, 1999.
credit: J. Plotz

Our goals at Providence Circus School are multi-layered. *Our first goal is to have fun!* Other goals for our students: 1) to learn skills in strength, dexterity, rhythm, concentration of attention, and stage presence, 2) to learn to work collaboratively, and 3) to have a community in which it is OK to be silly or eccentric; and for our School: 1) to bring the pleasure of circus shows to audiences of all ages, and 2) to keep alive circus traditions. We hope by our example to encourage young people to follow their own dreams and work for accomplishment in whatever field interests them.[203]

Skylight Circus Arts

Jim Riley, its Artistic Director, founded Skylight in 1988 in Rochdale, UK. Skylight is a circus school and a performance company; it also maintains a variety of outreach programs. Its efforts to enrich Rochdale through circus arts have been supported by the National Lottery of the Arts Council of England, the Northwest Arts Board, the Rochdale Metropolitan Borough Council and private sponsors. In 1997, Skylight was awarded lottery money to establish three outreach clubs - one a voluntary youth club, the second for young people with special needs, and a third all-inclusive group.

The Skylight Cross Curricular Teaching Pack sets forth the group's philosophy.

Circus Arts are an exciting new blend of traditional circus skills and other art forms such as mime, dance, theatre and music. Using human skills, everyone is given the chance to perform and participate. In a supportive, non-competitive environment, it's amazing how quickly students learn to juggle, spin plates, walk on stilts or the tightrope and throw diabolos. . . .

Learning, practicing and performing circus skills is a great exercise in itself and also conveys other benefits. Juggling and diabolo can improve throwing and catching skills and general coordination. Walking on stilts helps with posture, balance and body awareness. Students with concentration problems often cooperate well in this novel situation and focus for longer periods. Few of your students will have had the opportunity to build circus skills, so they'll all start at the same point, discovering their own strengths and limitations in this area. . . .Group activities give students a chance to see themselves as part of a team, each person's input as valued as anyone else's, communication and cooperation being key factors for success. The performance of circus skills can give a tremendous sense of achievement and confidence.[204]

Skylight won another National Lottery award for two Developmental Community/Professional Circus performances: *Shifting Bounds,* a theatre-based show combining circus and Asian dance for Easter, 1999; and *The Bridge,* presented on a Rochdale waterside venue for the millenium in May, 2000.

Other Skylight projects include five youth circus groups for youngsters 9-16 in Rochdale as part of its Initiative by Skylight Circus for Young People (**ISCAYP**) and half-hour shows for unusual venues such as youth clubs that are followed by skills workshops. Skylight also works on "instant" parades that are the culmination of six weeks work with community artists.

Zip Zap Circus School

The Zip Zap Circus School in Capetown South Africa promotes "the development of children from all walks of life free of charge." The school, which serves children age six to 20, was founded in 1992 by Brent van Rensberg and his wife, Laurence Esteve. Brent had performed in circuses around the world and served as an instructor at Ringling Brothers and Barnum & Bailey's Clown College; Laurence's background includes a French Masters Degree in Business and Management and extensive work as a circus aerialist. She recalls,

In the beginning we had no funding. In fact, we trained children in backyards, from trees, wherever we could hang a trapeze. As our reputation grew, we began to receive funding from the government and the corporate sector. At present we have two corporate sponsors, Caltex and Computer Associates. We have also received funding from the city and from the National Arts Council. The funding we receive doesn't cover our expenses, but together with the revenue from performances, we get by.

We present public performances frequently as the children love an opportunity to showcase their talents. In October we performed on an opera stage with a local dance company and Sibongile Khumalo, a well-know South African singer, as well as her son, a famous jazz violinist. It was a theatrical performance integrating the seemingly disparate art forms. This month we have been hired to perform at a wedding and we will be hosting a corporate Christmas party in our venue, a former warehouse. In September we performed in a community centre in the townships for school children. As you can see, our shows cover a broad range, depending on the audience. We are almost fully booked and this year we have done over 150 performances.[205]

At present we have 45 students on a regular basis. Training takes place after school and on weekends. We also liaison with schools and perform at school fundraisers. Circus practice occurs Saturdays and Sundays, 12:30pm to 5:30pm. Our school is open to any child who wishes to learn. Our only requirement is enthusiasm and motivation.

Our purpose is to introduce children to the magic of circus and through play and fun to create bonds that transcend the socio-economic barriers which, unfortunately, still exist in South Africa. We boost children's sense of self-worth and introduce them to the arts and, perhaps, a career in the arts or related fields.[206]

The Zip Zap staff consists of Brent van Rensberg, Artistic Director; Laurence Esteve, Managing Director; and Rodleigh Stevens, who toured over 25 years as a trapeze performer, is Trainer and Technical Director. Zip Zap hopes to establish a National School of Circus Arts that will include drama, dance, music, and mime as well as welding, wood work, music editing, design, set and costume design and stage management. Architect Pancho Gueddes has developed plans for the school.

Zip Zap, like the Belfast Community Circus School, Cirque du Monde and other groups working with children in stressful situations, demonstrates how Circus Learning can enrich the lives of these children.

Unlike visiting circuses that pitch their tents for a day and create a magical world before moving on to the next town, year-round, independent Circus Learning programs enable youngsters to master the magic without leaving home. Residencies and other short term exposures are valuable, but no substitute for having Circus Learning part of a community's life.

IX
College Circuses

EXTRACURRICULAR

Circus Learning was a tradition at some colleges before the revived interest that began when Hovey Burgess brought Circus Skills to New York University's School of the Arts as counter-cultural enrichment in 1966. The older programs started as competitive gymnastics; extracurricular activities sponsored by Physical Education departments. When funding was tight during the Great Depression, competitive gymnastics - a poor cousin to activities like football, transformed into Gymkana, a more theatrical form that could attract paying customers. The Gymkana program at the University of Maryland College Park has continued while the Flying High Circus at Florida State University and the Gamma Phi Circus at Illinois State University developed from Gymkana.

The Gymkana Troupe

The tradition that produced The Gymkana Troupe of the College of Health and Human Performance of the University of Maryland at College Park is described in one of its printed programs.

Exhibitional Gymnastics was introduced into this country in the early 1900s by Dr. Leslie Judd at Springfield College, Massachusetts. Several years later, a similar program started at the University of Illinois under the direction of Dr. Hartley Price. Exhibitional Gymnastics became very popu-

Vaulting at a Gymkana show.
Credit: Gymkana Troupe

lar in this country during the early 20s, 30s and 40s, but unfortunately experienced a decline with the introduction of American sports, recreation and competition. However the dream to keep Exhibitional Gymnastics alive was achieved by Dr. David A. Field who started the Gymkana Troupe at the University of Maryland in 1946.

. . .Today, after fifty years, Gymkana continues the tradition of presenting exhibitional gymnastics and healthy living to audiences everywhere.[207]

The fifty-member Gymkana Troupe, a co-ed, extracurricular gymnastics club, presents about ten touring shows each year for schools in Maryland, nearby states, and at military bases. The season ends with a Home Show on the College Park campus. Performances include traditional gymnastics - handbalancing, balance bar, parallel bars, pyramids, horse, tumbling, ladders, rings, high bar and vaulting augmented by juggling, chair balancing, dance and magic. The shows are characterized by the energy and enthusiasm associated with *Up With People* musicals as the performers, each of whom has taken a pledge to avoid drugs, demonstrates what clean living can achieve. When the Student Government Association accused the Troupe of discrimination in 1990 because of its anti-drug policy and threatened to withdraw Student Government funding, the troupe decided to forgo the funding.

A Gymkana Summer Camp for children 5 through 16 began in 1986.

Gymkana Summer Camp extends the philosophy of the Gymkana troupe by providing a wholesome opportunity for boys and girls to learn gymnastics while at the same time stressing healthy, drug-free living. One of our primary goals is to show the youth of the nation that they can say "No to Drugs" through sports and activities. Another important goal is to offer a camp where young people can learn and participate in gymnastics without the pressure of competition, while at the same time having fun and enjoying themselves.[208]

The Gymkana Troupe shared a stage at the Astrodome in 1996 with Senator Phil Gram, a candidate for the Republican nomination for President, and Dr. William Bennett, author of *The Book of Virtues* and former Education Secretary. In his keynote address, Bennett said:

It's a tremendous tribute to our young people that you've shown today by having Gymkana here and showing America what our young people are capable of. I was thinking while they were performing of how it is that young people will get together, join in a group, gravitate towards each other, and share a common set of values. . . .Our children will form into groups. Whether these groups become the Gymkanas of the world, the Boy Scouts of the World, or the Bloods and Crips of the world, depends an awful lot on what we do.[209]

It is fascinating to note again how the values of Circus Learning are invoked by right wing ideologues, such as Dr. Bennett, and left wing ideologues such as Wavy Gravy, hero of Woodstock.

The Gamma Phi Circus

Like the Circus City Festival in Peru, Indiana; the Gamma Phi Circus benefited from the many circus performers who lived in the Midwest. Male Physical Education students from Illinois State Normal University participated alongside circus professionals in the Bloomington YMCA circus in the 1920's. "The Gamma Phi gymnastic fraternity was struggling to organize a national organization. When the organization failed to generate enough interest nation wide, [Coach] Horton

Gamma Phi Circus Gym Wheel.
Credit: Gamma Phi Circus

kept it alive at I.S.N.U. by participation in the YMCA Circus. Soon Horton began to organize a separate circus for his talented gymnasts."[210] Females have participated since 1940 and the Gamma Phi Circus program now includes clowning, tightwire and other circus disciplines. Until recently, the program was entirely extra-curricular. While participants now receive one hour of academic credit for each year's participation, the focus remains extra-curricular. Students are discouraged from letting their circus work interfere with their studies and practice times are limited.

The original rolling globe and revolving ladder acts were brought to us by circus families here in the Bloomington/Normal area. Each year members of the Gamma Phi Circus perform two on-campus shows. The Gamma Phi Circus is open to all full time students at Illinois State University as well as all faculty and staff of the university. Practices are every Monday evening from 7:00-9:00 PM in Horton South Gym. Anyone interested in joining the circus is encouraged to come and see what it is all about. No experience necessary.[211]

The director of the Gamma Phi Circus, Jerry J. Polacek, Assistant Professor in the Physical Education Department, is a Gamma Phi alumnus from 1967. A Gamma Phi Circus Home Show involves seventy-five to eighty brightly costumed performers accompanied by a live band. The 1997 acts were

acrosport, gym wheel, women's rings and ladders, tightwire, trapeze and cloud swing, juggling, trampoline, clowns, Spanish web, high cradle and hanging perch and sky walk, vaulting, rolling globes, adagio, Russian bar, roller skating, teeterboard and unicycles.[212]

Prospective members of the circus are introduced to the acts when the school year begins. Students who come to the college because of the Circus and arrive with skills are encouraged to develop additional skills. Illinois State maintains a female gymnastics program which feeds the circus and shares rehearsal space with it. Since the University discontinued male gymnastics, the Circus provides an outlet for male gymnasts. At the first circus tryouts in November, students audition for a minimum of two acts. Captains for the individual acts base their evaluations on skill - each act has been broken down into a series of specific criteria, and on attitude. By December's final tryouts, the students have had time to condition themselves and practice. Selections are based on present and potential skill and "providing opportunity." This means that students with many skills may be replaced in some acts so other have a chance to perform. While students try out for some acts, others are cast by invitation based on demonstrated potential. Specialty acts are reserved for students with experience and outstanding ability.

In addition to Polacek, Wayne Wright, a former professional circus performer, coaches. They are assisted by experienced student members of the circus who mentor newcomers. Tom Romance, who is in charge of the Junior Gamma Phi Circus that is part of the University's schools program, helps with juggling. Gamma Phi also operates a summer circus camp that is staffed by Polacek, Wright and Wright's wife Carol, another veteran circus performer who used to join her husband as a projectile in Hugo Zacchini's cannon act.

Like the Circus City Festival in Peru, the Gamma Phi Circus, its summer camp and Junior Circus, are established parts of the Midwest landscape.

The Flying High Circus

The Flying High Circus at Florida State University in Tallahassee also operates as an extracurricular activity although the college offers a one-credit introductory circus course. The Circus is self-supporting; no state or college funds are used. The University offers no tuition waivers or

Flying High Circus logo

scholarships to Circus participants who must maintain a C average to appear in the Home Shows and a C+ to participate in the road shows performed during the year in the Southeast.

> Grades are not a problem, their collective average has always been one of the highest for students in any extracurricular activity in the University even though many of the students are in demanding fields such as pre-medicine, nursing, computer science and accounting."[213]

> The Home Show takes place the first two weeks of April in the FSU Big Top that is erected each February on the south side of the campus. The Show is three ring affair that includes 18-20 acts. "This is the one show that every circus participant will perform in if they stick with the circus through the spring."[214] The Big Top is used in some of the road shows; most present about ten acts.

> The Flying Trapeze is featured in the Flying high Circus and sometimes includes triple somersaults. Other acts are Perch Pole and

> Swing Pole
> for Swing Pole, one man holds up a steel pole about twenty feet long as his partner climbs to the top. As she fastens herself to the top of the pole with a neck loop, he spins the pole around as fast as possible until she is swinging out almost parallel to the ground

> Quartette Adagio
> which fosters teamwork between circus newcomers and old-timers alike. It requires three strong men and one small and flexible woman. The main portion of the act consists of the men throwing the

girl into the air and catching her after she completes her trick. Men are often combined into a quartette team to teach them timing and coordination while increasing their muscular development. Women are added to the teams to foster their confidence in trusting others to catch them when they are flying through the air and to develop the quickness, limberness and coordination required to perform more complex acts such as the cradle acts and flying. Quartette is an act in which the three men are totally responsible for the woman's safety. There are no safety nets or lines in quartette and when she goes high in the air, the men must catch her when she comes down to avoid some painful injuries if she hits the ground. One highlight of the act is the straight pitch, when the men try to throw the girl as high into the air as possible, then catch her as she falls back down. Another is "jump rope," a trick in which two men swing the girl around like a jump rope while the third jumps over her at the bottom of the swing. Timing is especially crucial here.[215]

Other acts are sky pole - which is like Russian bar, cloud swing, Spanish web, hand balancing, juggling, bicycle, unicycle, low casting and teeterboard.

The performing company for the Home Show numbers over 75. During the summer, 25-28 of them work at Florida's Callaway Gardens performing eight shows a week and acting as recreational counselors teaching circus skills.

In 1997, the Flying High Circus celebrated its fiftieth anniversary during the Golden Anniversary of the institution's transition from Florida State College for Women to Florida State University. As part of the celebration, Floyd Jordan, a former FSU clown, donated money to develop a production that would combine the resources and talents of the FSU Circus and its School of Theater. Others joined in and the result was *The Elemental Circus*, a project of the Flying High Circus, the School of Theatre and the School of Music. Danny Mordujovich, School of Music graduate student, wrote an original score and Circus Director Richard Brinson created new routines for the show. Leslie Grasia, a graduate student in the School of Theatre, wrote the script which dealt with Alia and her perilous quest to find and conquer the four demons who had destroyed her homeland.

The story will be told entirely through music and visual effects - there is no spoken dialogue. Because the cast includes trained circus performers, Elemental Circus will include acrobatics, stunts and optical illusions that usually cannot be performed in a play. At the same time, the presence of actors and a consistent story line will give the show greater continuity than a traditional circus show.[216]

Because of its size, the many years it has been in operation, and the excellence of its training, the influence of the FSU Flying Circus is extensive. Students, particularly flyers, have gone on to be professional performers. Teachers, like Bruce Pfeffer and his Circus of the Kids,[217] use techniques learned at FSU where safety nets and safety lines are employed in many acts. The casting acts that have become a feature of the Peru Amateur Circus were instituted the year Peru had a head trainer, Larry Camp, who came from the Flying High Circus. The experiment with *The Elemental Circus* indicates that Flying High is not only associated with traditional circus, but with the *new* circus which often uses quest themes to integrate a variety of theatrical elements.

CURRICULAR
Circus Works

Circus Works at Bloomfield College in Bloomfield, New Jersey is a curricular part of Bloomfield College's Arts as Catalyst program. Circus Works was created by faculty member John Towsen, a former student of Hovey Burgess. The class teaches skills and develops a Circus Troupe that performs in the community as part of the college's commitment to community service.

Fred Collins and program director John Towsen teach slackwire, Bloomfield College, 1997.

Circus Works is a circus troupe that gives Bloomfield College students a chance to master the art of juggling, tumbling, wire walking, balancing and more. In the process of sharpening these physical skills, students from diverse cultural and ethnic backgrounds
  - learn to collaborate with and trust one another
  - develop greater self-discipline and self confidence
  - experience the power of success.

Circus Works has proved to be an effective educational tool empowering Bloomfield College students to succeed in other areas of learning and, ultimately, in the workplace.[218]

The program was described by Lisa Farese, director of Arts as Catalyst.

The college was established in 1868 as a seminary for German Presbyterians when German immigrants could not get into what is now Montclair State University, which was also a seminary when it started, because it didn't teach classes in German. This college had its start serving a disadvantaged population and has continued doing so throughout its 125 years. We are now a four year Liberal Arts college. The Circus Troupe fits with the mission and philosophy of the college - "to prepare students to function at the peak of their potential in a multiracial, multicultural society" - because the idea of the Circus Troupe isn't just to teach circus skills; it's to teach students other things they're going to need the rest of their lives. Most are not going to become circus performers, but they learn to collaborate with others, they learns self-discipline, a fair amount of aesthetic appreciation and they get critical thinking.

The last time I checked, over 75% of those who joined the Troupe were either still in college or had already graduated; that's better than the retention and graduation rate for the rest of the college. When students gets into circus class or the Troupe, they learn what it takes to get something right. We believe they carry that over into their other classes. When students walk into circus class the first day of the semester, they think, "I'm never going to learn to juggle." Then they learn how. They have to persist because they can't pass the course without learning it. They find it's not as hard as they thought it would be because everyone in the class is pushing them along to do it. We believe this is something they carry over to say - chemistry, where they think, "I'm never going to be able to do these kind of calculations," but because they made it through another class where they thought something was equally impossible, they might think, "Maybe I can do it."

I believe that if students don't experience success somewhere in their schoolwork, they're not likely to keep trying. Some of the students who were in the Circus Troupe and persisted long enough to get through all their courses and graduate were not good academic students and might not have stayed otherwise. They struggle, but they kept struggling and that's the point.[219]

John Towsen, a Ph. D. from New York University is also a graduate of Ringling Bros. and Barnum & Bailey Clown College. He has been a professional clown, acrobat and juggler. His book *Clowns,*[220] a history, is based on his doctoral dissertation.

I started teaching here in 1986 when I started having kids and had to have health insurance and all that and a non-touring job. I started in the Performing Arts program. I was doing theatre which is my main background. When I started teaching circus skills, I taught everything for the first four or five years, but there are so many things I also have to do here including directing theatre productions. Performing Arts expanded into Creative Arts and Technology and now we're doing multi-media and video and theatre and circus and I'm head of the program and I can't be everywhere at the same time.[221]

When visited in 1997, Towsen was actively involved in the Circus Skills class, but was assisted by Fred Collins who teaches circus arts workshops in the New York City area in conjunction with the Guggenheim Museum, and juggler Ned Gelfars.

Each Circus class has about 12 students who meet in a large, high ceilinged, wood paneled room with tall, stained glass windows. The class members do not bring to the work the exemplary bodies and conditioning of extra curricular gymnasts. One of the lessons learned watching the class is how satisfying mastering circus skills can be for members of the general population.

Classes visited in September 1997 began with extensive stretching warm-ups after which students practiced a variety of tumbling tricks - somersaults, back shoulder rolls, cartwheels, stride somersaults, etc.. Each student then did a presentation for the class that combined four tricks. There was applause and encouragement for each person's achievement. Towsen commented:

This is only their fifth class, so they're into basics. When we get to December, they'll be performing. Some are better than others, but we gear it that way so they can go at their own tempo. As the equipment comes out in the room, it's transformed. We have a slack wire on the hooks here and we have a portable standing tightwire we take over and use in the theatre. We have all kinds of stilts and unicycles. We don't have aerial stuff basically because of the high ceilings, but we have plenty to keep them busy.[222]

The class broke into smaller groups to work on wire, diablo, rolla bolla and stilts. At the wire, Fred Collins encouraged students to experience the activity rather than rush through it. "The object isn't getting across, it's staying on," he told them.

After completing the class, students may join the Circus Troupe and take it twice for credit. Some continue to work with the Troupe as an extracurricular activity. Lisa Farese described what the Troupe does.

We've had ongoing workshops for kids from schools in Newark and we'll be continuing that next Fall. It's a grant from the Victoria Foundation that is based in Newark. We also started something else without grant money. I hooked up with a person at a local homeless shelter in East Orange, Isaiah House, and they brought some of the kids here for a series of workshops that included a literacy component. The kids got an hour of circus workshop and then the Circus Troupe members sat down with the kids and they read books together. It was great. The person I was working with wanted to get the kids to read more. It was hard because the shelter in East Orange is in a truly terrible neighborhood.

The kids couldn't even go outside to play. They'd be in school all day and they'd come back to the shelter where they couldn't go outside. They were bouncing off the walls so she hit on this idea - what about giving them time to run around and work off their energy and then sit down and read because that's something they need to do. One of the circus directors noticed incredible improvement in the reading skill of one of the kids over the course of six weeks. That was nice. We'll continue that. Sometimes there are as few as four kids, sometimes as many as eight. In essence we're combining community service and the arts.

When John Towsen formed the first Troupe, it was a performing troupe. He would get them rehearsing and about half way through the semester they'd be ready to go out. The college had a bus and they'd load it up with their equipment and they'd go to place like a Cerebral Palsy Center and they'd go to schools and give performances. Then the college didn't have a bus anymore and I hit on the idea of bringing small groups here. I found that schools had as much trouble with transportation as we did. Teachers have to come up with a good educational justification to get money for a bus. Coming to see a bunch of people perform wasn't enough so we hit on the workshop idea. We started that in 1992.[223]

Circus Learning has, for some time, been part of extra curricular activities attached to college Physical Education programs. More recently, Circus Learning has become part of curricular programs that meet needs of diverse student populations, introducing them to the challenges and satisfactions of learning.

IX
Case Histories

Learning is complicated. The learner brings to the process the inherited and acquired elements of his or her life. Finally, there are the circumstances under which the learner encounters the material. The child learning to walk is, again, a good example. Is the child endowed with a good sense of balance? How is its vision? Does it feel secure enough to venture into the unknown?

So far, we have examined organizations that provide Circus Learning. Perhaps we can gain additional insight by looking at Circus Learning from the viewpoint of the learner. In this chapter, we meet four circus professionals from different backgrounds who tell how they acquired their Circus Learning. One grew up in a touring circus family and developed his skills with them; the second had no experience with circus or any athletic activity until she married into a circus family that provided on the job training; the third grew up with state support for her acrobatic training and Circus Learning; the fourth became involved with a youth circus that took root in her home town and, after graduating high school, postponed college to attend a circus school.

Armando Cristiani

Armando Cristiani, when interviewed in 1997, was a circus performer whose primary acts were solo trampoline and juggling; he also did sword balancing and trapeze. His Circus Learning had taken place at home and on the road with his parents who were members of circus families. Lucio Cristiani, Armando's father, "one of the greatest bareback riders in history was the great grandson of the first Cristiani to enter the European circus world."[224] Armando Cristiani's life as an eleven year

Armando Cristiani juggles, Lili Cristiani styles.
credit: Circus Hall of Fame.

circus professional was the subject of a book.[225] He had begun appearing in his family's acts when three and practiced four years before making his juggling debut in the ring.

As an adult, Armando does solo acts assisted by his wife, Lili, who also does single trapeze and sword balancing. Armando is three years younger than his brother, Tino, who does trampoline with his two sons. Tino's wife Mara, like Armando's wife, does solo trapeze. Armando and Tino Cristiani's training started young.

We were about five or six years old. Dad knew gymnastics; if you're doing any kind of riding act, gymnastics are always involved. He taught us the basics - back bend and handsprings and things like that. We never got interested in doing anything with the riding act even though my parents were on the Beatty show into the mid-seventies doing it. My cousins, the Zamperlas on my mom's side, were renowned for doing trampoline and my brother and I wanted to do that. We learned a lot of it watching, then we worked with safety harnesses. We didn't just go out there and throw something; we took all the safety procedures.

With gymnastics, once you learn the basics of turning, everything begins to fall into place. My dad did the riding act and the teeterboard act, but a lot of the tricks my brother and I went on to do later on, my dad taught us. When my brother and I were doing the trampoline, we used to do the four twist to the shoulder. Once I learned one twist and the basics, everything else followed. After that, you sort of teach yourself.

My dad always pushed us doing comedy. I think he was afraid of doing a lot of tricks where we might get hurt. He would say, "You're doing enough. Do more comedy!"

We were always competing with our cousins the Zamperlas and the Canestrellis. The Fornasaris did a trampoline act, too, and it was all among the family because we're all related. We would hear that a person did a trick so we would want to do it.

A lot of kids I knew when I was growing up, as soon as school started, they would leave and go back home. We were so much a part of the acts we were doing, it was almost impossible. We were doing the trampoline; we were part of the riding act. We were schooled on the road. Our folks encouraged us. They would sit down and take the books out. It's hard because when you're on the road, your attention goes in all different areas. You want to play and you want to go out and do this and that, but our folks would say, "You have to sit down and take three or four hours a day and do your school work." My brother is very good with that with his kids. They don't go out of the trailer until they do their school work.

I tried to keep up as much as I could, but I didn't quite finish high school. I would still like to get my GED; it's sort of like unfinished business. It's important to be educated because you have to have businesses smarts. Circus is a business. It's hard. As a performer, it's getting to the point where you've got to have some talents to fall back on.

My primary act now is trampoline, but I'm a frustrated juggler. I love juggling. When I was a kid, I would commit myself to practicing all the time. I got so consumed by it, I wanted to do everything, but I realized my limitations. I'm definitely not an Enrico Rastelli. He was fantastic.

Right now I'm trying to keep myself in shape and trampoline gets hard as you get older. I'm only 35, but you start feeling it. If I lay off three months and think I'm in shape, I go back and I'm not. My legs hurt and I'm huffing and puffing. It's hard now because I do the trampoline act alone and I don't have a breather. I go out there and do about eight minutes; I'm out there by myself doing comedy and comedy tires you out. I do a lot of running around and the comedy puts more pressure on me than when I was doing the trampoline with my brother because you're always afraid of that rejection. Are you going to get a bad crowd? Are they going to respond? It makes me nervous. Once you go out and you feel the crowd's a good crowd, you relax right away. Sometimes you go out and people aren't in the mood to laugh. It doesn't matter what you do, but you have to say in character and do the work.[226]

Armando Cristiani grew up before the *new* one ring, theme-oriented circuses took hold and he has continued to perform in traditional shows, but when he discusses his work he sounds like performers in the *new* circuses.

It's like quality isn't as important as quantity. A lot of the shows that are out there today ask, "How many acts can you do?" And a lot of them don't want you to repeat the following season. You have to have a number of acts and I think it ends up hurting any one act that you want to focus on. For example, I want to be a good juggler and that's not enough unless you get into the night club scene or you get into something like Cirque du Soleil.

You can't do a lot of work on your act with the amount of traveling that some shows do. You get there after doing five hundred miles, pull in, set up your stuff and then you have to go out there and work. It takes away. I think that's why you see the quality hurt - and I'm not trying to be negative. I'm not saying everything. Even a lot of the Russian acts I've seen that first came here and just blew your mind. After they've been here a while, they begin to realize that one act isn't enough so I've seen some of them start putting together whatever. I think after a while you spread yourself too thin.[227]

As for the format of performances, Armando prefers one ring shows where

everything you do is center stage and you have to produce as a performer. I saw a Russian juggler with Ringling four or five years ago and he was in the center ring, but he was in a display. He did incredible tricks. He juggled on an unsupported ladder and he was juggling five clubs. He did seven hoops. He finished off at nine hoops, but it was the way he did the tricks. It was as if he could do them with his eyes closed. Even though he was center ring, half the stuff he did got lost. That takes a lot out of you as a performer.[228]

Armando Cristiani raises important issues about the adaptation of Circus Learning to the world of circus performance. A performer must continually adapt the work to the demands of the circus marketplace; in some situations that may mean compromising the artistic elements in the act. Another option is that taken by the performers in Cirque Eloize who created their own circus. Armando's father and his uncles did that for a while, but that, too, has its problems.

Shirley Earl and her favorite ringmaster, Brian LaPalme.

Shirley Earl

Shirley Earl had an unlikely background for a circus acrobat. In grade school, she was a straight A student except for Physical Education in which she regularly had a D. Things changed when she married Eddie Earl, a member of the family that owns and operates Roberts Brothers Circus. Shirley was not unfamiliar with circus; she grew up in Venice, Florida near the Ringling Brothers and Barnum & Bailey winter quarters, but she had no interest in circus as a youngster.

When she joined the Earl family, she joined the show. During her first year, she sold tickets and worked the Snake Show on the circus midway. Even before going on the road, she had decided to become a performer, but was thin and weak. In her words,

I couldn't do anything. I had no physical ability, no coordination, not a muscle in my body and I had to start from scratch. To build up my strength, Leanne (Earl) had me going up ropes every hour on the hour. We hung a web at Winter Quarters and it was every hour on the hour as many times as I could do it. On the road, they put up a ladder in the tent and I started working with that when I decided I really wanted to perform.

When I started, it was, "I'll see if I can do it; it looks like fun." And of course it doesn't get to be fun for quite some time because you're building callous and everything hurts and I had no strength and couldn't do anything. But if I saw something that interested me, I wanted to learn it and I'd say, "OK, how do I do that?" And Leanne would say, "Well, you do this and this and this."

A lot of it was being a member of the family - it was whatever they needed. From year to year, whenever they needed a new act that was within my abilities at all, they would teach it to me. And with every animal I ever presented, I started out taking care of it. The dogs or the horse became my responsibility prior to my learning how to do the act. I knew the animals and they would look to me for food and water.[229]

Along the way Shirley became a circus mom and tutored her daughter, Stacy, on the road. Shirley became a strong performer, especially on the trapeze, and her exuberant presentation of her acts made her a Roberts favorite. After fourteen years, she decided on a career change; she and Stacy stayed home while Eddie went on the road in 1998. Shirley wanted to become a lawyer and devoted the effort to those studies she had given to her Circus Learning. At the end of 1998, she received her Associate Degree with a 4.0 average and moved on to pursue her Bachelor's Degree, then her law degree. After a summer's separation, Eddie decided to leave the circus and find work that would enable the family to stay together year round.

Shirley Earl's experience suggests that the Circus Learning that goes into creating a circus career provides a method of work that is adaptable to other areas. Shirley Earl looks back on her circus career with the same clear eyed vision that led her to pursue it.

It was time for me to go after fourteen years. I have no doubts about my showmanship, but I'm never going to have Dolly Jacobs' ring act or even a version of it that's that good. I've always been a really good showman, but basically, as far as the acts went, I've always been a mechanic. I have no creativity in me. My sister is the creative one. I can not look at a blank anything and come up with any ideas, but if you tell me what you want, I can find a way to do it. And I didn't have the guts to do the really scary stuff. I never did a back balance, I never did a toe hang or a heel hang. None of the real scary stuff. I did stuff that looked good. I did a lot of drops that were safe, but they looked good and I presented them. I had the showmanship, but I didn't have the other stuff to become really good.[230]

During her final season with Roberts in 1997, Shirley worked with ringmaster Brian LaPalme and assisted in his magic act.

It was fantastic to be working with him my last year. He is my favorite ringmaster and my favorite magician to work with. What a perfectionist. That was a fantastic way to go out. At the end of the year, he and I did a tour out west. We went on John Strong's Christmas tour. Ten days, three shows a day, 300 mile minimum jumps. No rest. It was the hardest I've ever had, but with Brian - as much fun as he is to watch, he's that much fun to work with. He taught me so much about presentation. He and Buddy Manley who had an organ on the Roberts show one year. Buddy was brutally honest. He'd yell at me, "Why the Hell did you come in and jump on your own entrance?" He taught me timing the hard way, but I learned and I owe a lot to him.[231]

Ekaterina Odintsova

Ekaterina Odintsova, Katya, was a featured soloist in the Ringling Brothers and Barnum & Bailey Red Unit on its 1998-1999 tour. Katya started as a child gymnast in Russia. Alla Youdina brought her to the United States and trained her for her solo act which features a cloud swing and concludes with the one-arm *planges* (swings) Lillian Leitzel did on the Ringling show in the 1920's.

credit: Ringling Brothers and Barnum & Bailey

I started gymnastics when I was six and after seven years I switched to diving in the water. I got a master of Sports in Diving certificate so I didn't have to take an exam for college after Sports High School. But when the Cranes invited me into the circus - I was crazy about the circus, I quit everything.

The Cranes were going to start another act. It was like the Cranes - like a bird, but I am too short at five feet one for flying. I like the Cranes. They were my friends, all those guys. That was my first act.

Then I developed a cradle act with a Russian guy. It was just the two of us. It wasn't like the Spider Web; Alla brought me to the United States for that three years ago. My partner in the cradle act got married and now he works with his wife.[232]

In The Spider Web, Katya was the butterfly who emerged from a cocoon on a rope high on the air to stretch her wings. She then flew on a cloud swing before getting involved in a cradle act with a spider, Oleg Sergatchiov, on the thirty foot vertical spider web. Katya's butterfly then was trapped in the web. The climax of the act was her escape with a back dive to the floor, the fall broken by the safety belt attached to her waist.

Katya enjoyed being a soloist completely responsible for her act in the next show. She drove her car alone between dates and worked to maintain her personal space in a show where

> for two years we see every single person every single day. You know for two years you're going to wake up in the morning, go to the building, practice, do a show and come back to the train.
>
> I like Ringling. This year it's going well because I kind of know about working here, about what you have to do. It would be hard to go away from Ringling - it's kind of a home now; it's like a big family. I don't think it's going to be easy to finish the two years and just go. So this year working here is easier, but the act is harder. But I like it. I like working by myself.[233]

One thing complicating the *planges* for Katya was Ringling management's decision to have her go from the cloud swing that begins the act into the *planges*. To make this possible, the rigging for the *plange* was not hung from a static base as is traditional in the act, but from rigging which moves. Katya had to practice in each auditorium to find a new tempo for the act. She could have greatly increased the number of *planges* if the rigging had been different, but rigged as it was, the act was uninterrupted by her moving from one apparatus to another.

At that point, Katya had been in the United States for three years. She had a married sister in Cincinnati, but her brother and mother were in Russia. Like many Russian performers working in the United States, Katya sent money home regularly. "I have a paycheck every Friday, my mother does not."[234]

The Circus Learning that prepared Katya for the act includes Russian gymnastic training, work with the Russians of The Flying Cranes, work in the cradle act, work with Alla Youdina and advice Katya received from retired

American circus star Mickey King whom the author saw do the one arm *planges* in the 1940's.

I was so excited meeting her. I can't believe. She is 92 years old. She still has a good memory and she remembers all the streets in Sarasota. She still exercises. At 92 I hope I can look like her. I really wish that she could see my act.

She told me about Lillian Leitzel and the whole story about her and Alfredo Codona.[235] She told how she trained the actress to do the one arm swing for The Greatest Show on Earth movie. She did only five and they did a movie trick to make it look like more.[236]

As she toured, Katya Odinstova's Circus Learning continued.

I still have to practice. Somebody said in Russia, professionals don't have to practice; that's not true. I have to practice or I will lose the trick. I would like to do it a couple more years after Ringling. I worked really hard; I don't want to give it up. Then - sometime, I would like to be a coach.[237]

Molly Saudek

Molly Saudek's tightwire act would not have been featured in the 1999 Big Apple Circus if Rob Mermin had not established Circus Smirkus near the Saudek home in Vermont. Saudek, a delightfully levelheaded young woman, was interviewed in September 1997 in Montreal when she was studying at the National Circus School. She was asked if she would have gone into circus without Smirkus. "Of course not. And now circus is my life's work. You get this and this leads to this and that leads to that."[238]

credit: Big Apple Circus

Molly Saudek's mother

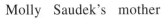

remembers how accidental Molly's initial involvement with Circus Smirkus was.

Molly was ten or eleven years old and was scheduled to go to Ireland with her flute teacher who was taking her students over for a competition. At the last minute, the trip was canceled and Molly was disappointed. We were casting about for a summer experience for her that would be as much fun and would keep her busy when we ran into a neighbor who said, "Have her try out for Circus Smirkus." I said, "Yes, she's a pretty good gymnast; I bet she'd be good at it." And so we did.[239]

The daughter of a lawyer and a Blue Cross-Blue Shield executive, Molly Saudek completed her secondary education at Phillips Exeter Academy. After graduation, thanks to her eight summers with Circus Smirkus, instead of accompanying her Exeter classmates to college, she went to the National Circus School. She had learned about it from Jade Kindar-Martin, a friend from Smirkus, who had attended.

I made the choice to do this now; I may do college later. If I went to a university now, it would just be doing this and that. I have many things I want to do that I couldn't focus on now. This I want to focus on. I want to do it 'til it's done.[240]

Her mother's memory of Molly's decisions to go to Exeter and then to the National Circus School reveal a good deal about the kind of person Molly Saudek is.

When Molly was in High School, she did gymnastics to keep herself energized and happy and excited. She taught gymnastics two nights a week and Saturday mornings and she did dance. She was really into dance. She probably took dance classes four nights a week. When she wasn't in the gym, she was taking dance class.

She was very serious about it and very good and that's what made high school sustainable for her. One summer she didn't do Circus Smirkus; she went to a dance program at Bates College and came back really energized. As she headed back to her Junior Year at Union School 32, she looked around and said, "I don't want to do this. This is really boring."

I said, "It's September and you have to go, but we can look at Prep Schools for your Senior Year." She interviewed at Andover and Exeter and was accepted at both and decided on Exeter. That year at Exeter was mind blowing for her. Previously, what had sustained her in High School had been dance and gymnastics; it hadn't been academics at all. At Exeter she adored calculus, she adored Shakespeare, she adored Zen. It was like a sea change for her and I remember asking her if she was doing any dance, any movement. She said, "Mom, that's not why I'm here." Then, when it came time to apply for colleges - and of course everybody at Exeter was applying for colleges, she said she wanted to go to circus school. I said, "Mol, you know you've had a terrific fall semester at Exeter, just go through the college application process because who knows who you'll be by the end of the year. You may want to go to college."

She said, "I want to go to circus school." I said, "Fine, apply, but also apply to college so you have options." She did and was accepted at most of the colleges she applied to. She decided if she was going to college, it would be Barnard. I said, "Defer it for a year. Go to circus school if that's what you want, but do the deferral."

I remember a phone conversation that spring where she said, "Mom, think about where I am - Exeter. Think about the kinds of people I'm surrounded by. This is not an easy decision for me; you've got to support me." I said, "OK, if you can be that articulate about it, we can do this." She never wavered. That's what she wanted to do and that's what she did.

I remember so clearly, leaving her off - almost on the curb in Montreal when she was 17 or 18. It's not like putting your kid into college where there are dorms. She wasn't sure where she was going to be living. She was just a kid. She moved in with three or four circus guys from the school from all over the world and went from there. She found her own apartment and really grew up fast. It tested us. But Molly was so focused and so clear about where she was headed. First of all, there was no denying her, but second of all, we had to trust her.[241]

Molly Saudek's brother, Richard, also spent a number of years with Circus Smirkus and their mother thinks Smirkus had a great influence on both her children.

Any kid who goes through that comes out at the end feeling they can do almost anything. Any of those chores challenges kids in profound ways. Being in front of audiences is part of it and for Molly it was physical things she had never tried before.

You go to some of those shows that are almost washed out by rain. I remember one when Rob carried Molly out and put her on her wire so she wouldn't get her feet wet. I remember a night where she did a trapeze act when all the electricity had gone out. We had a bunch of Russians that year and they all stood on the ring holding torches while she did the trapeze.

Some of the other values at Smirkus are making friends, having coaches and peers from all over the world. But mostly it's the idea that "I can do it." It's not easy, but it's a lot of fun.[242]

Molly Saudek stayed focused. She left the School after a year and half to tour the Far East for six months with Cirque Du Soleil's *Alegria*, then returned to the School to refine her act. In January 1998, Saudek's act won a Silver Medal at the 21st *Festival Mondial du Cirque de Demain* in Paris. She was booked for a three and a half month run at the Tiger's Eye circus cabaret in Frankfurt, Germany from which many outstanding circus performers have emerged. She also received a contract from Big Apple for 1999.

According to Rob Mermin, "Molly Saudek has the natural talent, intelligence and ambition for excellence to succeed in any chosen field. She came to us a giggly waif with glasses. Her self-discipline in gymnastics and dance fused with her artistic spirit and finally blossomed in a graceful and intelligent style on the low wire."[243] She joined Smirkus in its first year, 1987 and participated in the Smirkus 1990 Russian tour that had been arranged the previous year when Mermin visited Moscow to meet Alla Youdina, then an official at *RosGostCirk,* the Russian Circus monopoly.

The Russian connection is important to Saudek's story for among the instructors Youdina brought to Smirkus was Nina Malashikhina who helped Saudek integrate her interests in dance and the tightwire. Like many Smirkus troupers, Saudek had been introduced to the wire by long time Smirkus coach, Stuart Lippe who also has served as the show's Technical Director. Lippe, a multi-skilled circus and sideshow performer, was founder-director of The Franzini Family Circus, a traveling stage company in Florida. It was

Malashikhina who connected Saudek to the Russian tradition of tightwire dancing Youdina recalls, "There was a period in Russia when we had many great dancers on the tightwire."[244]

Interviewed shortly before she was invited to participate in the *Festival Mondial,* Saudek had a good deal to say about her developing career. She began by contrasting the learning she had done at Exeter to the learning she was doing at the National Circus School.

Actually, it's very much the same for me. In one, you have to make connections with the physical part of your body and it's all patterns. It's all based on progressions and you have to learn the patterns physically. When I was at Exeter, I was very much into calculus which is very logical. There are progressions you go through; you learn a systematic way of thinking. It's not just free thought and it's the same when you're working with your physical body. Your mind has to play a game to get into the system. You have to say, "OK, I agree that I'm going to follow these rules of thinking, these rules of logic, to get from point A to point B" instead of just saying anything goes to get to point B. It's the same with your body. If you want your body to be able to do a triple flip in the air, it has to know the rules of going up; it has to know the rules of turning, it needs to be able to work within that perspective.

For me, tightwire is very mental. There's a specific kind of concentration that you have to work on and that's true of every kind of circus art. There's a specific way of training your mind. Last night I started doing Zen archery. The mind training is very much the same as what I use on the wire.[245]

She contrasted her work on the low wire to that of Jade Kindar-Martin, the Smirkus colleague who had preceded her to the National Circus School and went on to do skywalks around the world.

My theory about the difference between what Jade does and what I do is that Jade is in love with the air. I mean, if you take him up on top of a twenty story building, you have to hold on to him; he might walk off. Whereas me - I'm much more focused on the wire than on the space around it. It's a different kind of concentration. When I walk on the wire, it's very much just me and the wire.[246]

The previous summer Saudek had toured with Cirque Eloize and found it very different from her tour with Cirque du Soleil.

Cirque Eloize, which has a company of about twelve, performs in theatres. The core group that started it is from the Isles d'Madeleine that are in upper Quebec. They were all students at the National Circus School; they came out of the School and started the circus. It's a good show, very good performers. Lots of talent. It's the most fun I've ever had. With Eloize, because of its intimacy, I could know everybody and my work was important. I work on a six or seven foot wire that's twenty feet long. That's my tool. Give me 6,000 people in a three ring show and they're going to get something out of my performance, but they won't get anything unless other people are doing exactly the same thing. Then, what's the point? You have something special to say and you have an identity as an artist, but in a three ring show the only way anyone is going to see you is if there are carbon copies of you. That's about the show, not about the individual performer.[247]

Saudek has been defining for herself what being a professional circus performer means.

What I've gotten out of it about the professional in this business is that there are certain things that are business, but you make a very clear separation between what's business and what's your work. There are things you are required to do - especially as a soloist because you have to be very demanding on yourself because there's no one there with a whip telling you what to do. And you need to search inside yourself to find why you're doing it and what's special about it.

For me, Cirque Eloize was special because it was small enough that I could focus on what I had to say. I had my space. It was my act; decisions made in that act were mine. It was small enough that if I needed lighting changed or sound changed, I knew who to talk to. And the group was small enough that before a show and during a show you had a real feeling of what was going on. You felt the difference between a bad show and a good show.

I also did acrobatics here and there. Pulling ropes and stuff. In a small show like that, everybody does everything. But you really feel what's happening in the show and there's a difference. When you're working on a very big show and your act goes badly, the rest of the show goes on. When you're working with a small group, if your act goes badly, the show goes badly. Or the show goes great and you can feel a good energy everywhere. There's an energy that goes throughout the show. In Cirque Eloize, I felt when we did a great show the finale would spark and everybody would be - wow! You could feel it.

For me that's very important because you're doing the same thing, the same act, every day, and you have to have choices. You have to have these differences. Which doesn't mean I wouldn't do the large shows, but it would be a different kind of experience. I learned a lot on *Alegria*. I learned about kicking myself in the butt instead of waiting for someone else to do it.[248]

At the time of this interview, negotiations for her joining Big Apple were in a preliminary stage. Saudek was handling them herself.

I haven't had any trouble finding jobs up to now so why pay for somebody else to find them? If you want a lawyer in Montpelier, there's a lot of people to choose from. If you want an equilibrist from North America at a certain level who can do a back salto - that's me. Even in Quebec, if somebody wants a tightwire walker, there are three of us who have our equipment and a certain level of technique. In Canada, there are four. In Europe there are a lot more. But if in Portugal they want a tight wire walker and they want specific things, they're going to have to go out of Portugal.

Everybody in circus is individual; everybody has something special. It's not like being a ballet dancer where for every tiny spot in a ballet there are many dancers who could easily do it. That makes our jobs secure, if not physically secure. I've only had twisted ankles or wrists. I haven't broken anything. (Knocks wood.)[249]

Molly Saudek is one of the new generation of North American circus performers who see themselves as Circus Artists. Influenced by coaches from the Russian system that treated circus as an art, trained in conservatories, skilled and tough minded, they demand artistry of themselves and of the circuses in which they work.

These four interviews suggest the variety of ways professional Circus Learning can be pursued. Today, those who are not born into or marry into circus families, have opportunities to encounter Circus Learning in recreational and school programs and then continue their studies in a professional school.

XI
Conclusions

With the recognition that there are circus *arts* as showcased in the *new* circuses, Circus Learning has moved into conservatories. Because Circus Learning empowers young people, it is being incorporated into recreational programs, human service programs and educational systems. But what is Circus Learning?

On the most basic level, it involves mastering traditional circus skills - tumbling, balance, juggling. For this to happen, bodies must be prepared so Circus Learning is healthy. This is no small matter at a time when obesity and underutilized muscles are growing concerns. Circus Learning involves not just physical dexterity, but intellectual mastery of integrated operations just as when a child takes its first steps. Because Circus Learning is difficult, it requires good work habits and cooperative relationships with those who share the learning. Circus Learning is open ended; each skill mastered is the basis for further learning. Carried far enough, skills can transform into art.

We now know people learn in different ways. Those who learn best through their bodies adapt easily to Circus Learning and develop confidence and work habits they can apply to other learning. Circus Learning is also important for those who need to become more comfortable with their bodies and to use them more effectively. Because Circus Learning includes a variety of skills that can be dealt with on many levels, it, unlike competitive athletics, can be adapted to the needs of all students. Circus Learning permits boys and girls of different ages to work together and escape the usual segregation.

The ancient idea of a healthy mind in a healthy body is important in an era when the media encourage passivity and technology offers enticing virtual realities. Circus Learning provides authentic experience in the physical world. It offers strategies to defy the limitations of time, space and gravity. One flies from a mini-tramp or trapeze; balances on a slender wire. Juggling, one momentarily transcends limitations; the juggled objects fly before they return to earth. Is it too much to suggest that this defiance of the inevitable is analogous to the defiance of mortal limitations that is the basis of tragedy? At any event, Circus Learning is a holistic engagement with one's environment.

Certain requirements are necessary for Circus Learning to take place. Because one is battling physical limits, the environment must be safe. Mentoring must assure that the learner is warmed up, prepared and employing appropriate equipment. It helps if the coach is sensitive to the uniqueness of the learner for Circus Learning, at its best, is an interactive process involving learner, coach and skill.

Such interaction does not always exist. In China students confront rigid expectations for their work; individuality is not a consideration. Rob Mermin noted this when young Chinese performers and their coaches joined his 1998 Circus Smirkus.

I had an interesting discussion with our guests. They come from a long tradition of Chinese acrobats. It is very disciplined, very structured, and the acts are very similar to each other. The children are trained to do the same acts over and over in the same style. The Chinese performers here with us this year have been learning a little about how to bring out their personalities a little more. We talk about their smiling at the end of the act when taking their bows and bowing to three sides of the audience all around. They are used to performing on a stage. In contrast, we try to find ways of helping our performers make a connection with the audience.

I have noticed that after they do their act, the Chinese performers sneak back around and catch the rest of the show. They seem particularly interested in the juggling act and the clowns.

One of the boys does a comedy acrobatic act. It is very Chinese and every single movement is always exactly the same. It never changes regardless of the reaction. In America and the West, we make changes to react to audience response. We've learned the rhythm of the audience, whereas the Chinese have choreographed their comedy so the timing is always the same instead of altering it to the audience response. They watch our clowning and the way we connect. They are having discussions in China now about how to be more open to the audience.

The same thing happened with the Russians. Very stiff. Heavily coached to do everything always the same. We try to loosen them up, not change the act. Get them to stop and look at the audience and smile. Here's how to take a bow to make the audience friendlier. Without changing the act, we change their style for our show.[250]

What does happen when learned skills move into performance? Circus is live; audiences and performers - even in the largest shows, interact. Whatever the performers' training, audiences respond. In the youth programs examined in this study, the most effective presentations theatricalize skills. Theatricalization can involve making skills part of a story or relating them to a theme; it can also be as simple as having a personality engaged in the drama of demonstrating a skill. A clown who seems unfamiliar with the materials of an act, conquers its difficulties; a sparkling girl shares with the audience her joy as she masters difficulties with grace. Programs that do not theatricalize their presentation feel mundane to audiences because the skills are presented as just that - skills.

Circus Learning offers lessons for other kinds of learning. While physical safety is necessary in the rigors of Circus Learning, a secure academic classroom environment makes it easier for students to confront the unknown. Sensitive mentoring is as important in the classroom as the gymnasium. Difficult material in both places is best presented when broken down into components.

This raises the question of the best circumstances for Circus Learning. Residencies and camps provide occasional enrichment to the lives of participants. How much better when Circus Learning is a continuing part of a community's life. Afterschool programs are useful; more effective are programs integrated into a school's curriculum that are available to all.

This study attempts to demonstrate the value of Circus Learning and make a case for it being more integral to our lives. The study has tried to suggest the diversity of the burgeoning Circus Learning programs. Doing the study, the author noted how poor communication is, especially in North America, between programs. Maybe this is because the programs are new. Several directors noted that they have been so busy building their programs they haven't had the opportunity to find out about others.

Perhaps this study, along with the new American Youth Circus Organization (AYCO), will encourage program directors to become better acquainted to discuss teaching methods, establish standards for work, share resources and provide opportunities for students to experience a variety of programs. All the programs already have one thing in common; they teach people to fulfill themselves through integrating mind and body in truly satisfying work.

PROGRAM LITERATURE

Excerpts from Brochures and Training Manuals

ACTORS GYMNASIUM CERTIFICATE
Students receive a multidisciplinary education in the field of circus arts. Over a two year period, certificate students take four classes per week. These are: Circus Arts (twice weekly), Gymnastics (once a week), and one of eight required courses as their fourth weekly class. Open gym time is also made available every week for students to practice on their own.

Each year culminates in a final performance created by the students in conjunction with our circus faculty. The second of these performances is an original act in the student's chosen field of specialization. Graduates leave this program with a basic proficiency in trapeze, web, stilt-walking, tightrope, unicycling, juggling, gymnastics and teeterboard. Students must pass a final examination in each of these disciplines before graduating.[251]

CIRCUS ARTS AND ACROBATICS, Inc.
Professional Program
Our new Circus Arts Professional Program (CAP Program), a forty week "college like" training curriculum for those seeking intense training in the areas of Aerial Arts and/or Acrobatic Arts. This program is designed for those individuals who want to train intensely in circus arts (whether you desire to become a professional performer or not.)

The program is broken down into four ten-week sessions beginning with Intro to Circus Arts and ending with portfolio development, performing opportunities, auditions and a possible career in the circus arts industry. No prior experience is necessary to enter the program and advance placement is available for those students who have already ventured out into the performance world.

Our price buys a student a single session of 40 hours a week training with our world class staff, lodging at our student apartments, student medical insurance, field trips, performances, auditions, act development and more. An enrollment package is available for those interested in this opportunity.[252]

THE CIRCUS SPACE

The BTEC National Diploma, Performing Arts Circus, includes:

Aerial Awareness and Techniques - introducing the trapeze, corde lisse[253] and other aerial equipment, and exploring their use in performance.

Acrobatic Techniques and Performance - developing acrobatic techniques and their performance potential.

Manipulation and Equilibristics - exploring a variety of juggling and balancing disciplines.

Language of Circus - gaining an overall understanding of circus. You will also study more general aspects of the performing arts.

Arts Administration - administrative, business, financial and legal aspects of performance.

Arts in Society - historical development of the performing arts, and the way in which they influence society.

Production Techniques - understanding the working practices of a venue and gaining experience of basic stagecraft skills.

Movement Studies - developing skills in physical expression.

Performance Workshop - provides opportunity for devising and performance throughout the course, as well as learning specific skills such as clown.

Performance Project - towards the end of the second year devising and performing an ensemble final show.

In addition there are regular tutorials. The course is taught through a programme of assignments. There are no final examinations but progression through the course will depend on successful completion of each module. There are also two short work placements during the course.[254]

The BA (hons) Theatre Practice (Contemporary Circus) program is an accelerated 2-year vocational course which aims to equip students to find employment with existing performing arts companies or to establish new companies of their own. Students undertake an intensive training which is equivalent to a 3-year degree but which is delivered over two years, each of 45 weeks, to ensure a sustained physical progression. This unique degree will appeal to those with some experience in circus, performance or dance who would relish the opportunity to experiment, cross-fertilize and create new work with other talented performers.

The course aims to enable students to gain an understanding of, and experience in, the broad range of skills needed to create innovative and excellent circus, while achieving a high level of individual expertise and performing ability in a particular circus discipline such as trapeze, tightwire, juggling or clown. However, the course also encourages the exploration of new ideas and the creation of a new skill type or discipline would also be considered. Common to all students will be practical classes in physical conditioning, theatre, circus and movement, leading to solo and ensemble performance projects. Alongside the physical skills development, there is a strong focus on artistic exploration and creativity, as well as the historical, critical and business aspects of circus.[255]

SAN FRANCISCO SCHOOL OF CIRCUS ARTS
Advice for individuals creating their own programs:

We encourage you to take a broad range of classes, either to have a greater experience of circus or if you are working towards a professional career. To make this easier, we offer special discounts if you take more than one class. Your second and third class each receive a 20% discount. If you register for four or more classes, all your classes receive a 20% discount and a monthly payment plan is available.

Private Instruction

The school offers specialized training for aspiring or established performers of all ages. Private classes are available in many disciplines including:

+Chinese Acrobatics
+Trick Roping
+Adagio Hand Balancing
+Mini-tramp and trampoline
+Juggling
+Wire
+Contortion
+Spanish web and rope
+Chair balancing
+Swinging trapeze[256]

SAILOR CIRCUS
RULES AND REGULATIONS
I Attitudes and Behavior

A. Students must have a high moral code and maintain good citizenship at all times. The use of tobacco, alcohol or any illegal drug is cause for dismissal.

B. Students must have and maintain a minimum 2.0 grade point average to be in Sailor Circus. Report Card must be attached to registration forms. Students must also maintain a 2.0 or above in all P.E. classes.

C. Report cards must be turned in to the office each grading period. A copy will be made and the original returned to you. Failure to do so after two practice days will result in off grounds suspension. Suspension time will be made up with work detail at the convenience of the coach.

D. Students falling below 2.0 grade point average will result in off grounds suspension and students will have two weeks to show grades have improved. A parent/student conference will be held with the director and a member of the staff. The director has final decision as to satisfactory improvement made and may dismiss student from circus at that time.

E. Children in special classes or with learning disabilities will be evaluated individually. It is the responsibility of the parent to advise Sailor Circus of these special circumstances when enrolling their child.

F. Student tutors may be available for a small fee.

II Discipline

Discipline is very important in keeping Sailor Circus a safe activity. Having to deal with impossible behavior will not be tolerated.

Conduct Rules

1. **Follow directions**. Not following directions could cause injury to yourself or fellow students.
2. **Keep hands and feet to yourself unless practicing an Act.**
3. **Show respect to coaches and fellow students at all times.**
4. **Foul language will not be tolerated.**

III Attendance

Sailor Circus has received local, state and international acclaim for its outstanding achievement. It is necessary for us to dedicate our leisure time to maintain this high standard of entertainment. Some students like to become involved in various outside activities. **We insist that Sailor Circus must come first if there is a conflict of interest.** This also pertains to school activities (i.e. sports, music, field trips, religion, etc.) . . .

GIRLS must wear required unitard practice uniform. Proper undergarments are a must. Inexpensive low cost tennis shoes are recommended. Dance girdles are recommended for practice. Girls with long hair must have it out of their faces at all time. No outlandish or fad hairdos will be tolerated. No exceptions will be made.

BOYS must wear required practice uniform of shorts and tee shirt. Proper undergarments are a must. Girdles are recommended for practice. Inexpensive low cost tennis shoes are recommended. Boys must be clean shaven at all times. No long hair, pony tails, braids or shaven heads will be allowed. No outlandish or fad hairdos will be tolerated. No exceptions will be made.

No jewelry may be worn by any student on any part of his/her anatomy. This includes post earrings. . . .

All Senior High and Middle School students will assist with rigging and spotting of other students.[257]

SAILOR CIRCUS GYMNASTICS PROGRAM
Course Objectives – each objective is worth a possible 5 points
Strength building, Flexibility, Basic Gymnastics, Rigging equipment, Spanish Web, Juggling, Clowning, Unicycle, Handbalancing, Teeterboard, Globes, Stilts, Rolla Bolla, High Wire, Trapeze, Flying Trapeze, Circus History, Costume Design, Marketing, Concessions/Operations.
GRADE
50% Participation/Attitude; 30% Class Objectives; 10% Show Preparation; 10% Project/ Final Exam

CIRCUS OF THE KIDS (brochure)
Step Right up to the Circus of the Kids Cafe
The Mini Circus Appetizer. Our most popular selection. A one-day activity beginning with a series of juggling workshops for various grade levels and culminating in a forty-minute school-wide afternoon assembly featuring a variety of juggling acts and simple circus routines.

The Two-Course Luncheon Special. This tasty choice features two days of circus activities. The first day is devoted to teaching acrobatic routines through your school's regular physical education program. The second day begins with rehearsals and ends with a 40-minute circus performance starring **Circus of**

the Kids staff and 12 students of your choice. Another 6-7 of your school's youngsters act as roustabouts.

The Ready for Prime Time One Ring Circus. In this weekend selection, a number of circus activities intermingle to create an exquisite dish. The week begins on Sunday with parent/student orientation and ends the following Sunday with several live performances. Sandwiched between are two days of circus arts activities taught through your regular physical education classes, five days of more intensive after school instruction for 50 youngsters selected on a first-come, first-served basis and three all-star performances featuring a delightful variety of ground acts.

The Two Ring Blue Plate Special. This menu includes both ground and aerial acts taught to your entire student body for one week through your regularly scheduled physical education classes. The second week consists of an intensive after school program geared for 100 students. At the end of the residency, students as well as the public are treated to five 90-minute shows.

The Three-Ring Chef's Delight. Our *Piece de Resistance* is a delectable combination of ground and aerial acts made to order for the elementary and middle school set. Either three or four weeks in duration, it includes an expanded physical education circus program and after school performance program. This multi-course event can include instruction on our 32-foot high regulation-size flying trapeze. At the end of the residency, **Circus of the Kids** staff and students present six two-hour performances.

SIDE DISHES

Circus Across the Curriculum. This tasty treat makes learning fun! A series of materials designed to supplement the regular curriculum, it incorporates circus-related information into various academic disciplines. Free with all residency programs. Not available as a separate item.

Trapeze for Everyone. This flavorful dish is almost a meal in itself. Community citizens get to try their hand at the flying trapeze. Usually open after a performance or in conjunction with a school carnival.

Refreshments and souvenirs are available at all performances.[258]

NATIONAL CIRCUS PROJECT (brochure)
Programs

The *First of May* program is the most popular offering.

What is the "First of May: program?

The "First of May" program is an introductory circus arts residence. The program places two of our professional artist/instructors in your school for one or more full school days. It begins with a spectacular circus assembly performance attended by your entire student population. The performance is then followed by "hands-on" workshops for your students in a variety of age-appropriate circus skills.

Tell me about the circus assembly performance.

Each "First of May" residence includes one 45-55 minute performance. For schools with larger populations, multiple assemblies may be arranged. The performance is presented in an exciting and entertaining format with plenty of audience interaction. It features circus skills from around the world, including juggling, unicycling, balancing, clowning, and object manipulation. All of the skills introduced in the workshops are demonstrated during the performance, showing the high level of skill and artistry that can be achieved with patience and practice.

What happens in the "hands-on" workshops?

The workshops take place in your gymnasium or large all-purpose room. Our workshop activities are safe, "ground" based circus skills such as juggling, balance skills and object manipulations. The following selection of workshop activities by age/grade level is based on the motor skill levels of the participants. We can also accommodate physically challenged, adaptive and special needs children.

+ Primary Ages (K-2): Class-wide instruction includes scarf and/or ball juggling and feather balancing.

+ Intermediate grades (3-6): Classes are divided into smaller rotational units to work in three skill areas: scarf/ball juggling, plate spinning and devil stick manipulations. A brief lecture/demonstration at the beginning of each class period explains how the skills are accomplished, and then the groups are circulated among the three work stations for personal skills development.

+ Middle and Jr. High School: Older students are introduced to ball juggling, plate-spinning and devil stick manipulation, with greater autonomy in their personal skills development time. Advanced tricks with the introductory skills are presented to students who accomplish basic steps.

+Senior High School: At the high school level, the assembly program is eliminated in favor of an advanced lecture/demonstration at the beginning of each workshop period. The balance of the workshop is spent in "hands-on" practice. In addition to the basic skills, advanced skills such as ring and club juggling, diabolo spinning and rola bola (balance board) may be introduced.[259]

CARRIE HELLER'S TRAINING MANUAL (First page)

Therapeutic base to EVERYTHING - we know this and teach under this premise, but don't discuss it with the students unless it comes up.

GOALS

1. Increase self-confidence/self-respect.
2. Help students to move through their fears. When someone moves through a fear of doing a cradle on the trapeze, this experience is transferred to their everyday life.
3. Tap into the body/mind connection.
4. Love of self and one's own body.
5. All "tricks" are taught at each student's individual pace. As often as possible, students are grouped into classes with their age appropriate group as well as their rate of physical learning; however, this is not always possible.
6. Circus Camp is a NON-COMPETITIVE environment. Although there are Beginner, Intermediate and Advanced "tricks" - these levels of progress can be pointed out; however it is done in a non-competitive way.
7. We help students to take risks physically and emotionally (for example, try a trick that they previously thought they could not do) in a safe environment.
8. Help each student tap into the SOURCE OF UNLIMITED CREATION that everyone has access to.
9. Circus Camp teaches balance, timing, flexibility, strength building, acrobatics, creative movement, and tricks on the equipment. This is all done in a FUN and safe environment.
10. Safety *is always stressed. This is the #1 priority in Circus Camp because if someone gets hurt no one has fun!!*[260]

everyday circus (brochure)

EVERYDAYCIRCUS is a multi-talented company dedicated to bringing the excitement of the circus to your school, home or special event. We can supply you with everything from one clown to a complete circus. We can teach a one-class workshop or a whole semester of circus skills.

EVERYDAYCIRCUS can provide any type of circus-style entertainment. Our specialty is the Participation Circus where audience members can star in the show along with the everydaycircus dogs, birds and monkey. We have a variety of Moon Bounces for hours of safe, high-bouncing fun. Kids also love our new kiddie rides. We have a wide variety of carnival games suitable for all ages. We can add the taste of circus to your event with our cotton candy, snow cones, popcorn, nachos, hot pretzels or funnel cakes. And we can keep children busy and supply them with a souvenir with our variety of Kids' Crafts activities.

EVERYDAYCIRCUS has provided entertainment for an array of local events to schools, parks and homes throughout the St. Louis area.

EVERYDAYCIRCUS' staff has taught circus skills to people ages 5 to 75. . . . We teach basic tumbling, juggling, clowning, wire-walking, single trapeze, stilt-walking, rolla bolla, partner acrobatics and pyramids.[261]

Resource Guide

This list, far from exhaustive, contains information available to t author at the time of publication. Included, wherever possible, are nan address, country, phone, FAX, Email, web site, contact person, description the activity, and a listing of certificates or diplomas offered. The Guide arranged alphabetically by country and alphabetically within each country.

Argentina

LA ARENA
Charcas 5058 Capital Federal
Argentina
011 54 1 4777-8920
galacirco@infovia.com.ar
Contact: Ariel Pitluk
Circus School

CIRCO CRIOLLO (HERMANOS VIDELLA)
Chile 1584 Capital Federal
Argentina
011 54 1 4382-5017
Contact: Nestor Martellini
Circus School

CIRCO SOCIAL "ESCALANDO ALTURA"
Argerich 1141, Timbre 2 Capital Federal
Argentina
011 54 1 4637-1145
marianluna@yahoo.com
Pablo Holgado, Mariana Luna Rufolo, Artistic Directors
Circus School

ESCUELA MUNICIPAL DE BERAZTEGUI
Gimnasio Municipal de Berazategui
Subsecretaria de Deportes

Calle 18 y 148
Berazategui, Provincia de Bueno Aires, Argentina
011 54 11 4256-4659
Mario Prez, Director
Free Bi-weekly program serving 2 children annually

ESPACIO CIRCO
Espacio Circo Building
Soler 4635, Capital Federal
Argentina
011 54 11 4832-6777
gabriela@espaciocirco.com
www.espaciocirco.com
Gabriela Ricardes and Mario Per Directors
Private Circus School, Child and Adult

TALLERES DE CIRCO, del Centro Cultural Ricardo Roja
Universidad de Buenos Aires
Corrientes 2038, Capital Feder Argentina
011 54 1 4954 5527/4954 552
FAX: 011 54 1 4954 8352/495 2947
rojas@rec.uba.ar
Mario Perez, Director
Private, afterschool Circus Progr serving 20 college students.

Australia

THE CIRCUS FEDERATION OF AUSTRALIA
PO Box 1002
Springwood. QLD. 4127 Australia
011 61 7 3287 7255
FAX 011 61 7 3287 7244
circfed@powerup.com.au
www.angelfire.com/az/AustCircus/fed.html
Professional organization of Australian circus owners.

DUBBO WEST PUBLIC SCHOOL
North Road
Dubbo West 2830
NSW Australia
pgwoodhead@yahoo.com
Paul Woodhead, Assistant Principal
Curricular school circus program, Circus West touring group.

FLYING FRUIT FLY CIRCUS
609 Hovell Street
Albury, N.S.W. 2640 Australia
P.O. Box 479
Wodonga, Vic. 3689 Australia
011 61 60 217 044
FAX 011 61 60 217 238
acroarts@albury.net.au
www2.tpgi.com.au/users/acroart
Trevor Matthews, Coordinator
Touring youth circus; its school is part of the public school system.

NATIONAL INSTITUTE OF CIRCUS ARTS (NICA)
144 High Street, Prahran
Victoria 3181
Australia
011 61 3 9214-6975
FAX: 011 61 3 9214-6574
Nica@groupwise.swin.edu
www.nica.swin.edu.au
Pamela Creed, Project Director
Professional training.

NATIONAL CIRCUS FESTIVAL
355 Simpsons Road
Bardon Q 4065 Australia
011 61 7 3369 2003
Tony Rooke
Advanced training project followed by festival.

PLAYSPACE STUDIO
18A Enmore Road
Sydney 2042
Australia
011 61 2 9557-7837
artmedia@one.net.au
www.artmedia.com.au/playspac.htm
Alan Clay, Director
Professional full-year training in Circus, Clown and Acting.

SUITCASE CIRCUS
272 Walcott Street, Mt. Lawley
West Australia 6050
rbolton@iinet.net.au
www.circusshop.net
Reg Bolton, Director
Circus classes, shows, resources, shop, archive, assistance.

SYDNEY AERIAL THEATRE ASSOCATION (SATA)
Hut 24
Addison Road Community Cenbtre
142 Addison Road
Sydney

Australia
011 61 2 4132 17309
Aimee Thomas, Shelalagh
McGovern, teachers
satassociation@hotmail.com
www.artmedia.com/au/aerial.htm
*Afternoon and evening workshops
and performances in trapeze, rope
and aerial skills for adults and
children.*

Belgium

**ECOLE DE
CIRQUE DE BRUXELLES**
Chaussée de Boondael, 104
1050 Bruxelles, Belgium
011 32 2 640 15 71
circusarts.org@infonie.be
www.circusarts.org/
*Training in circus arts for children,
adolescents and young people. Has
a program for people with special
needs.*

**ECOLE DE
CIRQUE DE HONNELLES**
Mail Address: rue des Juifs 29
Onnezies B-7387
Honnelles, Belgium
Location: rue de l'Abreuvoir, 13 à
Onnezies
Phone/Fax: 011 32 65 75 93 68
Guy Hénaut, President
*Circus School, sponsors European
Circus Festival "to promote and
encourage circus art; it is a friendly
gathering of young people from dif-
ferent horizons wishing to share
their passion."*

**ECOLE SUPÉRIEURE DES
ARTS DU CIRQUE (ESAC)**
25, rue Williame.
B - 1160 Auderghem
Belgium
011 32 2 675 68 84
FAX: 011 32 2 662 11 79
Mme. Christine Decker, Secretary
the School, Philippe Haenen,
Director
Three year professional program

ESPACE CATASTROPHE
Rue de la Glacière, 18
1060 Bruxelles, Belgique
Phone and FAX: 011 32 2 542.541
Email: catastrophe@skynet.be
*Circus arts training; creates show
circus festivals and events.*

**EUROPEAN FEDERATION O
CIRCUS SCHOOLS (FEDEC**
6 rue de la Limite
1210 Bruxelles Belgium
011 32 2 227 4060
FAX 011 32 2 227 4069

Brazil

**ESCOLA NACIONAL DE
CIRCO**
Praça da Bandeira, 4
Rio de Janeiro RJ Brazil
20270-150
011 55 21 273-2144
escolacirco@funarte.gov.br
Carlos Cavalcanti, Director
Professional Circus School

ESCOLA CIRCO DE BELÉM
Travessa 14 de Abril, 1127 – São
Bráz
Belém/PA 66040-460
Brazil
Contact: Sandra Helena Cruz
Social service circus program.

ESCOLA PICOLINO
DE ARTES DO CIRCO
Av. Otávio Managabeira, s/n –
Pituaçu
Salvador/BA 41740-000
Brazil
Contact: Anselmo Serrat
Social service circus program

ESCOLA ZOIN DE CIRCO
Rua Sete de Setembro, 1787 – Vila
Operária
Teresina/PL 64002-260
Brazil
Contact: Frank Mamu
Social service circus program.

FABRICA DE SONHOS – ESCO-LA DE CIRCO
Rua Carlos Seidl, 813 – Caju
Rio de Janeiro/RJ 20930-690
Brazil
Contact: Telma Martins
Social service circus program.

PICADEIRO CIRCO ESCOLA
Av. Cidade Jardim, 1105 – Itain-Bibi
São Paulo/SP 01453-000
Brazil
Contact: Jose Wilson Leite
Social service circus program.

SPASSO – Escola Popular do

Circo
Av. Francisco Sá, 16 – Prado
Belo Horizonte/MG 30410-060
Brazil
Contact: Rogério Sette Câmara
Social service circus program.

Canada

BIG TOP SCHOOL
OF CIRCUS ARTS
1131 Gorham Street
Units 14 & 15
Newmarket, ON L3Y 5GD Canada
905 898-0699
Yurii Nadtotchii, Founder
Child and adult classes.

CIRKIDS
5995 Prince Albert
PO Box 60022, Fraser RPO
Vancouver, BC Canada V5W 4B5
604 737-7408
Mischa_Sandberg@telus.net
www.cirkids.org
Mischa Sandberg, Managing
Director
*Childrens' afterschool circus
program.*

CIRQUE DU SOLEIL/CIRQUE
DU MONDE
8400, 2 Avenue
Montreal (Quebec) H1Z 4M6
Canada
514 722-2324
FAX 514 722-3692
www.cirquedusoleil.com
Circus with permanent and touring

companies worldwide.
*Cirque du Monde establishes circus
programs for at risk youth in many
countries.*

THE GREEN FOOLS
PHYSICAL THEATRE
1046 18th Ave, S.E.
Calgary, Alberta T2G 1M6 Canada
403 237-9010
FAX 403 266-1508
Grnfools@cadvision
Xstine Cook
*A physical theatre company that
does circus skills residencies on
First Nations reservations.*

MAIN SPACE
283B Queens Quay West
Toronto ON M5V 1A2 Canada
416 935-0037
FAX: 416 935-1308
mainspace@sympatico.ca
http://www.mainspace.com
*Yearround circus training; communi-
ty circus resource.*

NATIONAL CIRCUS SCHOOL
(ÉCOLE NATIONALE DE
CIRQUE)
417, rue Berri
Montreal, Quebec H2Y 3E1 Canada
514 982-0859
FAX 514 982-6025
www.enc.qc.ca
Professional School
Academic Degree

Ethiopia

CIRCUS ETHIOPIA
Addis Abba, Ethiopia
Also has other troupes: Circus
Jimma, Circus Nazret, Circus Tigra
(Mekele) and Circus Nazareth
(Nazareth). Each has a performing
group and a school.
www.leforneau.com/artistes/circus
Aweke Emiru, Director
Touring youth circus.

Finland

FINNISH YOUTH CIRCUS
ASSOCIATION
Newsletter: *Sirkus Pyramidi*
Kalliotie 9
33610 Tampere Finland
kimehy@uta.fi
Merja Hyodynmaa, Editor-in-Chie
*Sponsors national circus competite
and summer circus camp.*

SUVELAN SIRKUS
Liisa Liuhto
Tuikkukua 3
FI-02770 Espoo, Finland
Phone and FAX: 011 358 9 855
2859
suvelan.sirkus@co.inet.fi
Juha Korhonen, Executive Directc
http://personal.inet.fi/yhdistys/suv
lan.sirkus
*Youth circus school, touring circu
circus festival.*

France

ARC EN CIRQUE
9, rue de Genevois
73000 Chambery-le-Haut
France
011 4 79 60 09 20
FAX 011 4 79 60 08 94
aec@arc-en-cirque.asso.fr
www.arc-en-cirque.asso.fr
*Prepares students for the Centre
National des Arts du Cirque; recreational and youth programs.*

**CENTRE NATIONAL DES ARTS
DU CIRQUE**
1, rue du Cirque
51000 Châlons en Champagne
France
011 33 3 26 21 12 43
FAX 011 33 3 26 21 80 38
Bernard Turin, Director
National professional circus school
Academic Degree

**ECOLE NATIONALE DU
CIRQUE ANNIE FRATELLINI**
2, rue de la Clôture
75019 Paris France
011 33 148 45 58 11
FAX: 011 33 148 40 20 66
*Children, adult; professional train-
ing in association with the
Education Ministry.*

**FÉDERATION FRANÇAISE DES
ÉCOLES DE CIRQUE (FFEC)**
3, rue du Département
75019, Paris France
011 1 40 35 44 89

FAX: 011 1 40 35 01 13
*Organization of French Circus
Schools under the supervision of the
Ministry of Culture and the Ministry
of Youth and Sports.*

Germany

CIRCUS CALIBASTRA
Othellostrasse 5
70563 Stuttgart
Germany
011 49 711 7 19 91 13
FAX: 011 49 711 7 19 91 12
susanne.durchdewald@calibastra.de
www.calibastra.de
Susanne Durchdewald, President
Youth circus.

CIRCUS-ALFREDO
Rubensstr. 136
D-48165 Munster
011 41 2501 8566
FAX: 011 251 9723912
thomas@circus-alfredo.de
www.dental-technik-ms.de/alfredo/
Thomas Egbers, Cirkusdirector
Youth circus.

The Netherlands

Circusshool DE HOOGTE
Haniasteeg 18
8911 BX Leeuwarden
The Netherlands
phone/FAX 011 31 582 16 22 36
E-mail: circusschooldehoogte@
compuserve.com
http://huizen.dds.nl/~dehoogte/info

The only Dutch circus academy;
three year training program.

YOUTHCIRCUS BOMBARI
P.O. Box 124
9400 AC Assen
The Netherlands
Phone: 011 31 592 374 445
Email: bombari@hetnet.nl
Contact: Anneke Koster
Youth program established
September 2000.

New Zealand

CIRCOARTS
Faculty of Media Arts
Christchurch Polytechnic
Institute of Technology
P.O.B. 22 095
Christchurch, New Zealand
011 64 3 364 9063
FAX 011 64 3 364 9079
www.chchp.ac.nz/polyinfor?CircoArts
Godfrey Sim, CircoArts Course
Coordinator
One year course.
CircoArtsCertificate

Northern Ireland

**BELFAST COMMUNITY CIR-
CUS SCHOOL**
23-25 Gordon Street
Belfast, Ireland BT1 2LG
Will Chamberlain, Director
011 44 28 902 36 007
Non-Sectarian youth workshops,

adult training, summer camp.

CIRCUS 1 TO 3
St. Patricks Training School
Glen Road
Belfast BT11 8BX Northern Irelan
Pat Duggan, Project Leader

Portugal

CHAPITO
Colectividade Cultural e Recreativ
de Santa Caterina
Rua Costa do Castelo 1/7
P-1100 Lisbon, Portugal
011 351 1 8878225-8861410
FAX 011 351 1 8861463
Teresa Ricou, Director
Two and three year course.
Secondary Degree

Russia

**STATE COLLEGE OF CIRCU!
AND VARIETY ARTS**
5 Ul. Yamskogo Polya, 24
125124 Moscow, Russia
011 7 095 212 7121
Degree Program.

South Africa

ZIPZAP CIRCUS SCHOOL
1A Verbena Street
Paarden Eiland
Cape Town
South Africa

Brent van Rensberg, Laurence
Esteve-van Rensberg, founders.
Phone/FAX: 011 27 21 790 1673
zipzap@iafraca.com
www.zip-zap.co.za
Afterschool program for youth 6-20.

Sweden

CIRCUS MAX
Uppsala, Sweden
m97mlu@student.tdb.uu.se
www.privat.katedral.se/~nv95pesa/m
ain.htm
Marcus Lundwall, Instructor
One of Uppsala's two circus schools.

LUDVIKA MINICIRCUS
Gamla Bangatan 55
S-771 53 Ludvika Sweden
Phone/FAX 011 46 240 140 56
larserik.bang@kommun.ludvika.se
www.ludvika.se/lmc
Barbro Nordstrom, Artistic Director
School and touring youth circus.

NORSHOLMS YOUTH CIRCUS NORRKOPING
Norrkoping, Sweden
011 12 1545
FAX 011 18 7566
ulf.nersing@
norrkoping.mail.telia.com
www.angelfire.com/biz/
Ungdomscirkus
Youth circus; sponsors international youth circus festival.

Switzerland

JUGENDZIRKUS ROBIANO
c/o Fredi Furer
Im Langen Loh 241
4054 Basel
Switzerland
011 41 61 302 39 93
www.robiano.ch/informationen
Youth circus.

United Kingdom

CIRCOMEDIA
Centre for Contemporary Circus &
Physical Performance
Brittania Road
Kingswood, Bristol, BS15 8DB, UK
Phone/FAX T/F 011 44 117 947
7288
info@circomedia.demon.co.uk
www.circomedia.demon.co.uk
Bim Mason, Course Director
Fulltime One year Course.
Diploma

THE CIRCUS SPACE
Coronet Street
London N1 6HD UK
011 44 171 729-9522
FAX 011 44 171 729 9422
enquiries@the circusspace.co.uk
www.thecircusspace.co.uk
Charlie Holland, Program Director,
Deputy Chief Executive
Professional and Recreational School.
Four year degree sequence

NATIONAL ASSOCIATION OF YOUTH CIRCUS (N.A.Y.C.)
1 Moorgate Rise, Kippax
Leeds LS25 7RG UK
Phone/FAX 011 44 113 287 6080
Steve Ward, Secretary

THE SERIOUS ROAD TRIP
8, Westgate Street
Hackney, London E8 3RN UK
Phone/FAX 011 44 181 806 3533
srt@roadtrip.demon.co.uk
http://www.roadtrip.demon.co.uk/
Uses circus to help children affected by war, poverty or natural disasters.

SKYLIGHT CIRCUS ARTS
Broadwater Centre
Smith Street
Rochdale OL16 1HE UK
011 44 1706 650676
FAX 011 441706 713638
www.skylight-circus-arts.org.uk
Training courses; outreach programs.

ZIPPO'S ACADEMY OF CIRCUS ARTS (ZACA)
174 Stockbridge Road
Winchester, Hants SO22 6RW UK
011 44 7050 247 287
FAX: 011 44 7050 24 48 67
Zipposcircus@yahoo.com
www.zipposcircus.co.uk
Martin "Zippo" Burton, Director
Training with touring circus.

United States
California

CAMP WINNARAINBOW
Sep.-May
1301 Henry St.
Berkeley, CA 94709 USA
510 525-4304
FAX 510 528-8775
June-August
P.O. Box 1359
Laytonville, CA 95454 USA
707 984-6507
arainbow@well.com
http://users.aol.com/wgeneral/camp.html
Wavy Gravy, Director
Summer camp.

CIRQUE SAN JOSE
634 N. Eighth St.
San Jose, CA 95112 USA
Dan Hoff, Cheryl Taylor-Hoff, Directors
http://members.aol.com/Ashburner
Yearround youth circus program.

CONCORD SCHOOL OF CLOWNOLOGY
83 Donegal Way #2
Pleasant Hill, CA 94523
925 937-4004
Zipp, Director
Two month, twice-a-week introduction to clowning.

THE DELL'ARTE SCHOOL OF PHYSICAL THEATER
P.O. Box 816
Blue Lake, CA 95525 USA
707 668-5663

FAX707 668-5665
dellarte@aol.com
www.dellarte.com
Daniel Stein, School Director
One year program, master work-shops, summer programs in physical Theater; Dell'Arte Abroad: Bali Program.

FERN STREET CIRCUS
P.O.B. 621004
San Diego, CA 92162 USA
619 235-9756
FAX: 619 231-7910
John Highkin, Director
www.fernstreetcircus.org
Yearround youth training programs; touring show - adults and children.

FLYING TRAPEZE ASSOCIATION
P.O.B. 391593
MountainView, CA 94043
800 205-6888
FAX 650 968-7153
TrapAssoc@aol.com
members.aol.com/trapassoc
Maria Carrillo, Director
Dedicated to the promotion of trapeze and aerial arts.

THE GREAT ALL AMERICAN YOUTH CIRCUS
Community Circus Arts Corporation
P.O.Box 7941
Redlands, CA 92375
909 798-YMCA
circusdir@surfree.com
www.ycircus.org
Pete Wray, Director
Community circus.

THE L.A. CIRCUS
Los Angeles Foundation for the
Circus Arts (LAFCA)
Los Angeles, CA *USA*
213 751-3486
Wini McKay
Circus, outreach.

MAKE*A*CIRCUS
755 Frederick St.
San Francisco, CA 94117 USA
415 242-1414
booking@makacircus.org
www.makeacircus
Summer participatory circus, clown therapy, teen apprentice program.

SAN FRANCISCO SCHOOL OF CIRCUS ARTS (SFSCA)
755 Frederick St
San Francisco, CA 94117 USA
415 759-8123
FAX 415 759-8644
sfca@sfcircus.org
www.sfcircus.org
Professional and recreational training.

TRAPEZE ARTS, INC.
210 South Hill Court
Daly City, CA 94015 USA
Phone/FAX 415 337-1900
traparts@sirius.com
www.trapezearts.com
Stephan Gaudreau,
Executive Director

Colorado

DENVER FLYERS
Denver, CO USA

Trapeze@damnhot.com
www.damnhot.com/trapeze
Flying trapeze club.

Connecticut

**CHILDREN'S CIRCUS OF
MIDDLETOWN**
Oddfellows Playhouse
128 Washington Street
Middletown, CT 06457
860 347-6143
FAX 860 343-1592
oddfellows@wesleyan.edu
Dic Wheeler, Circus Director
Summer youth circus.

Florida
CAMP UNIVERSE
5298 cr 114
Wildwood, FL 34785
561 487-4457
FAX: 561 487-4809
campuniver@aol.com
www.camp-universe.com
Sheryl. M. Ryan
*20% of the program devoted to
circus.*

CIRCUS OF THE KIDS
926 Waverly Rd.
Tallahassee, FL 32312-2813 USA
800 881-SHOW
circusofthekids@aol.com
Bruce Pfeffer, President
Residencies.

CIRCUS SARASOTA
P.O. Box 18636
Sarasota, FL 34276 USA
941 355-9335

fax: 941 355-7978
ncspa@gte.net
www.circussarasota.org
Pedro Reis, Director
*Performing circus; schools out-
reach; summer clown training;
hopes to establish a professional
school.*

FLYING HIGH CIRCUS
Florida State University, Tully Gym
Tallahassee, FL 32306-3064 USA
904 644-4874
mfpeters@admin.fsu.edu
http://mailer.fsu.edu/~circus/
Richard Brinson, Director
Extracurricular circus.

SAILOR CIRCUS
2075 Bahia Vista Street
Sarasota, FL 34239 USA
941 361-6350
FAX: 941 361-6351
Community youth circus.

**TITO GAONA FLYING
TRAPEZE ACADEMY**
432 Spadaro Drive
Venice, FL 34285 USA
Phone/FAX: 941 488-2496
Tito Gaona

VERO BEACH
Recreation Department
1725 17th Avenue
Vero Beach. FL 32960 USA
561 567-2144
Summer circus camp.

WARD ALEXANDER'S COLLEGE OF COMPLEXES CARNIVAL AND CIRCUS STUDIO
P.O.B. 159
Newberry FL 32669 USA
352 472-6103
coccircus@aol.com
Ward Alexander
Flying and other circus training on ad hoc basis.

Georgia

CARRIE HELLER CIRCUS ARTS, LLC
206 Rogers Street N.E., Suite 211
Atlanta, GA 30317 USA
404 370-0001
FAX 404 370-1659
Carrie Heller, Director
Yearround circus training.

Hawaii

HICCUP CIRCUS
R.R. 2, Box 4524
Pahoa, Hawaii 96778 USA
808 586-8675
FAX 808 586-8685
juggler@aloha.net
http://hiccupcircus.com
Graham Ellis, Director
Touring youth circus.

Illinois

ACTORS GYMNASIUM
Circus and Performing Arts School
Noyes Cultural Arts Center
927 Noyes Street
Evanston, IL, 60201 USA
847 328-2795
actorgym@enteract.com
www.enteract.com/~actorgym
Sylvia Hernandez, co-founder, teacher
School of circus and physical theatre.
Two Year Certificate

GAMMA PHI CIRCUS
Illinois State University
Normal, IL 61761 USA
309 438-2690
jpolacek@ilstu.edu
www.its.ilstu.edu/gpcircus
Dr. Jerry Polacek, Director
Extracurricular circus.

THE MIDNIGHT CIRCUS
2233 West Cullom Ave., #2
Chicago, IL 60618
773 583-2222
FAX 773 583-6768
mncircus@aol.com
www.midnightcircus.net
Jeff Jenkins, Julie Greenberg co-directors
Circus that integrates theatre. Offers child and adult circus classes.

Indiana

CIRCUS CITY FESTIVAL
154 N. Broadway
Peru, IN 46970 USA
765 472-3918
www.perucircus.com
Linda Cawood, Office Manager
Annual community circus.

Maine

CELEBRATION BARN THEATER
190 Stock Farm Rd.
South Paris, ME 04281 USA
207 743-8452
FAX: 207 743-3889
Info@celebrationbarn.com
www.celebrationbarn.com
Carolyn Brett, Executive Director
Summer professional workshops.

Maryland

MARYLAND GYMKANA TROUPE
College of Health and Human Performance
Building #255, Valley Drive
University of Maryland
College Park, MD 20742 USA
301 405-2566
Dr. Joseph Murray, Director and Head Coach
Extracurricular gymnastics program.

Massachusetts

BERKSHIRE KIDS CIRCUS
Berkshire Community College
1350 West Street
Pittsfield, MA 01201 USA
413 499-4660, Ext. 379
Alexandra Warshaw, Director of Community Services
Camp.

Minnesota

CIRCUS OF THE STAR
P.O.Box 16284
St. Paul, MN 55116 USA
651 699-8229
info@circusofthestar.org
www.circusofthestar.org
Dan and Betty Butler, co-Directors
Yearround youth program.

Missouri

everyday circus, inc.
3340 Oxford Ave.
St. Louis, MO 63143 USA
314 645-4445
FAX 314 645-4277
circuslady@everydaycircus.net
everydaycircus.net
Jessica Hentoff, Mike Killian, Directors
Yearround youth circus training, community circus resource.

New Hampshire

PINE HILL WALDORF SCHOOL
P.O.B. 668
Abbot Hill Rd.
Wilton, NH 03086-0668 USA
603 654-6003
Jackie Davis, Director, Hilltop Circus
jackie@schoolshows.com
Annual middle school curricular circus.

New Jersey

BLOOMFIELD COLLEGE
Westminster Arts Center
Bloomfield, NJ 07003 USA
973 748-9000, Ext 343
FAX 201 743-3998
lisa_farese@bloomfield.edu.
Chenara Yancey, Director of Arts as
Catalyst
www.bloomfield.edu/bc_main.htm
Curricular and extracurricular circus program.

New Mexico

ALBUQUERQUE SCHOOL FOR CIRCUS ARTS
PO Box 11172
Albuquerque, NM 87192
505 362-0278
Abqsdca@aol.com
Rosalinda Rojas, Director
Afterschool program, summer camp.

New York

AMERICAN YOUTH CIRCUS ORGANIZATION (AYCO)
215 West 88th St., #12G
New York, NY 10024
212 679-7575
kevcircus@aol.com
New organization for youth circuses.

BIG APPLE CIRCUS
Beyond the Ring'
505 Eighth Avenue
19th Floor
New York, NY 10018-6505 U.S.A.
212-268-2500, Ext. 137
FAX 212-268-3163
vgardiner@bigapplecircus.org
www.bigapplecircus.org
Viveca Gardiner, Director of Special
Projects
School residencies, afterschool program.

CIRCUS MINIMUS
215 W. 88th St., #12G
New York, NY 10024 USA
212 679-7575
kevcircus@aol.com
www.circusminimus.com
Kevin O'Keefe, Director
Residencies, afterschool programs, camps; One man Circus-in-a-Suitcase.

NATIONAL CIRCUS PROJECT
56 Lion Lane
Westbury, NY 11590 USA
516 334-2123
FAX 516 334-2249
Circusproj@pb.net
JeanPaul Jenack, Executive Director
School and camp residencies.

NEW WAY CIRCUS CENTER, Inc
Russian American Kids Circus
1202 Ave. P
Brooklyn, NY 11229 USA
Ph/FAX: 718 266-0202
nycircus@hotmail.com
www.rakidscircus.org
Regina Berenchtein, Founder and
Creative Director
Yearround youth training; touring youth circus.

NY GOOFS
126 1st Place, #1
Brooklyn, NY 11231
718 797-2331
FAX: 718 797-2343
NYGOOFS@aol.com
Nygoofs@aol.com
Dick Monday, Founder
Performing group, clown workshops.

TRAPEZESCHOOL.COM
P.O. Box 299
Tillson, NY 12486
914 658-8540
Jonathan Conant, Director
Info@trapezeschool.com
http://trapezeschool.com/
Flying trapeze on 350 acre farm.
Also rock climbing and horseback
riding.

Pennsylvania

SPORTS AND ARTS CENTER
AT ISLAND LAKE
Island Lake Road
Starrucca, PA 18462 USA
717 798-2550
FAX 717 798-2346
Winter Office
P.O.Box 800
Pomona, NY 10970 USA
914 354-5517
FAX 914 362-3039
ISLNDLAKE@aol.com
www.islandlake.com
Bev, Mike, Matt Stolz, Directors
Summer camp with circus program.

CAMP WESTMONT
Summer Address (6/15-9/1):
P.O. Box 15
Poyntelle, PA 18454
Winter Address:
14 Squirrel Drive
East Rockaway, NY 11518
516 599-2963
FAX: 516 599-1979
westmont4u@aol.com
www.campwestmont.com
Jack Pinsky
Trapeze, web, unicycle, trampoline,
juggling. Clowning when available.

Rhode Island

PAN-TWILIGHT CIRCUS
"Rhode Island and the Nation's
ONLY Circus of the Arts"
http://users.ids.net/~tomss/ptc/index.
html
Bob Colonna, Director
1997 Production: a circus version of
Shakespeare's Tempest.

PROVIDENCE CIRCUS
SCHOOL
104 Eleventh Street
Providence, RI 02906
401 861-0892
FAX 401 331-1987
jplotz@aol.com
Judith Plotz, Director
Yearround youth program

Texas

BOERNE GYMNASTICS
CENTER
105 Stonegate Rd.

Boerne, TX 78006
830 816-9496
FAX: 830 249-3550
Info@boernegym.com
www.boernegym.com
Lorna Spellman, Owner
Full time gymnastics school that is expanding its current 25% focus on circus skills. Summer Circus Arts Camp, Resident and Day.

Vermont

ALLA YOUDINA
P.O. Box 83
Greensboro Bend, VT 05842 USA
Phone/FAX: 802 472-6964
uralhill@aol.com
Aerial and ice skating instruction.

CIRCUS SMIRKUS
1 Circus Rd.
Greensboro, VT 05841 USA
802 533-7125
Fax 802 533-2480
smirkus@together.net
www.circussmirkus.org
Rob Mermin, Director
Touring youth circus, circus camp, residencies.

VAN LODOSTOV FAMILY CIR-CUS
POB 624
Hartford, VT 05047 USA
Phone 802 296-2927
FAX 802 295-3312
drquark@sover.net
Ted Lawrence, Director/Head Coach
Circus camp.

Virginia

CIRCUS ARTS WORKSHOP
1153 Bellview Road
McLean, VA 22102 USA
703 759 9496
FAX 703 759 2521
info@circusarts.com
http://home.circusarts.com
Summer flying trapeze training.

RINGLING BROTHERS AND BARNUM & BAILEY
Feld Entertainment, Inc.
8607 Westwood Center Drive
Vienna, VA 22182 USA
703 448-4000
www.Ringling.com
Two units of the circus, each tours for two years; educational program.

Washington

CASCADE ELEMENTARY SCHOOL
16022 116th Ave S.E.
Renton, WA 98055
425 204-3350
Jerry Burkhalter, Physical Education Specialist
Curricular circus program.

CASCADE YOUTH CIRCUS
P.O. Box 857
Maple Valley, WA 98038
425 432-9999
FAX 425 432-5269
Adjmaus@aol.com
http://summit-kidnastics.tripod.com/CYC/

Debbie Johnson, Director
Afterschool programs, residencies.

CIRCUS CAMP '98
c/o The WAIL Collective
PRAG Tree Farm
13401 184th St. NE
Arlington, WA 98223 USA
306 403-0185
wisefool@hooked.net
Summer camp, may not continue.

WENATCHEE YOUTH CIRCUS
1918 5th Street
Wenatchee, WA 98801 USA
509 662-2489
Phone/FAX 509 662-0722
Paul K. Pugh, Managing Director
Touring youth circus.

West Virginia

GESUNDHEIT! INSTITUTE
HC 64 Box 167
Hillsboro, WV 24946 USA
Phone/FAX 304 653-4338
oma00445@mail.wvnet.edu
www.well.com/user/achoo
Patch Adams, Founder
Community working for social change, uses clowning.

Wisconsin

GREAT YOUTH CIRCUS
P.O.B. 661
Baraboo, WI 53913 USA
Phone/FAX 608 356-2375
Tim Tegge, Director
Circus Residencies

Web site

TEACHCIRCUS.COM
Website dedicated "to helping teachers, recreation professionals and performers give effective instruction in Circus Arts"
Jason Catanzariti
www.teachcircus.com

GLOSSARY

Acrobatics Circus style gymnastics.

Adagio Two person balancing, one supporting the other. See **Quartette Adagio.**

Aerials All acts in the air. See **Trapeze, Cloudswing.**

Balance and Equilibre. Balance acts involving the body alone, as in **Adagio,** or using props, as in **Tightwire, Slack Wire** and **High Wire.**

Balance Beam Horizontal beam mounted on legs; used in gymmnastics.

Bicycle Specially built bicycles support large numbers of performers and permit them to do tricks. There are also solo and duet bicycle acts.

Bungee Elastic straps that permit performers to leap from heights and return to their original position. Can be combined with **Trapeze.**

Casting A person is thrown from one person to another, often those casting hang upside down. Sometimes called Flying Trapeze in Miniature when it is **Low Casting.** The same thing done higher is **High Casting.**

Chinese Hoop Diving Jumping forwards and backwards through vertical hoops; sometimes two or three hoops are mounted on top of each other.

Chinese Pole Stationery vertical pole on the floor on which acrobats climb and do tricks. Also called **Russian Pole.**

Cloudswing Swinging on a loose horizontal rope. Tricks done are similar to those done on **Swinging Trapeze.**

Clown Performer specializing in physical humor. Clowns can appear in their own acts or as part of other acts. In American circuses they are often non-verbal. European clowns are often musical and the masters of many circus skills. Traditional makeups include Whiteface, Auguste (ridiculous), and Hobo.

Corde Lisse Acrobatics on a vertical rope. Vertical **Strap** or fabric can be used. **Tissu** performers work with two vertical pieces of fabric.

Cradle   One person hanging by his/her legs supports another with his/he
arms. May be done in multiples.

Cylinder Balancing   Also called **Rolla Bolla.** A performer balances on
short board balanced on an unfettered horizontal cylinder. A series of cylin
ders may be used.

Devil Sticks   A stick about three feet in length manipulated by two simila
sticks held in the performer's hands.

Diablo   A spinning spool, narrow on the middle, is manipulated on a strin
that runs between two wands held in the performer's hands.

Equilibre   Acts involving balance with the human body.

Flying Trapeze   Also called **High Flying Trapeze.** A performer swings fror
a trapeze to a catcher hanging from another trapeze. Always done over a net

German Gym Wheel   Also called **Gym Wheel.** A circular apparatus con
sisting of two rings joined together. Performers cling to the part that connect
the two wheels.

Giraffe Cycle   See **Unicycle.**

Gymnastics   Set acrobatic routines used in competiton.

Hand to Hand   See **Adagio.**

Hanging Perch   See **Perch Pole.**

High Bar   Elevated horizontal bar, used in gymnastics.

High Flying Trapeze.   See **Flying Trapeze.**

High Wire   A horizontal, heavy wire usually suspended at least twenty-five
feet in the air. Performers often use balance poles. When suspended betweer
buildings or in other outdoor venues, often called **Skywalk.**

Horse   Sturdy, static device used for vaulting in gymnastics.

Horse Acts Performers work on the backs of moving horses in **Bareback** acts. Riderless performing horses are **Liberty Horses**. A single rider controlling a horse with the rider's body is **Dressage**, sometimes called **High School.**

Juggling Usually hand manipulation of objects such as balls or clubs in the air or against the ground or an object. The mouth can be used with ping pong balls.

Ladder Traps Suspended ladder used like a trapeze.

Low Casting See **Casting**.

Lunge Also called **Mechanic, Safety Belt** or **Spotting Rope**. A performer's belt attached to a line to the ceiling and then to an operator on the floor/ground who can keep the performer from falling. The line may also be attached to the apparatus being used. Used in training and performance.

Lyre A trapeze that is circular or rectangular. Circular lyre is also called **Russian Ring**.

Mechanic See **Lunge**.

Mini-Tramp A small trampoline used for launching a perfomer.

Parallel Bars Horizontal bars on a secure base. Used in gymnastics.

Perch Pole Vertical pole supported on the shoulders or forehead of a person standing on the ground. Another performer climbs the pole to do tricks.

Plange The performer hangs by an arm from a ring or other device and swings so that the feet go over the head.

Pyramid Standing performers on the floor support one another in a formation. North African acts often end with all the perfomers being supported by one.

Quartette Adagio Three performers throw a fourth into the air who does tricks before being caught by the three. Sometimes the object is to throw the fourth as high as possible.

Rings The performer swings from one or two small circular rings suspended from above. Also called **Roman Rings**.

Russian Ring See **Lyre**.

Risley A performer lying on his/her back, manipulates objects and/or people with his/her feet.

Rolla Bolla See **Cylinder Balancing**.

Rolling Globes Large balls performers manipulate with their feet as the performers stand on them.

Roman Rings See **Rings**.

Russian Bar Sometimes called **Sky Pole**. Usually a pole of fiberglass or two poles taped together. The pole is supported on the shoulders of two performers at either end while a third works on the center of the pole.

Russian Pole See **Chinese Pole**.

Russian Swing A long swing that permits people to stand one behind the other. It is used to launch the person in the front as on a flying trapeze.

Safety Belt See **Lunge**.

Shoot Through At the end of a two person act on a rotating ladder, one person flies through the ladder.

Slack Wire A thin, loose wire securely attached at each end. The movement of the wire becomes part of the act. A low wire act like **Tightwire.**

Spanish Web See **Web**.

Spotting Rope. See **Lunge**.

Static Trapeze The performer works on a horizontal bar suspended from above. When the trapeze moves, it becomes a **Swinging Trapeze.** In either case, performers do not leave the trapeze as in **Flying Trapeze. Double** or **Triple Trapeze** are wider trapezes used by two or three people side by side.

Strap See **Cord Lisse**.

Swing Pole Performer on the floor supports a vertical steel pole. A second performer climbs the pole, attaches to the top with a neck loop and swings horizontally as the other performer spins the pole.

Teeterboard A sturdy board balanced in the middle like a see-saw. A performer standing on the end of the board on the ground is launched when one or more people jump on the other end of the board.

Tightwire Thin horizontal wire usually six or seven feet in the air.

Tissu See **Corde Lisse.**

Trampoline Taut horizontal canvas attached by springs to a frame. It gives great leverage to those who jump on it.

Trapeze See **Static Trapeze** and **Flying Trapeze.**

Tumbling Acrobatics involving rolls, hand stands and cartwheels.

Unicycle One wheeled cycles, Can be short or tall **GIRAFFE** cyclces.

Web Performer works on a vertical rope anchored above. The performer may be assisted by a person on the ground who spins the rope. Also called **Spanish Web**.

Bibliography

There is a library of materials about various aspects of the circus. These are most germane to this study.

Books

Albrecht, Ernest. *The New American Circus.* Gainesville: University Press of Florida. 1995.
Essential study of the New Circus Movement.

Bolton, Reg. *Circus in a Suitcase.* Bethel: New Plays Incorporated. 1982.
How to put together a children's circus.

Bolton, Reg. *New Circus.* London: Calouste Gulbenkian Foundation. 1987.

Cushman, Kathleen and Montana Miller. *Circus Dreams, The Making of a Circus Artist.* Boston: Joy Street Books, Little Brown. 1990.
Follows the first American to study at the Centre National du Cirque in France.

Gossard, Steve. *A Reckless Era of Aerial Performance, the Evolution of the Trapeze.* Normal, IL: Self Published.
History with a focus on training methods.

Harris, Leon. *The Moscow Circus School.* New York: Atheneum. 1970.
Record of Russian circus training for youngsters in the 1960's.

Keen, Sam. *Learning to Fly: Trapeze*
– Reflections on Fear, Trust and the Joy of Letting Go. New York: Broadway Books. 1998.
Theory and practice of the flying trapeze.

Machotka, Hana. *The Magic Ring: A Year with the Big Apple Circus.* New York: William Morrow & Company. 1988.
Record of Big Apple in the 1980's.

Mermin, Rob. *Circus Smirkus: A True Story of High Adventure and Low Comedy.* Greensboro: Circus Smirkus. 1997,
Record of the first 10 years of Circus Smirkus.

Powledge, Fred. *Born on the Circus.* New York: Harcourt Brace Jovanovich. 1976.
Armando Cristiani as an eleven year old performer.

Simon, Peter Angelo. *Big Apple Circus.* New York: Penguin. 1978
Account of the beginnings of Big Apple Circus.

Steele, Tony. *The A B Cs of Flying Trapeze.* Self Published.
Advice from an outstanding flyer and teacher of flying.

Supple, Todd R., Ed. *Gymkana Troupe: The First Fifty Years 1946-1996.* College
Park: College of Health & Human Performance. 1996.
A record.

Towsen, John H. *Clowns.* New York: Hawthorn Books, Inc. 1976.
Authoritative history of clowning.

Woodhead, Paul and Deborah Duffy. *Circus in Schools: An Innovative Approach to
Physical Education, Sport and Personal Development.* Dubbo, Self Published. 1998.
Account of a curricular circus program in Australia.

Videos

Belfast Community Circus
Circus of Hope. Susan Rosenkrantz. 1993

Circus City Festival
Circus Town USA. 1970.

1997 Peru Circus Commemorative Video: Mardis Gras under the Big Top. Marcus
Media. 1997.

Cirque du Monde
When the Circus Came to Town. Adobe Foundation. 1995
The first Cirque du Monde residencies in Rio de Janeiro and Montreal.

Flying High Circus
Fifty Years of Flying High Circus. Florida State University. 1997.

Magazines

arts de la piste. Circus Arts Quarterly. Formerly bi-lingual in French and English,
now only in French.
HorsLesMurs
68, rue de la Folie-Mericourt
75011 Paris, France

Bandwagon. Bimonthly Journal of the Circus Historical Society, Inc.
1075 West Fifth Ave.
Columbus, OH 43212-2691

Don Marcks' Circus Report.
Weekly Newsletter.
P.O. Box 2476
El Cerrito, CA 94530-5361.
eMail: marcksd@iopener.com

King Pole
Quarterly Magazine of the Circus Friends Association of Great Britain.
43 Waterloo Lane
Skellingthorpe, Lincoln LN6 5SJ UK
http://www.webcircus.co.uk/kingpole/
kingpole@webcircus.co.uk

Planet Circus. Bilingual Circus Arts Quarterly. German and English.
Circus Verlag
D. Kuik und H. Grosscurth GbR
Am Lautershof 6,
D-41542 Dormagen, Germany.

Spectacle: A Quarterly Journal of the Circus Arts.
Circus Plus Publications
P.O. Box 1420
Edison, New Jersey 08818-1420.
circusarts@aol.com
http://members.aol.com/circusarts/

The White Tops. Bimonthly Journal of the Circus Fans Association of America.
70 Dublin Ave.
Nashua, NH 03063

End notes

[1] Youdina interview, Ringling rehearsals, Tampa, FL, Dec 3, 1995
[2] Youdina interview, Bolton Valley, VT, Nov. 14, 1995.
[3] Ibid.
[4] Ibid.
[5] Youdina interview Tampa, Dec. 4, 1995.
[6] Ibid.
[7] Ibid.
[8] Ibid.
[9] See interview with Armando Cristiani, Chapter 10.
[10] Youdina interview Bolton Valley, Nov. 20, 1995.
[11] Ibid.
[12] Ariana rehearsal, Tampa, Dec. 3, 1995.
[13] See additional discussion of Chinese training in Chapter 11.
[14] Youdina phone interview, Jan. 20, 1996.
[15] Quoted in *White Tops*, Mar./Apr. 1998, 8.
[16] See Odintsova interview, Chapter 10.
[17] Clown College Graduation Program, 1996.
[18] *The White Tops*, Mar./Apr. 1998, 8,9.
[19] Peggy Williams Email to the author, Nov. 23, 1998.
[20] "A Little Town and the Big Top", *New York Times*, Sep. 19, 1998, B5. col. 6.
[21] *Big Apple Circus: Twenty Years! 1997-1998 Season* Program, 25.
[22] Ibid. 24.
[23] Quoted, Peter Angelo Simon, *Big Apple Circus* (New York: Penguin, 1978), unnumbered pages.
[24] Sylvia Hernandez FAX to the author, Jan. 1, 1999.
[25] http://www.arc-encirque.asso.fr/Pages/usloisir.html.
[26] Ibid.
[27] Ibid.
[28] http://www.arc-en-cirque.asso.fr/Pages/otrcirkus.html
[29] http://www.circusarts.org/handi.html. February 16, 2000. Translated.
[30] Centre National des Arts Du Cirque brochure. Undated.
[31] http://www.actech.co.nz/circoarts/circoarts.html. Dec. 26, 1998.
[32] http://www.circomedia.demon.co.uk/rabout.html. 1. Dec. 26, 1998.
[33] http://www.circomedia.demon.co.uk/rcourses.html 2. Dec. 26, 1998.
[34] Maria Carillo phone interview with the author, Jan. 17, 2000.
[35] Maria Carirllo phone interview. May 23, 2000.

[36] Maria Carrillo, Email on trapezegroups.com, September 23, 2000.

[37] Pedro Reis phone interview, Dec. 10, 1998.

[38] See Chapter Four.

[39] Sue West phone interview Jan. 26, 2000.

[40] http://www.circussarasota.org/Human_Services/human_services.html.

[41] Aaron Watkin phone interview, May 2, 2000.

[42] Charlie Holland interview, Circus Space, Feb. 18, 1998.

[43] http://www.dellarte.com Nov. 5, 1997.

[44] Ibid.

[45] Ibid.

[46] Patricia Martins, Emails to the author, October 20 and 30, 2000.

[47] l 'Espace Catastrophe brochure. Undated. Translated.

[48] See Molly Saudek interview, Chapter 10.

[49] Pierrette Venne interview, National Circus School, Sep. 25, 1997.

[50] Christiane Barette interview, National Circus School, Sep. 25, 1997.

[51] Ibid.

[52] Ibid.

[53] Venne interview.

[54] Daniela Arendasova interview, National Circus School, Sep. 25, 1997.

[55] Ibid.

[56] Ibid.

[57] Ibid.

[58] Barette interview.

[59] Pam Creed, "Message from the Director, NICA NEWS, Spring 2000.

[60] Dick Monday phone interview, Feb. 5, 1999.

[61] Ibid.

[62] Dick Monday Email to the author, Jan. 27, 1999.

[63] *Students Fly through the Air with the Greatest of Ease* by Peter Sciacca, Sunset Beacon, June 1996. Reprinted in San Francisco School of Circus Arts Web site.

[64] San Francisco School of Circus Arts *Winter Schedule 1999.* Brochure.

[65] Laura Hamburg, "Circus School" *Circus Report* Jan. 26, 1998, 8.

[66] John H. Towsen, *Clowns* (New York: Hawthorne, 1976) , p. 309.

[67] Ibid. , p. 315.

[68] FAX from the Moscow Circus School, March 7, 2000. Translated by Nicholas Fersen

[69] Leon Harris, *The Moscow Circus School* (New York: Atheneum, 1970.)

[70] Calvin Sima, "HighWire Feats Rule North Korea", *New York Times* 13 March 2000, E1, 2.

[71] Martin Burton Email Nov 25, 1999.

[72] http://www.lefourneau.com/artistes/circus/ethiopie/cirquesangl.htm 4. Jan.

11, 1999.
[73] Amanda Crockett Email to the author, Feb. 2, 2000.
[74] Karen Saudek phone interview, Sep. 27, 1998.
[75] Rob Mermin. *Circus Smirkus: A True Story of High Adventure and Low Comedy.* 1997. (Greensboro, VT, 1997), 21, 22.
[76] Ibid. 554, 55.
[77] *The Flying Fruit Fly Circus presents "Children of the Sun,* program, 6.
[78] Trevor Matthews letter to the author, Oct. 13, 1998.
[79] http://www2.tpgi.com.au/users/acroart.operat.htm. Oct. 4, 1998.
[80] http://www.democrats.org.au/democrats/parliament/old/0820/5vbqon.html Aug. 21, 1996.
[81] Graham Ellis phone interview, Aug. 13, 1998.
[82] Hawaii's Volcano Circus *Juggling for Success* brochure. Undated.
[83] Graham Ellis Email to the author, Apr. 3, 2000.
[84] Barbro Nordstorm letter to the author, Oct. 20, 1998.
[85] Ibid.
[86] Paul Pugh interview, Cleveland, Ohio, Jun 19, 1998.
[87] Ibid.
[88] Ibid.
[89] Ibid.
[90] Ibid.
[91] Steve Ward letter to the author, Mar. 17, 1998.
[92] Ibid.
[93] *Circus of Hope* Video, 1993.
[94] Ibid.
[95] See Chapter Three.
[96] See Chapter Seven.
[97] Will Chamberlain phone interview. Jan, 24, 2000.
[98] Steve Gossard, *A Reckless Era of Aerial Performance, the Evoluition of Trapeze* (Normal: Self Published, 1994).
[99] From a brochure for the First International Congress of Children and Youth Circuses, July 12-14, 2000 sponsored by Cabuwazi.
[100] "Children's Circus of Middletown: An overview and brief history." Oddfellows Playhouse FAX. Jan. 20. 2000.
[101] 1991 31st Annual Circus City Festival Program.
[102] 1997 38th Annual Circus City Festival Program.
[103] *Peru Tribune*, Circus Souvenir Edition, July 11, 1997. 20.
[104] 1997 Circus Festival Program, 41.
[105] Linda Caywood, CCFI secretary, phone interview. Oct. 14, 1998.
[106] "An Innovative program," *Cirque du Monde: A Cirque du Soleil Outreach Program*, undated, p. 7.

107 Paul Laporte, phone interview with the author, June 13, 2000,

108 Ibid.

109 "Educational Approach", *Cirque du Monde Handbook for Instructors and Partners,* Section 7, 1999, p. 1.

110 Ibid.

111 "An Outreach Program," *Handbook,* p. 2.

112 "Educational Approach," *Handbook,* p. 7.

113 www.mccrometer.com/sifft/gyc. Oct. 4, 1998.

114 *Sailor Circus in Retrospect,* flyer reprinted from the 1962 Sailor circus program.

115 Susan Loeffler, FAX to the author, Oct. 5, 2000.

116 *Sarasota Sailor Circus, The Greatest Little Show on Earth.* 1995.

117 Patricia A. Campbell, letter to the author, Nov. 5, 1998.

118 See Chapter 8.

119 See Chapter 1.

120 "A Word from the Director," Sailor Circus 1997 Program, 3.

121 Nat Hentoff, *Speaking Freely: A Memoir* (New York: Knopf, 1997) p. 260, 261.

122 See Chapter 8.

123 Mike Killian interview, Aug. 8, 1997.

124 Jessica Hentoff letter, undated.

125 http://www.arena.com/~/Imagine-Ere/campe.htm, 1. Mar.29, 1998.

126 http://www.imagine-ere.qc.ca/campe.htm. April 14, 2000.

127 http:/users.aol.com/wgeneral/camp.html. Oct. 5, 1998.

128 http:www.well.com/user/arainbow/inKIDS.html. Oct. 4, 1998.

129 htttp:www.mccrometer.com/sifft/gyc/. Oct. 4, 1998.

130 See Chapter 9.

131 See Chapter 8.

132 CircusCamp '98 brochure.

133 K. Ruby, Email to the author, Dec. 11, 1998.

134 Circus Minimus - A Circus Kids Create - Newsletter. Sep. 15, 1997.

135 Circus Minimus Newsletter, Dec. 1997.

136 Rob Mermin, phone interview. Oct. 22, 1998.

137 www@indian-river.fl.us. Nov. 2, 1997.

138 "Individualized Programming for Today's Child, Sports & Arts Center at Island Lake" brochure, 1998.

139 Ted Lawrence interview, Greenwich, NY, April 5, 2000.

140 Ibid.

141 Viveca Gardiner phone interview, Dec. 5, 1997.

142 Ibid.

143 Leslie Moore interview, November 20, 1997.

144 Ibid.
145 Gardiner interview. Nov 20, 1997.
146 Leslie Moore Interview, Nov. 20, 1997.
147 Ibid.
148 Ibid.
149 Beth LeCours phone interview, Nov. 2, 1998.
150 Ibid.
151 Promotional Packet for Circus Smirkus Residencies, 1998.
152 Tim Tegge phone interview, Sep. 29, 1998.
153 Tim Tegge phone interview, Nov. 2, 1998.
154 Xstine P. Cook, letter to the author, Nov. 1, 2000.
155 Xstine P. Cook telephone interview, October 19, 2000.
156 JeanPaul Jenack phone interview, April 17, 2000.
157 Jerry Burkhalter, phone interview. April 13, 2000.
158 Paul Woodhead and Deborah Duffy, *Circus in Schools: An Innovative Approach to Physical Education, Sport and Personal Development.* (Dubbo: Self published, 1998).
159 Ibid, p. 3.
160 Paul Woodhead EMail to the author, Nov. 20, 1998.
161 Ibid, p. 48.
162 Flyer for The Tenth Annual Waldorf Movement-Education Conference held at the Pine Hill Waldorf School, May 29-30, 1998.
163 The Hilltop Circus 1998 poster.
164 Jackie Davis interview, Pine Hill Waldorf School. Feb. 7, 1998.
165 Ibid.
166 Jackie Davis phone interview. Dec. 2, 1998.
167 Jackie Davis phone interview, Feb. 19, 2000.
168 Jackie Davis phone interview, Dec. 2, 1998.
169 Ibid.
170 Ibid.
171 Jackie Davis phone interview Feb. 19, 2000.
172 Ibid.
173 Rosalinda Rojas, phone interview with the author, May 3, 2000.
174 Carrie Heller phone interview, Mar. 24, 1998.
175 Horizons Circus Show *The Web of Life*, printed program, March 4, 14, 15, 1997.
176 Ibid.
177 www.creativeloafing.com. Mar.14, 1998.
177a http://summit-kidnastics.tripod.com/cyc/id2.html. September 12, 2000.
177b Phone interview, March 8, 2001.
177c Phone interview, April 10, 2000,

[178] Betty Butler phone interview. Dec. 1, 1998.

[179] *Circus of the Star: Raising the Big Top.* Capital Campaign brochure, 1998, 4.

[180] Dan Butler phone conversation with the author, April 5, 2000.

[181] Betty Butler interview.

[182] Dan Butler phone interview.

[183] http://www.cirkids.org/WhatIsCirKids.html

[184] Mischa Sandberg, Email to the author, April 29, 2000.

[185] everydaycircus Partnership Program brochure, undated.

[186] Jessica Hentoff phone interview, Dec. 30, 1998.

[187] John Highkin phone interview. Nov. 16, 1998.

[188] Sam Keen, Learning to Fly (New York: Broadway Books, 1998), jacket.

[189] Jonathan Conant phone interview, Jan 19, 2000.

[190] http://trapezeschool.com/ Feb. 4, 2000.

[191] Bernadette Pace phone interview, Feb. 8, 2000.

[192] Ibid.

[193] http://www.mainspace.com/history.htm. 3, Dec. 13, 1998.

[194] Ibid.

[195] Marsha Kennington phone interview, Dec. 13, 1998.

[196] Ibid.

[197] Ibid.

[198] Ibid.

[199] Regina Berenchtein interview. Brooklyn, Nov 16, 1998.

[200] Ibid.

[201] Ibid.

[202] Ibid.

[203] Providence Circus School Grant Application to the Youth in Philanthropy Board, Mar. 22, 2000.

[204] http://www.skylight-circus-arts.org.uk/whycpm.html. Jan. 12, 1999.

[205] Laurence Esteve Email to the author, Nov. 30, 2000.

[206] Laurence Esteve, Email to the author, Nov. 29, 2000.

[207] "1996 Gymkana Home Show Introduction," quoted in *The Gymkana Troupe: the First Fifty Years 1946-1996,* ed. Todd R. Supple (College Park: U. of Md, 1997) unnumbered.

[208] 1995 Gymakana Summer Brochure, quoted in *Gymkana Troupe,* 167.

[209] Quoted in *Gymkana Troupe,* 4.

[210] Steve Gossard, *A Reckless Era of Aerial Performance, the Evolution of Trapeze* (Normal: Self Published, 1994), p. 145.

[211] http:www.its.ilstu.edu/gpcircus. July 13, 1998.

[212] Jim Moyer, "Gamma Phi Circus," *Circus Report,* July 7, 1997, 16, 27.

[213] From the 43rd Home Show Program, quoted in the FSU Web site

http://mailer.fsu.edu/~mpeters/whatis.html. Nov. 5, 1998.

[214] http://mailer.fsu.edu/~mpeters/homeshows.html. Nov. 5. 1998

[215] Ibid.

[216] http://mailer.fsu.edu/-lag5439/plot.html. Nov. 5, 1998.

[217] See Chapter 6.

[218] *Bloomfield College Circus Works: A Well Balanced Act.* Brochure, 1997.

[219] Lisa Farese interview, Bloomfield College, Sep. 18, 1997.

[220] John H. Towsen, *Clowns* (New York: Hawthorn, 1976).

[221] John H. Towsen interview, Bloomfield College, Sep. 18, 1997.

[222] Towsen interview.

[223] Farese interview.

[224] Tom Ogden, "Cristiani, Lucio (1906-1992)", *Two Hundred Years of the American Circus* (New York, Facts on File), 1993, 118.

[225] Fred Powledge, *Born on the Circus* (New York: Harcourt Brace Jovanovich, 1976).

[226] Armando Cristiani phone interview, Nov. 28, 1997.

[227] Ibid.

[228] Ibid.

[229] Shirley Earl phone interview. Dec. 10, 1998.

[230] Shirley Earl phone interview. May 12, 1998.

[231] Ibid.

[232] Ekaterina Odintsova interview, Albany, NY, May 28, 1998.

[233] Ibid.

[234] Ibid.

[235] Leitzel married the great flyer. After her death from a performing accident, Codona's life fell apart; he later murdered his second wife and himself.

[236] Ibid.

[237] Ibid.

[238] Molly Saudek interview, Montreal, Quebec, Sep. 24, 1997

[239] Karen Saudek, phone interview, Sep. 27, 1998.

[240] Molly Saudek interview.

[241] Karen Saudek interview.

[242] Ibid.

[243] Rob Mermin, *Circus Smirkus: A True Story of High Adventure and Low Comedy"* . (Greensboro, VT, 1997) 33.

[244] Alla Youdina interview, Sugarbush Resort, Warren, VT, August 26, 1998.

[245] Molly Saudek interview.

[246] Ibid.

[247] Ibid.

[248] Ibid.

[249] Ibid.

[250] "The Magic Revealed," *Spectacle* Fall 1998: 11.

[251] *The Actors Gymnasium Circus Arts Certificate* flyer. Undated.

[252] Maria Carillo Email, Mar. 23, 2000.

[253] "A single hanging rope upon which a bewildering variety of moves can be done." Course description.

[254] Description in the Circus Space 1998 calendar.

[255] *The Circus Space: Powerhouse of Britain's Contemporary Circus.* 1999 Programme and Prospectus. Unnumbered.

[256] http://www.sfcircus.org/courses/advanced.html July 13, 1998.

[257] Sailor Circus - Rules and Regulations Handbook.

[258] *Step right up to the Circus of the Kids Cafe.* Brochure, 1998.

[259] The "First of May" Program, National Circus Project brochure, undated.

[260] Carrie Heller, *Aerial Circus Training Manual.* 1996

[261] everydaycircus flyer, undated.

Robert Sugarman

When Robert Sugarman was six years old, his father engaged legendary Ringling Brothers and Barnum & Bailey ringmaster Fred Bradna to stage the first Shrine Circus in Syracuse, New York. From then on, Sugarman and his father visited Fred and Ellen Bradna in their wagon on the circus lot when the Big Show pitched its tent in Syracuse. Sugarman was fascinated at the way the informal chaos of the circus backlot transformed into the wonderful performance presented in the tent. That interest was rekindled when Alla Youdina, then Creative Director-New Circus Acts for Ringling Brothers and Barnum & Bailey, invited him to watch her prepare The Spider Web Act for the show's Blue Unit in Vermont in 1995.

Sugarman has taught at Bennington, Cazenovia and Southern Vermont Colleges and at the State University of New York at Albany. His plays have been performed at theatres across the country. This is his first book. His next will be a mystery novel, *An Unusual August.*